THE FUTURE OF EVANGELICAL CHRISTIANITY

OTHER BOOKS BY DONALD G. BLOESCH

The Future of Evangelical Christianity

A CALL FOR UNITY AMID DIVERSITY

By Donald G. Bloesch

HELMERS & HOWARD

COLORADO SPRINGS

Abbreviations for scriptural references are as follows:

RSV	Revised Standard Version
NEB	New English Bible
GNB	Good News Bible
NKJ	New King James Version
KJV	King James Version
NIV	New International Version

Dr. Mark Noll's foreword, "The Surprising Optimism of Donald Bloesch," originally appeard as an article under the same title in *Center Journal* (Summer, 1984).

© 1988 by Donald Bloesch.

Published by Helmers & Howard, Publishers, Inc.,
P.O. Box 7407, Colorado Springs, CO 80933 USA.

First published in 1983 by Doubleday & Company, Inc.

FIRST PAPERBACK EDITION

Library of Congress Cataloging-in-Publication Data

Bloesch, Donald G., 1928-
    The future of evangelical Christianity : a call for unity
amid diversity / by Donald G. Bloesch.
       p.   cm.
    Bibliography: p.
    Includes indexes.
    ISBN 0-939443-10-4
    1. Evangelicalism.   I. Title
BR1640.B56 1988
270.8'2—dc19   88-11187
                                                     CIP

Printed in the United States of America

To Brenda,
My Partner in Ministry

Acknowledgments

I WISH TO ACKNOWLEDGE the substantial help that I have received from my wife Brenda, particularly in her role as a copy editor of this book. I am grateful to Joseph Mihelic and Donald McKim, my colleagues at the University of Dubuque Theological Seminary, and to Roger Nicole, Clark Pinnock, Gerald Sanders and Kenneth Kantzer for providing important information and advice. As usual, Edith Baule of our seminary library staff has given invaluable assistance in obtaining books and checking publishing data. James Gingery, our newly appointed seminary reference librarian, Mary Anne Knefel and Duane Cavins have also been immensely helpful in this area. Finally, I want to thank Peg Saunders, our faculty secretary, for her painstaking typing of this and many other manuscripts in the past.

Some of the material in this book has been presented in the form of lectures at a Presbyterian Pastors' Conference at Hope Presbyterian Church in Spicer, Minnesota; a workshop at the First Covenant Church in Omaha, Nebraska; a Reformed Pastors' Conference at Trinity Reformed Church in Fulton, Illinois; the Board of Directors' National Meeting of the National Association of Evangelicals in Chicago; and at the following schools: Gordon-Conwell Theological Seminary, Winebrenner Theological Seminary, Wheaton College, Asbury Theological Seminary, Rockford College, Central Baptist Theological Seminary and Northern Baptist Theological Seminary.

Contents

Foreword:
The Surprising Optimism
of Donald Bloesch

WITH *THE FUTURE OF EVANGELICAL CHRISTIANITY: A
Call for Unity Amid Diversity* Donald Bloesch, a minister in the
United Church of Christ and a professor of theology at the
Presbyterian University of Dubuque, continues his reflections
on a strand of Christian faith concerning which he has already
written several other substantial books.* Bloesch's definition of
"evangelical" is light on sociology, but carefully nuanced for
theology and religious practice: "An evangelical is one who
affirms the centrality and cruciality of Christ's work of reconciliation and redemption as declared in the Scriptures; the
necessity to appropriate the fruits of this work in one's own life
and experience; and the urgency to bring the good news of this
act of unmerited grace to a lost and dying world" (p. 17).
Bloesch makes a point of insisting that his subject is "evangelical Christianity" rather than "evangelical Protestantism" because he finds the resources of Roman Catholicism helpful at

---

*Among Bloesch's other books examining or expounding evangelical Christianity
are *The Ground of Certainty: Toward an Evangelical Theology of Revelation* (1971), *The Evangelical Renaissance* (1973), *The Orthodox Evangelicals* (1978), and the two-volume *Essentials of Evangelical Theology* (1978, 1979). Richard Lovelace used the occasion of the
1983 publication of *The Future of Evangelical Christianity* to review the contributions of
Bloesch's prolific pen in *Renewal*, vol. 3, no. 3 (Nov. 1983).

many points. It is this which leads him to the conclusion that "the evangelical message cannot maintain itself apart from the catholic concern with tradition and the means of grace." And it is why he claims that "the most authentic kind of evangelicalism is a catholic evangelicalism" (p. 5).

The most remarkable thing about this book is that Bloesch is optimistic about the future of evangelical Christianity. In this he runs counter to much of the recent serious literature on the subject. James Hunter, for example, concludes his pioneering sociological inquiry, *American Evangelicals: Conservative Religion and the Quandary of Modernity* (Rutgers University Press, 1983), by predicting the decline of evangelicalism. A canvass of popular books and an extensive study of survey data convinced Hunter that evangelicals are increasingly at ease with the antisupernaturalistic mindset of what he calls "modernity." By accepting modern education, modern economic assumptions, modern commitments in politics and personal values, evangelicals subject their worldview to "still further mutations that will make it even less similar to the historical faith than it already is" (p. 133). For him, the future of evangelical life and faith is "dubious."

From a different vantage point, the evangelist Francis Schaeffer and his publicist son, Franky Schaeffer V, also have little hope for evangelical prospects. In books whose titles understate the extent of their disillusionment, *The Great Evangelical Disaster* and *Bad News for Modern Man: An Agenda for Christian Activism* (both Crossway, 1984), the Schaeffers excoriate their fellow conservative Protestants especially for failing to mount a singleminded opposition to legalized abortion. Francis Schaeffer argues that only moral weakness and a misreading of history can explain the failures of his fellow evangelicals to apply the resources of their faith to the current crisis. Franky Schaeffer's polemic is even sharper, marked as it is by a pervasive distaste, one could almost say contempt, for a great range of evangelical institutions and individuals.

Another less than triumphalist reading of the situation comes from the historians who contributed to *Evangelicals and Modern America 1930-1980*, George Marsden, ed. (Eerdmans,

1984). They are not so much overwrought like the Schaeffers as simply quizzical. In their chapters on evangelical experience in politics, theology, the mass media, the study of the Bible, American democracy, and several other topics, these historians seem most impressed with the ironies of recent history. They see evangelicalism, claiming to represent a perennial biblical Christianity, regaining visibility in American public life by either adapting to cultural fashions of the late 20th century or reasserting the vanished certainties of the 19th century. Yet many of these historians, more bemused than angry, are apparently content to do their work within evangelicalism despite serious doubts about its continuing Christian vitality.

By way of contrast, Donald Bloesch is remarkably positive about the evangelical future. Even more remarkable is the kind of evangelicalism about which he is optimistic. Not for Bloesch are nervous readings of the public pulse, panicked contentions for reductionistic fundamentals, or slick pandering to the fickle tastes of the mass market. For Bloesch the future belongs to an evangelicalism which can relive the best of historic Christianity at the same time that it carefully reaps the harvest of modern thought. Bloesch's orthodoxy is historic, but does not lapse into nostalgia or fundamentalism. His modernity is genuine, but does not supplant the faith.

Bloesch pictures evangelicalism as a positive force which, though beset by dangers on every hand, retains a great potential integrity. Merely to list some of the elements which make up this evangelicalism is to appreciate both the breadth of vision which inspires Bloesch and the self-defeating sectarianism which he rejects.

• Bloesch believes strongly that the first Christian priority—intellectually as well as spiritually—is living faith in Christ. Yet this affirmation does not drive him to mysticism, anti-intellectualism, or irrationalism.

• He affirms the necessity of scriptural authority because the written word of God communicates the living Word of Christ and the Spirit. But he also gently deprecates the recent precisionism involving inerrancy as missing the point of the Bible's importance.

• Bloesch greatly values the riches of the past, but he also warns against enslavement to encrusted historical rigidities.*

• He believes the church should be writing contemporary confessions to restate the old faith for the modern world. At the same time he criticizes confessional bodies for exalting their historic confessions over the living word of Scripture and the present voice of the Spirit.

• He values highly the structures of church traditions, in both worship and theology, even as he warns against the dangers of formalism and hierarchialism.

• He calls for a revitalization of eschatological preaching and theology. For Bloesch, however, these activities should unify and inspire the church, not divide it or trivialize it as eschatology has so often done in American evangelical history.

• Bloesch believes that the church must take firm positions on modern ethical issues. As an example, he stands for the ordination of women, but against the feminist reconstitution of theological concepts.

• Bloesch does not apologize for his vigorous opposition to abortion-on-demand. At the same time, he sees no possibility of providing absolutely unequivocal guidelines for every facet of this problem, and he believes that prolife convictions must remain subordinate to even more fundamental beliefs in the atoning work of Christ.

According to Bloesch, an evangelicalism constructed from these elements will endure. He can say this even after a full recital of the maladies which bedevil contemporary evangelical churches and institutions. For one so confident in the strength of evangelicalism, Bloesch is in fact amazingly candid about its problems.

Bloesch perceives difficulties in nearly every area: thought, church, and life. Some of these arise out of evangelicalism's own past, such as "the tendency to absolutize the Bible as a book" which leads to "a new rationalism and biblicism" (p. xxi). More generally, evangelicals are always prey to the dangers of a "fundamentalism [which] as a folk religion elevates human

*The range of authorities whom Bloesch finds useful is staggering, from the right-wing theonomist Rousas J. Rushdoony to Karl Barth, from Mennonites to Catholics, Methodists to Fundamentalists, and many others along the way.

tradition to practically the same level as God's self-revelation in Christ" (p. 21).

Theological dangers are compounded by ecclesiastical weaknesses. Evangelicalism is "a movement rent by growing schism" (p. 5). Evangelicals display a "marked sectarian propensity" and are prone to "elevat[e] nonessentials" (p. 11). They tolerate "the growing worldliness of the church" and so manifest little concern for unity among Christians (p. 65). Also, they consistently undervalue the life-sustaining character of the sacraments.

For Bloesch, however, the most serious problem is captivity to modern culture. Evangelicals too often find themselves in "ideological bondage to technological materialism" (p. 6). They are suspicious of "original, creative scholarship" (p. 10). Certain "'young evangelicals' often display . . . uncritical fascination with left-wing ideologies" (p. 11). They divide into mutually antagonistic "feminists and patriarchalists" (p. 62). They are polarized on abortion and nuclear arms. They are preoccupied "with behavioral requirements for evangelical clergy and faculty" (p. 63).

Above all dangers is the temptation "to politicize the gospel, to show how faith in God undergirds the American Way of Life" (p. 22). Bloesch perceptively points out that evangelicals are especially vulnerable to the lure of ideologies because of their general naiveté concerning "the influences of historical and cultural factors on religious commitment" (p. 68). Thus, Bloesch finds evangelicals selling their souls to the political left or the political right, letting themselves be undermined by feminism, fascism, or secular humanism—even sometimes when stridently denouncing these very positions.

Bloesch realizes that ideologies influence everyone, that none of us preserves an acultural Christian faith untouched by the *Zeitgeist*. Yet he feels that insensitivity to such mingling of the gospel and contemporary convictions is a particular evangelical difficulty. He concludes that evangelicals who do not perceive the generic threat—subordinating the gospel to *any* political, social, cultural, intellectual, or economic position—compromise the integrity of the gospel. Yet even here Bloesch is not downcast, for he finds within the evangelical heritage itself resources to counteract ideological captivity: "the authority of the Bible, the uniqueness of Jesus Christ, the meaning of the cross of Christ, the decisive role of the sacraments and the [unifying, evangelizing, reforming] mission of the church" (p. 83).

Bloesch does not seem overly concerned that his evangelicalism is an ideal. Early in the book he makes an implicit distinction between "the movement that presently bears the name *evangelical*" and "the classical tradition of evangelicalism" (p. 3). The latter—embracing Athanasius, Augustine, a substantial dose of Aquinas, Luther, Calvin, Wesley, the Puritans, the early Pietists, and a broad range of the Christ-centered faithful in more recent centuries—is for Bloesch the key. In a footnote he admits that his optimism is for "evangelicalism in its ideal form, in what it seeks to be, in what it is at its best" (p. 156, n.19). The obvious question is whether such an evangelicalism as Bloesch describes actually exists.

A natural question this may be, but it is not an essential one for the purposes of the book. If Bloesch cannot identify fully realized expressions of his ideal evangelicalism, he is in much the same position as those who speak of "genuine" Lutheranism, Roman Catholicism, or Orthodoxy. Like the proponents of these other ideals, Bloesch can point to shadows and types, to moments of realization, or to individuals in whom the ideal comes closer to reality. It is certainly legitimate for him to gather these shadows, moments, and individuals into a conceptual ideal, especially since he is able to present that ideal as such a forceful, attractive, and faithful version of Christian faith.

A more germane question still remains, however. If Bloesch admits that "the movement that presently bears the name evangelical" is but a partial realization of the evangelical ideal, why does he continue to single out *this* imperfect contemporary expression as the hope of the future rather than some other imperfect contemporary expression of a more general Christianity or of some other ideal-variation of the faith? In an illuminating exchange over this book in a *TSF Bulletin*, Vernard Eller asked Bloesch why he set such store by contemporary evangelicalism. Since those who now bear the name fall so far

short of Bloesch's ideal, since some who bear other labels often
come closer to Bloesch's ideal evangelicalism than those now
known as evangelicals, and since Bloesch is really talking about
an ideal *Christianity* for which all party labels are inappropriate,
why continue to focus so narrowly on the contemporary
evangelicals?*

Catholics may have a similar question. Even granting significant differences between an ideal evangelicalism and an ideal
Roman Catholicism, might it not be the case that as much of
Bloesch's ideal evangelicalism is to be found today among
Roman Catholics as among theologically conservative Protestants? This is a particularly important question for this book,
since Bloesch draws so charitably upon Roman Catholic
sources to flesh out his picture of an ideal faith and since he has
been so honest in charting the follies of contemporary
evangelicals.

In making use of Roman Catholic resources, Bloesch directs
his readers to "the doctors of the medieval church . . . as
sources for evangelical renewal in our day" (p. 116). Although
these authorities must be read with "biblical discrimination" (a
caveat which Bloesch applies also to the Fathers and the
Reformers), they may instruct evangelicals in theology, spirituality, and worship. More particularly, Bloesch calls for a cross-
fertilization between forms of spirituality, with Catholics ap-
propriating insights from the Reformers, Pietists, and Puritans,
and Protestants recapturing such Catholic practices as voluntary celibacy, religious orders, spiritual retreats, silent meditation, the intercession of the saints (within the doctrine of the
communio sanctorum), and (with Luther) "a Christocentric form of
Marian devotion" (p. 134). In a rare feature for a Protestant
book, Bloesch even cites Sirach and The Wisdom of Solomon
to support one of his arguments (though these references do
not appear in the "Scripture Index.")

If Bloesch makes such charitable use of Roman Catholicism,
why does he not go further and align his ideal evangelicalism

---

*"'Evangelical': Integral to Christian Identity? An Exchange Between Donald
Bloesch and Vernard Eller," *TSF Bulletin* (Nov.-Dec., 1983), pp. 5-10. That Bloesch's
response to Eller ultimately comes around to the meaning of justification suggests
the reason for Bloesch's ultimate commitment to evangelicalism.

with an ideal catholicism? Bloesch's objections to Catholicism represent refined expressions of traditional Protestant opinions: the Catholic Church fosters a "heteronomy" that establishes the church as the mediator of salvation (p. xxi). It artificially restricts itself to only one tradition in the church: "The Church of Rome is not catholic enough" (p. 51). Its leadership, including John Paul II whom Bloesch otherwise admires, "is fixated on the past" in its stubbornness concerning birth control and the marriage of priests (p. 86).

Despite these weighty objections, Bloesch is consistent. He does not contrast Catholic practice with evangelical ideals. He concedes, for instance, that evangelicals have been as guilty as Catholics in their pretentious efforts to dictate terms concerning the treasures of the gospel. He is willing, with Bonhoeffer, to perceive the fellowship of the saints in the Roman Catholic Church as much as in the other sects. He cites with approval the judgment of Philip Schaff that the Reformation was "the legitimate offspring" and the "greatest act" of the Catholic Church (p. 113). Given Bloesch's willingness to concede so much to Roman Catholicism and given his own admission that he is describing an evangelical ideal found only imperfectly among Protestants, what reason can he offer for championing an evangelicalism open to catholicism, instead of the reverse, as the most faithful way of following Christ in the late 20th century?

The answer takes us back to the basic optimism of this book. Bloesch prefers the evangelical ideal, even while drawing much from Roman Catholicism, because everything hangs for him on the work of Christ. Questions for which Roman Catholics provide more definite answers than do Protestants—on how that work is communciated in the present, how it is transmitted through history, how it unites believers into agents of a common kingdom—remain subordinate to the one great reality, "the irreversible victory of Jesus Christ and the continuing life-transforming reality of Pentecost, which confirms this victory in the hearts of all who believe" (p. 152). For Bloesch, the center and sum of the Christian message is the gospel, the evangel. For him it is classical evangelicalism which best proclaims that message.

It is also this same evangel which makes Donald Bloesch confident about the future, a future which will ultimately draw together the best that can be found in Roman Catholicism, Orthodoxy, and the Protestant bodies. For Bloesch this future is secure, not because of the feebleness of Christian effort, but because of "a centripetal power drawing evangelical Christians from all communions into a deeper unity—namely the movement of the Holy Spirit in these last days" (p. 152).

Donald Bloesch may overestimate the possibility of actually realizing the evangelical potential. He may underestimate the difficulties in moving from ideal to practice. But he has not misconstrued the liberating power of the gospel which unifies Christians even as it draws them from darkness to light. His unwavering fidelity to that power adds edification to the hopes of this fine book.

MARK A. NOLL
Professor of History
Wheaton College

Preface

I HAVE BEEN LED to write this book for several reasons. First, I wish to defend the thesis that evangelicalism today exists as a cohesive, growing movement and must therefore be taken seriously by the church at large, both Catholic and Protestant. Despite its tensions and schisms, it has an inner theological unity in the midst of external theological and cultural diversity. Those who claim to be evangelical today generally have a solid historical basis for doing so. At the same time, they tend to exclude some who also have biblical credentials and to include some whose fidelity to the faith of the Scriptures and the Reformation is suspect.

Most people who stand in the heritage of the Reformation have at least one foot in evangelicalism. Yet many of these people are unwilling to associate themselves with the evangelical renewal movement. Some are undoubtedly reluctant because any show of support for the evangelical cause might result in the loss of academic or social respectability. Others, who have a genuine fear of sectarianism, see the evangelical movement as promoting divisiveness in the churches.

I identify myself as an evangelical because I definitely share in the vision of the Reformers, Pietists and Puritans of a church under the banner of the gospel seeking to convert a world under the spell of the powers of darkness to the kingdom of our Lord and Savior, Jesus Christ. I have moved in this direction from an earlier fascination with existentialism, for I believe that the rediscovery of the gospel is the key to the renewal of the church in our day. Though painfully aware of the current heterodoxies which give a distorted picture of evangelicalism, I am happy to note that the greatest theologians of Protestantism in the twentieth century have identified themselves as evangelical: P. T. Forsyth, Benjamin Warfield, Karl Barth, Helmut Thielicke, G. C. Berkouwer and Emil Brunner. The obvious disagreements among these giants of modern evangelicalism are overshadowed by what they have in common: an unswerving commitment to the biblical message of salvation through the grace of God revealed and fulfilled in Jesus Christ, in his sacrificial life and death and in his glorious resurrection.

It is possible to speak, as does Clark Pinnock, of a growing divide in theology today between a reborn evangelicalism and a chastened liberalism, paralleling the conflict between fundamentalism and modernism in the earlier part of this century.[1] We certainly need to remember that not all theology accepts the gospel as a revelation of God; instead, it is often understood as the product of human faith and experience. I do not agree with some of my neoevangelical friends, however, when they argue that the gospel needs to be shored up or validated by external evidence. The Word of God is self-authenticating, though its claims can be made more clear and intelligible by an enlightened reason in the service of faith.

The common distinction today between "mainline" and "evangelical" is sociological, not theological. I myself stand in a mainline Protestant denomination, but I am committed to evangelical theology.

A growing number of Roman Catholics wish to be known as evangelical, theologically speaking, but culturally and sociologically they belong in another camp. I agree with Howard Snyder: "Evangelical Christianity today is more than a group of theologically conservative churches. It is decreasingly a specific branch of Western Protestantism and increasingly a transconfessional movement for biblical Christianity within the worldwide Church of Jesus Christ."[2] In this book, I try to show that the evangelical movement has a distinctive theological thrust and undergirding.

A second reason for writing this book is to warn my fellow evangelicals of dangers that could disrupt and splinter this renewal movement. I explore the openness of a growing number of Protestant evangelicals to Catholicism,* seeing in this reason for hope as well as for uneasiness. I have no compunction in referring to myself as a catholic evangelical, because I recognize the need for cultus, liturgy and sacraments in addition to personal piety and a love for the Scriptures. The current fascination with Catholicism among many evangelicals is an understandable reaction against individualism and rational empiricism. Yet there is the everpresent danger of a new heteronomy, of viewing the church as a mediator of salvation, of making church tradition equal to Scripture. We would be wise to maintain a certain critical stance toward catholicizing tendencies within Protestantism; at the same time, we are called to discover anew the catholicity of Protestantism.

I also address myself to the other kind of heteronomy, which is more germane to Protestantism than Catholicism—the tendency to absolutize the Bible as a book. When an absolute equation is made between the words of the Bible and divine revelation, the Word of God is placed in the power of man, since words and propositions can be mastered by reason. I do not wish to deny the propositional dimension of revelation; the divine meaning shines through the propositions set forth in Scripture, but it is not encased in these propositions nor in any human formulas. Many evangelicals, in their antipathy to mysticism and existentialism, are hardening into a new rationalism and biblicism. A. W. Tozer has ventured to predict that the conflict in the future will be between evangelical rationalism and evangelical mysticism.

I am not among those who wish to give up inerrancy and infallibility when applied to Scripture, but I believe that we need to be much more circumspect in our use of these and related terms. Scripture is without error in a fundamental sense, but we need to explore what this sense is. Evangelicalism must not be confused with an obscurantist fundamentalism, though all evangelicals should be fundamental in the sense of holding to the fundamentals of the historic faith of the church.

Finally, I try in this book to build bridges between the various strands of evangelicalism and also between evangelical Protestantism and the Catholic churches. At the same time, I point out where

---

* Whenever the word Catholicism is used, it refers to the beliefs and practices shared by the Roman, Eastern Orthodox, and Anglo-Catholic churches, unless the context indicates otherwise.

bridges cannot be built, where compromise is out of the question. I write with the firm conviction that evangelicalism can have a bright future if it seeks to be a unifying rather than a divisive force within world Christianity. Yet I recognize the fact that real unity entails an accord on doctrinal essentials as well as fellowship in the spirit. Love and truth need to be united, and we should not rest until we reach this goal.

There is an unfortunate tendency among some of us to "look down" upon theology and theologians! . . . I have heard some young people say: "I don't need any theology!" How ridiculous! They don't need to study about God?

GEORGE VERWER

Evangelicals are to be known in the world as the bearers of good news in message and life—the good news that God offers new life on the ground of Christ's death and resurrection. . . . The apostles did not go out into the world preaching . . . scriptural inerrancy, or a premillennial kingdom, or some of the other things that are made the foremost issues today.

CARL HENRY

There is hardly a Church that has not suffered from its success. And when I say suffered, I mean it has suffered in its power of witnessing [to] the Gospel. It has gained comfort, affluence, and influence, but it has lost its prophetic soul, it has fallen from its apostolic insight and succession.

P. T. FORSYTH

There can only be a church as a Confessing Church, i.e. as a church which confesses itself to be for its Lord and against its enemies. A church without a confession or free from one is not a church, but a sect, and makes itself master of the Bible and the Word of God.

DIETRICH BONHOEFFER

I

Introduction

For I am not ashamed of the Gospel. It is the saving power of God for everyone who has faith . . . because here is revealed God's way of righting wrong, a way that starts from faith and ends in faith; as Scripture says, "he shall gain life who is justified through faith."

ROMANS 1:16, 17 NEB

Every true progress in theology is conditioned by a deeper study and understanding of the Word of God, which is ever . . . renewing the Church, and will ever remain the infallible and inexhaustible fountain of revealed truth.

PHILIP SCHAFF

Some even talk of being saved by Christianity, instead of by the only thing that could possibly save us, the anguish and love of God.

WILFRED CANTWELL SMITH

Christianity can endure, not by surrendering itself to the modern mind and modern culture, but rather by a break with it: the condition of a long future both for culture and the soul is the Christianity which antagonizes culture without denying its place.

P. T. FORSYTH

IT IS COMMONPLACE, especially in establishment circles, to label any resurgence of biblical Christianity as "fundamentalist." Fundamentalism is a clearly defined movement within the church, and it is on the uprise today. Yet what is occurring as well is a reemergence of classical evangelicalism, and this poses a definite threat not only to fundamentalism but also and even more to liberalism.

Liberal religion is on the defensive today, despite the fact that its hold on the divinity schools of the great universities and the seminaries of most mainline denominations remains virtually intact. Even in these bastions of higher theological education, there is unquestionably a mounting interest in orthodoxy, particularly among the students. As a spiritual movement within the churches, liberalism is slowly but surely giving way to both classical evangelicalism and fundamentalism. The spell that it casts over the secular culture is still significant, though that too is eroding.

Evangelicalism is making a dramatic comeback in the mainline churches, but shadows loom on the horizon. A backlash against the evangelical boom is painfully evident. Among Lutherans, there is an increasing emphasis on baptismal regeneration, thus downplaying the need for personal decision. Among Reformed and Presbyterians, being born into the covenant community is often accorded greater value than either baptism or conversion. A bias against evangelicalism is also apparent in the new interpretation of mission as the self-development of deprived peoples or simply as the announcement of unconditional grace rather than the conversion of the spiritually lost. Reformed Christianity stresses *ecclesia semper reformanda* (the church always being reformed), but unless this is constantly seen in the light of the gospel, it invariably leads to latitudinarianism. Other ominous signs are the retreat into liturgy, the emphasis on the experiential over the cognitive in Christian education and the elevation of community consensus over biblical authority.[1]

Such developments only serve to intensify the growing reaction in lay circles against creeping formalism in church life and worship as well as against narrow denominationalism. The attraction for the electronic church among laity in the mainline churches is due in part to a thirst for biblical truth and even more for the spiritual reality that underlies this truth. Unfortunately, the hopes of many have been disappointed by the abysmal lack of solid biblical teaching on the part of the media preachers.

Evangelicalism as a spiritual renewal movement in the churches today cannot be adequately understood apart from its uneasy relationship to liberal Christianity. Religious liberalism, with its roots in the Renaissance and the Enlightenment, stresses the infinite possibilities of man. It sees the Christian life as a process of growth into salvation, which is redefined as spiritual maturity. Evangelical Christianity, on the contrary, which is anchored in Paul, Augustine and the Reformation, underlines the total depravity of man, his utter helplessness to save himself in the face of the vitiating power of sin. It regards salvation as a crisis by which one is transported from spiritual death into spiritual life.

One of the chief spiritual mentors of modern liberalism in its American guise is Ralph Waldo Emerson, with his romantic, optimistic view of human potentiality. A leading figure in the modern age who reflects the concerns of historical evangelical religion is Søren Kierkegaard, with his emphasis on Christ as both Savior from sin and Pattern for righteous living.[2] There is no doubt that Emerson's influence far exceeds that of Kierkegaard in popular American religion and culture, even among many of those who call themselves evangelical. Yet this may be changing, as the children of the evangelical revival are beginning to dig into the historical sources of their faith and rediscover the saints of biblical Christianity—Athanasius, Augustine, Calvin, Luther and Wesley.

In my opinion, the movement that presently bears the name *evangelical* stands in unmistakable continuity with the classical tradition of evangelicalism. At the same time, this is a broken continuity, for some are included as evangelical who are really Pelagian or semi-Pelagian, and some are excluded simply because they doubt the appropriateness of the term "inerrancy" when applied to Scripture. The word "evangelical" needs to be deepened and expanded if we are to do justice to the rich heritage it represents.

Evangelical, as used in this book, signifies an emphasis within Christendom or historic Christianity, one that intends to include as well as exclude. Its specific reference is to the doctrinal content of the gospel itself, with the focus on the vicarious, atoning sacrifice of Christ, on the unsurpassable grace of God revealed in Christ, which is laid hold of not by works of the law but by faith alone (Rom.

3:21–28; Col. 2:11–14; Eph. 2:4–8).[3] All Christianity will contain an evangelical element; otherwise the very claim to be Christian would be suspect. At the same time, the word "evangelical" is best reserved for that segment of Christianity that makes the proclamation of the biblical gospel its chief concern, that appeals to this gospel in its biblical setting as the final arbiter for faith and practice. Only the kind of preaching that celebrates the victory of Christ over sin and death and calls people to repentance and decision in the light of this victory can appropriately be designated as evangelical.

Today the battle is over biblical authority. Because Holy Scripture in all its parts witnesses to God's self-revelation in Jesus Christ, because the gospel of what God has done in Christ comprises the divine content of Scripture, evangelicals stress Scripture in its unity with the Spirit as the ruling norm (cf. John 5:46; 10:35; Rom. 16:25, 26; I Cor. 15:3, 4; I Pet. 1:10–12; II Pet. 1:20, 21; II Tim. 3:15, 16). All other norms—church councils, papal decrees, confessions, conscience and religious experience—are derivative from this higher norm. All are subordinate to the living Word of God attested to and revealed in Scripture.

Liberal Christianity, on the other hand, tends to read Scripture in the light of the wisdom and experience of modern culture. The truth of Scripture is judged on how it accords with the spirit of modernity. As a result, attention is focused no longer on the remission of sins through the atoning death and glorious resurrection of Christ but on any number of other things—character development, the cultivation of God-consciousness, salvation through education, psychological wholeness, existential commitment, social revolution, etc. The question is: Can this in any way be included under the rubric of evangelical religion, the faith of the apostles and Reformers? I am convinced that religious liberalism is basically incompatible with evangelical Christianity, though this is not to deny that it contains Christian elements. I also do not wish to preclude the very real possibility that some liberals who entertain a philosophy that stands at variance with biblical Christianity may still have an evangelical heart, i.e., they still may be in inward communion with the Christ whom they misunderstand. It is well to note that a growing number of revisionist theologians, including David Tracy[4] and Rosemary Ruether, readily acknowledge the tensions between their positions and historical evangelical religion.

I prefer the term "Evangelical Christianity" over "Evangelical Protestantism," because the evangelical thrust cuts across all denominational and confessional lines. Evangelical Christianity is not the only form of Christianity, but it is the truest and purest form. Yet it cannot stand by itself. The evangelical emphasis is not complete apart from structure and cultus. The evangelical message cannot maintain itself apart from the catholic concern with tradition and the means of grace. This is why the most authentic kind of evangelicalism is a catholic evangelicalism, and the purest form of catholicism is an evangelical catholicism.

An attempt is made in this book to differentiate the transcendent content of evangelical Christianity from its ideological form. Just as the gospel transcends and negates every formulation and witness to it,[5] so the true evangelicalism transcends and negates evangelicalism as a movement or party within the church. The gospel stands in judgment over all human ideologies, including the ideology of cultural evangelicalism.

In its ideal form, evangelicalism is a movement that points beyond itself to the gospel, a movement whose primary concern is to glorify not itself, its forms of worship, its doctrinal platform, its leading personalities but instead the message of the cross. The apostle Paul expresses what should be the sentiments of all evangelicals: "God forbid that I should glory except in the cross of our Lord Jesus Christ, by whom the world has been crucified to me, and I to the world" (Gal. 6:14 NKJ).

Evangelical Christianity is the true orthodoxy. Yet it is not an orthodoxy bent on preserving its own sacred traditions but one that uses these traditions to advance the cause of the gospel in the world today. Evangelical Christianity, in contrast to formalistic orthodoxy, seeks to lose itself for the sake of the salvation of the world.

Evangelicalism today presents the paradoxical picture of an emerging alliance of born-again Christians drawn from all communions and a movement rent by growing schism. Yet although there are centrifugal forces pulling evangelicals apart, there is also a unifying power bringing them back together. The key to evangelical unity lies in a common commitment to Jesus Christ as the divine Savior from sin, a common purpose to fulfill the great commission and a common acknowledgment of the absolute normativeness of Holy Scripture. Evangelicals of all stripes confess to an underlying affinity with their fellow believers no matter what their ethnic, denominational or confessional background. Evangelicalism may indeed be the ecumenical movement of the future because of this capacity to transcend age-old denominational and creedal barriers.

In the area of ethics, there is a developing consensus among evangelicals concerning the critical moral issues of our time. From the far right to the left, evangelicals find themselves in an unforeseen unity in their opposition to abortion on demand, pornography, euthanasia, and homosexuality as a valid alternative life-style. They are also increasingly acknowledging the sinfulness of divorce, a malady that has penetrated the evangelical as well as the secular world, though not to the same degree. Moreover, there is a growing agreement on the evils of nuclear and biochemical warfare. Billy Graham has become one of the leading voices on behalf of world peace.

A persistent temptation of modern evangelicalism is to rely on human strategy and technique in carrying out the great commission to make disciples of all nations (Matt. 28:18–20). Evangelicalism needs to break out of its ideological bondage to technological materialism and affirm once again the freedom of the gospel. The Word of God makes its own way in the world. It calls for our acclamation and honor but not for any undergirding to insure its success.

Jesus Christ does not need our aid, but he wishes to enlist us in his service. He does not need to be bolstered by our feeble efforts, but he invites us to share in his victory. He alone procures the victory over sin and death, but we can proclaim and celebrate what he has done. We can also cooperate with the Spirit of God in manifesting and extending this victory. We are the beneficiaries, not the causes, of this victory; at the same time, we can be instruments of the Spirit as he carries the impact of the reconciling and redemptive work of Christ into the world.

Even more dangerous than the desire to accommodate to worldly patterns of success is the pretension to possess the treasure of the gospel. The evangelical church has been as guilty of this as the Roman Catholic Church. We need to recover the biblical truth that we as Christians can never be masters but only servants of the Word. We can prepare the way, but we cannot force God to yield the treasure of salvation (neither through importunate prayer nor meritorious works). God will act in his own time and way, and sometimes he will act despite, even against, all our efforts and strategies.

Evangelicals today can best serve the cause of the gospel by refusing to join their liberal colleagues in trying to make the Christian religion credible or palatable to the "man come of age." Instead, they should try to regain the robust confidence of Calvin, Wesley and Whitefield, a confidence in the gospel itself to convert and renew. This does not mean that the gospel should be thrown at the world like a stone (an accusation leveled at the early Barth), but it does mean that the gospel should not be converted into a bridge that rests partly on worldly wisdom. The message of the cross will always confound the wisdom of the philosophers. As Paul so dramatically put it: "Jews demand signs and Greeks seek wisdom, but we preach Christ crucified, a stumbling block to Jews and folly to Gentiles, but to those who are called, both Jews and Greeks, Christ the power of God and the wisdom of God" (I Cor. 1:22–24 rsv; cf. 17, 18).

Rather than a bridge, the gospel is more appropriately likened to a battering ram that breaks down the defenses of the city of the world. It employs, moreover, a definite strategy and has a specific aim. Those whom the Word commissions do not hesitate to make use of the prevailing thought forms and symbols of a culture in order to challenge its pretensions. There cannot be theological points of contact between the gospel and the world, but there must be sociological and cultural points of contact. We must speak the language of our age even while seeking to overthrow its follies and superstitions.

The question today is what branch of Christendom can best survive in the uncertain future before us. Much conflicting advice is being given. Some counsel that we as Christians must learn to bend with the times. Others advise a retreat to a confessional stance of the past. Still others advocate a minimizing of doctrine and an elevation of liturgy and priestly ministrations.

It is my position that the future belongs to that branch of Christendom that is willing to make itself expendable for the sake of the evangelization of the world to the greater glory of God. This may well involve the death of denominations, even of mission boards and agencies, for the life of the paganized masses in the West and East.

II

The Problem of Evangelical Identity

Between the man who is bound to a God in heaven, and another who knows nothing of this bond, there is a contrast deeper than all other contrasts which separate men from men.

KARL HEIM

Christianity is not the sacrifice we make, but the sacrifice we trust; not the victory we win, but the victory we inherit. That is the evangelical principle.

P. T. FORSYTH

What disturbs me most about modern fundamentalism is its lack of spirituality, its utter carnality.

D. MARTYN LLOYD-JONES

Fundamentalism and orthodoxy in general are a petrification of Christianity; and modernism and all doctrines of immanence are its dissolution.

EMIL BRUNNER

EVANGELICALISM IN CRISIS

THE EVANGELICAL RESURGENCE forges ahead as conservative Protestant bodies gain in membership while the mainline denominations, including Roman Catholicism, barely hold their own in the light of the population increase or actually suffer losses in membership. Evangelicalism had one of its own in the White House in the person of Jimmy Carter, and its influence is also discernible in the Reagan administration.

While the evangelical renaissance continues, the term "evangelical" remains fluid. Even in the ranks of the far right, there is an amazing lack of consensus on what "evangelical" really implies.

In some strands of evangelicalism, there is an emphasis on experience over doctrine. We hear much of the "born-again experience" or the "experience of Pentecost," but very little of the need for correct theology and sacramental integrity. Evangelicals associated with the "New Pietism" frequently denigrate scholarship, especially in the area of theological and biblical studies. What they value is "relational theology," which focuses on cultivating a personal awareness of God and growing toward psychological and spiritual maturity.

Quite common in experientialist religion is a stress on extraordinary signs of having received the Holy Spirit. Miracles of healing, speaking in tongues, and prophecy are considered integral aspects of the life of a church based on the "full gospel." Where these extraordinary gifts are lacking, it is said, there is no fullness of the Spirit.

In other branches of evangelicalism, the focus is on biblical inerrancy and the need for rational corroboration of the claims of faith. Thus epistemology, not soteriology, becomes the watershed of evangelical faith.[1] Such a position betrays its distance from the Protestant Reformation, from early Protestant orthodoxy, and also from Pietism and Puritanism.

Modern evangelicalism is confronted with the embarrassing fact that its special emphases reveal considerable theological immaturity and even theological heterodoxy rather than dynamic, vibrant orthodoxy. Many of the cults and sects claim the signs, the special experiences, even inerrancy, yet their doctrines are manifestly unbiblical. The United Pentecostals, the Way, the Jehovah's Witnesses, the Moonies, and the Christadelphians are obvious examples. Several of these groups are avowedly anti-Trinitarian. A further cause for embarrassment is the number of celebrities who claim the so-called evangelical experience and yet whose lives testify against the truth of their experience.

Although evangelicalism constantly warns against the encroachment of worldliness, its accommodation to cultural norms and values is almost as noticeable as in liberalism. While it has been eager to maintain sharp lines of distinction from liberal theology, it has been too ready to come to terms with the technocratic mentality of our age. Busyness is considered more important than being in the truth, activism more commendable than contemplation. Evangelism is regarded as a technique to be mastered, not as a surprising movement of the Spirit into which one is caught. Teachers in evangelical colleges and seminaries are esteemed more as transmitters than as thinkers. Original, creative scholarship meets with suspicion in many of these circles. Significantly, many evangelical institutions of higher learning do not even grant sabbaticals to their faculties.

The electronic church, which is consciously evangelical, generally features those who are seen as successful according to the standards of a consumerist, technological culture. Sin is often portrayed as failure to make something of oneself rather than as revolt against God. With their emphasis on happiness and prosperity through faith in God, the electronic preachers tend to confirm the bourgeoisie in their complacency rather than convert people to a new way of thinking and living that calls into question the commonly accepted values of the technological society.[2]

The alliance of a major segment of evangelicalism with the political right is likewise a cause for concern on the part of those who affirm biblical Christianity.[3] Here the principal enemy is secular humanism, but there is no comparable prophetic indictment of technological materialism or nationalism. Far-right evangelicals often assail humanism as antifamily and propornography, but they tend to overlook the fact that at least some so-called secular humanists are actively engaged in combating evils of this kind.[4] Because of its stress on the autonomy and infinite possibilities of mankind, secular humanism (a life- and world-view having its roots in the Renaissance and the Enlightenment) does pose a serious challenge to the Christian understanding of life and traditional Christian values.[5] But secular humanism is not the only enemy, and it may not always be the principal enemy.[6]

Those who are sometimes known as "young evangelicals" often display a similar imbalance in their uncritical fascination with left-wing ideologies. For them the enemy is big business and capitalism; the shortcomings of socialism remain virtually unheeded. Their tirades against Anglo-American imperialism, without any comparable indictments of international Communist subversion, can only give comfort to the Soviet Union and its allies. This one-sided approach can also destroy the impact of their sometimes valid critiques of Western society.

Evangelicalism is in crisis not only because of its theological immaturity and isolation and its ideological coloration but also because of its marked sectarian propensity. It is inclined to function as a party within the church that promotes its own particular interests rather than as a genuine movement of renewal that is ready to sacrifice itself for the good of the wider church. A sectarian mentality exacerbates the tensions within the church by elevating nonessentials, whereas a catholic mentality binds the wounds of the church by focusing attention on essentials. Ideally, evangelicalism should be a spiritual movement of purification and renewal that breaks down ideological polarization, party division and class distinction within the church universal. In practice, evangelicalism has too often been an ideological movement of reaction which polarizes rather than unites and which fortifies rather than overcomes ethnic and class loyalties and biases. It should be recognized that in some periods of history evangelicalism has indeed approached the ideal of being a unifying and renewing force within world Christianity. If it could disengage itself from those forces that pull it in an ideological and sectarian direction, it might yet become the spiritually revolutionary and dynamic movement that it essentially was and is.

CURRENT MISUNDERSTANDINGS

Today, some of the definitions of what it means to be evangelical are too narrow. To equate evangelicalism with a belief in biblical inerrancy is to leave out many in the past and present who staunchly affirm the gospel in all its breadth and depth and yet who recoil from applying the term "inerrancy" to Scripture. "Inerrancy" can indeed be used to describe Scripture, but even many of its supporters acknowledge that it is an ambiguous term capable of lending itself to various interpretations. The term "infallibility" is stronger, in my estimation, but it, too, is not without ambiguity, since it can be used to denote quite different understandings of biblical authority. This does not mean that neither term should ever be employed, but it does mean that the essence of being evangelical must not be tied to any one symbol or slogan.

The experiential criterion is also too narrow in determining the substance of evangelical faith, particularly where this means a datable, rapturous experience. Even Philip Spener and Count Nikolaus von Zinzendorf, two of the luminaries of German Pietism, did not claim this kind of experience as integral to their faith.

Some scholars limit the term "evangelical" to eighteenth- and nineteenth-century revivalism and its descendants. But this disregards the awakening movements within Reformed and Lutheran churches in the late sixteenth and seventeenth centuries. It overlooks the resolute evangelical witness that has continued within Anglicanism from the sixteenth century on. Worse still, it leaves out the Protestant Reformation of the sixteenth century, which can only be rightly understood as a rediscovery of the biblical gospel in an age dominated by formalism, scholasticism and superstition.

Even if we included the whole of the evangelical tradition within Protestantism, this would still be too limiting. An evangelical thrust has not been entirely lacking in the Catholic and Orthodox churches. Cyril Lucaris, Orthodox Patriarch of Constantinople in the seventeenth century, vigorously affirmed the priority and sovereignty of grace, though his teachings were condemned by synods held at Constantinople (1638, 1642), Jassy (1642) and Jerusalem (1672). Russian Orthodox bishop Tikhon in the eighteenth century based his spirituality almost exclusively on the Scriptures and had a warm sympathy for German Pietists and English Evangelicals. A number of Roman Catholic theologians, notably Augustine, Ambrose, Ambrosiaster, Pascal[7] and in our own day Hans Urs von Balthasar and Ida Friederike Görres, are identified with such evangelical themes as divine election, the radical pervasiveness of sin, the sovereignty of grace, the cruciality of faith for salvation, and the substitutionary atonement. One could also make a case that there is a definite evangelical strand in Thomas Aquinas[8] and in some of the Catholic mystics (though not in all).[9]

In some circles today, evangelicalism is virtually equivalent to premillennialism and even to dispensationalism. One of the key issues is whether the rapture of the saints will occur before or after the great tribulation at the end of the age. Such a position connotes a sectarian mentality, for it reduces evangelicalism to a sect or party within the church, sadly out of contact with the broader stream of Christian tradition.

At the opposite extreme, we find those who conceive of evangelicalism in too broad or inclusive a way. Some argue that anyone can be called evangelical who acknowledges Jesus as Savior and Lord. But this would include many Unitarians and Arians, who clearly stand outside the mainstream of evangelical, catholic faith. Others contend that anyone who experiences forgiveness or inner peace must be an evangelical Christian. This would then open the door to any number of cults that deny the basic precepts of historic Christian faith. A similar problem arises with those who base the case for evangelicalism on the reality of a personal communion or personal relationship with Jesus Christ. To make evangelicalism roughly tantamount to Christian supernaturalism or classical theism is to risk confusing evangelical theology with a philosophy of religion in which the saving work of Christ plays no crucial role.

There are many who define "evangelical" on the basis of a particular approach to Holy Scripture. Some hold that the hallmark of evangelical Christianity is an affirmation of the divine authority and inspiration of the Bible. Yet this could include sacramentalist Roman Catholics, Moonies, Mormons, the Local Church of Witness Lee, the more tradition-bound Eastern Orthodox, and many others who would find it difficult if not impossible to accept the basic message of the Protestant Reformation.

In an illuminating and provocative article in *The Christian Century*, Peter Schmiechen maintains that all Christian theology is by definition evangelical and that it is wrong for any particular theological movement to claim the word "evangelical" for itself.[10] Yet this is to overlook the fact that many theologians, though speaking out of a Christian orientation, tacitly if not explicitly deny the motifs that have characterized evangelical Christianity in the past—*sola gratia* (salvation only by the grace of God), *sola fide* (justification by faith alone), *sola scriptura* (Scripture as the final arbiter for faith and practice).[11] We can certainly consider a theology that does not incorporate these themes as deficiently Christian, but can we condemn it as non-Christian? Pelagius in his battle with Augustine surely cannot be described as evangelical, but he can still be regarded as representative of a continuing theological position in the church.[12] Similarly, Erasmus, who was drawn into a conflict with Luther on the sovereignty of grace and the bondage of the will, was still writing Christian theology, albeit not evangelical theology. Albert Schweitzer could accept neither the deity of Christ nor his vicarious, substitutionary atonement; it was the mystical Christ that was the focus of his concern. His admirers claim that he was a model Christian, but he certainly stood outside the circle of evangelical faith.[13] There are theologians in the contemporary period who underline the need for an existential encounter with Christ and yet view the Bible as a basically unreliable witness. Can they in all honesty be included under the rubric of evangelical?

Dietrich Bonhoeffer is instructive in this connection. Though acutely aware of the dangers of religious triumphalism, he nonetheless held that some communions are closer to the truth of the gospel than others. In his view, the Evangelical church, the church that stands in the tradition of the Reformation, is "the true one," even though it cannot claim to be in and of itself "the essential church."[14] It can claim, however, to be "the church of the Gospel," for, despite its faults, it can be deemed a more fitting instrument of the grace of God than the church that rejected the Reformation. Yet Bonhoeffer readily acknowledged that the fellowship of the saints (*sanctorum communio*) was also present in the Roman Catholic Church and in various sects.

For Bonhoeffer, the Evangelical church exists in tension not only with Catholicism but with liberal Protestantism as well. He contrasted "the church of the Gospel" with the hodgepodge of voices in the ecumenical movement:

> The churches included in the World Alliance have no common recognition of the truth. It is precisely here that they are most deeply divided. When they say "Christ" or "Gospel," they mean something different.[15]

REDEFINING "EVANGELICAL"

Before redefining "evangelical," it is necessary to explore the historical background of this word. It was not used in a partisan or polemical sense until the sixteenth century when the Reformers increasingly designated themselves as Evangelical as opposed to Roman Catholic.[16] As early as 1520 Luther referred to "those who boldly call themselves Evangelicals" and in 1522 to "this common Evangelical cause." Several years later Erasmus acknowledged the common usage by describing "some who falsely boast they are Evangelicals." When the Reformers called themselves Evangelicals, they did not think of themselves as a schismatic group within the church but as representatives of the true church—the church founded by Jesus Christ and based on the biblical gospel.[17]

In the spiritual movements of purification subsequent to the Reformation, Pietism and Puritanism, the term "evangelical" became further refined to include the necessity for the personal appropriation of the gospel. The so-called Evangelical movement in eighteenth-century England, Scotland and Wales associated with the names of George Whitefield, John and Charles Wesley, Daniel Rowlands and Howel Harris gave special emphasis to the new birth without intending to minimize or downplay justification (though the dialectic between justification and regeneration was not always maintained).[18]

"Evangelical" is derived from the Greek word *evangelion*, meaning the gospel or message of good news concerning what God has done for us in Jesus Christ. Because this message is the dominant theme of the New Testament and is indeed present in anticipatory form even in the Old Testament, evangelicals maintain a high view of Scripture as well as fidelity to the gospel. Because the gospel focuses upon God's free, unconditional grace rather than on human achievement or merit, evangelicals steadfastly affirm *sola gratia* (salvation by grace alone).

"Evangelical" can therefore be said to indicate a particular thrust or emphasis within the church, namely, that which upholds the gospel of free grace as we see this in Jesus Christ. An evangelical will consequently be Christocentric and not merely theocentric (as are the deists and a great many mystics). Yet it is not the teachings of Jesus Christ that are considered of paramount importance but his sacrificial life and death on the cross of Calvary. The evangel is none other than the meaning of the cross.

Evangelicalism may take the form of a particular party within the church, but its intention is not to remain a mere party but instead to

serve as a catalyst that unifies the whole church under the gospel.[19]
Today, as in the time of the Reformers, the Pietists and the Puritans, evangelicalism is best understood as a movement of spiritual
renewal within the wider church. Its purpose is not simply to enhance the spiritual life, moreover, but to renew the church by calling it back to its theological and biblical foundations. It is a movement based on and reformed by the gospel as attested in Holy
Scripture. It seeks not to advance itself but to serve the cause of
Jesus Christ and his kingdom. Though ready and willing to challenge heresy, its basic orientation is positive, since it focuses on the
glad tidings of God's act of reconciliation and redemption in Jesus
Christ. Unlike ideological movements, it is willing to sacrifice or lose
itself for the truth of the gospel and the well-being of the church. It
seeks to confess not a party line (a characteristic of sects) but the
holy catholic faith, the faith shared by the entire church.

The substitutionary atoning work of Christ on the cross has special significance for evangelicals. This is not the whole of the gospel,
but it is the essence of the gospel. A key verse is I Cor. 15:3:
"Christ died for our sins according to the scriptures" (KJV). What is
at stake in the battle that evangelicals wage is not only the
significance of Christ and the meaning of his salvation but also the
integrity of Holy Scripture. Scripture's account of Christ's life, passion, death and resurrection must be seen as trustworthy and reliable.

In stressing the vicarious atoning death of Christ for our sins,
evangelicals see this as an act performed not simply by Christ as
man but by Christ as God. Various cults incorporate theories of
penal redemption and substitutionary atonement but deny the deity
of Jesus Christ. The Jehovah's Witnesses are a contemporary example of this aberration.

In evangelical theology, Scripture is the source; the atonement or
message of the cross is the central content. Later Protestant orthodoxy referred to the first as the formal norm and the second as the
material norm of faith. The incarnation of Christ is, of course, also
vigorously affirmed, but always the incarnation seen in the light of
the cross. As opposed to the mystical tradition in Catholicism, evangelicalism subordinates the incarnation to the cross, not vice versa.
Christ came into the world to save humankind through his dying

and rising again. It is not simply the event of the incarnation but the purpose of the incarnation that is decisive for our salvation.

From the evangelical perspective, true Christianity entails *doctrine, experience* and *life*. Whenever any one of these elements is underplayed or denied, something crucial to the faith of the church is lost. The great luminaries of evangelical Christianity—Irenaeus, Augustine, Luther, Calvin, Pascal, Forsyth and Karl Barth—sought to do justice to all these elements, though some assigned more importance to one than to another. It can be said that we are deficiently evangelical if we emphasize the *person* and *work* of Christ and treat lightly the *effect* of Christ in the lives of his people. Evangelicals, particularly in the tradition of Pietism and Puritanism, have underlined the need for regenerate theologians as well as correct theology. Here we see the difference between a formalistic orthodoxy and a vital, biblical faith.

At this point it is appropriate to define *evangelical* more precisely: An evangelical is one who affirms the centrality and cruciality of Christ's work of reconciliation and redemption as declared in the Scriptures; the necessity to appropriate the fruits of this work in one's own life and experience; and the urgency to bring the good news of this act of unmerited grace to a lost and dying world. It is not enough to believe in the cross and resurrection of Christ. We must personally be crucified and buried with Christ and rise with Christ to new life in the Spirit.[20] Yet even this is not all that is required of us. We must also be fired by a burning zeal to share this salvation with others.[21] To be evangelical therefore means to be evangelistic. We are not to hide our light under a bushel but manifest this light so that God might be glorified in the world (Matt. 5:15, 16).

If asked to list the key elements in a vital Christian faith, an evangelical in the classical sense might well reply: biblical fidelity, apostolic doctrine, the experience of salvation, the imperative of discipleship, and the urgency of mission. Holding firm to the doctrine taught by the prophets and apostles in Holy Scripture, evangelicals stress the need for personal experience of the reality of Christ's salvation as well as the need to carry out the great commission to teach all people to be his disciples and to call all nations to repentance.

Undergirding this whole pattern of discipleship and mission is a further element in the evangelical vision: the eschatological hope.

Evangelicals affirm as belonging to the essence of faith not only belief in the first advent of Christ but also hope for his second advent.
While the messianic kingdom is already present in the community
of faith, this kingdom is yet to be consummated and fulfilled in the
kingdom of glory. Evangelicals look forward not to a gradual evolution of humanity into a kingdom of freedom (the Enlightenment position) but to a cataclysmic intervention of the Son of God into
human history at his second coming. Yet this eschatological vision
not only has an apocalyptic dimension (dualism, supernatural intervention) but also includes elements of the prophetic hope—an earth
transfigured by the glory of God.

Evangelical theology not only entails the explication of the message of Scripture, but it is done by those who have experienced the
Holy Spirit as the interpreter of Scripture. This means that theology
is not only the language about faith but also the language of faith. It
cannot be stressed too often that true theology presupposes converted
or regenerate theologians.

Evangelicals maintain a high view of Scripture. They affirm its divine authority and its full inspiration by the Holy Spirit. They do
not hesitate to speak of the inspiration of words as well as of authors,
though this does not commit them to any theory of mechanical inspiration or dictation. They acknowledge Scripture as the medium by
which those who earnestly seek hear the voice of the living God (cf.
Rom. 16:25, 26). With St. Paul they regard Scripture as "the sword
of the Spirit" (Eph. 6:17), the sword by which the powers of sin
and death are routed and lives are renewed. Scripture is more than
edifying religious literature: It is the divinely chosen vehicle of
redeeming grace.

Furthermore, evangelicals have a high view of God. They affirm
his sovereignty over the world he created. In contrast to many im-
manentalist theologians today, they have no difficulty in addressing
God as "Lord" and "Master," even though they also see him as Savior and Friend, but he is Lord before he is Savior, Master before he
is Friend. What Kierkegaard called the infinite qualitative distinction between God and humanity, eternity and time, is integral to
evangelical faith. Even when they speak of the mystical union between Christ and the believer, they are acutely aware that this union
does not obliterate but instead more fully reveals the abysmal gulf
between deity and humanity. In upholding the sovereignty of God,

evangelicals also affirm the sovereignty and sufficiency of his grace. The word of God goes forth from him mightily and does not return to him void (Isa. 55:11).

Similarly, evangelicalism emphasizes the sovereign love of God, the love that conquers and does not simply accept. This love, moreover, is a holy love, since God is infinite majesty and holiness as well as boundless compassion. These attributes are inseparable, yet distinct. They were fully reconciled in the incarnation and cross of Jesus Christ where God both satisfied the demands of his holy law and demonstrated his incomparable self-giving love that goes beyond the law.

Despite a profound sense of absolute dependence on God, evangelicals are reluctant to speak of God's absolute power, since this connotes arbitrariness or lawlessness. They prefer to speak of God's sovereign will and to understand this as a will to love. Instead of focusing on the power of God's eternal decree, they dwell on the power of his suffering yet conquering love. In contrast, theologies that concentrate on the unrestricted, absolute power of God as well as those that posit a secret will of God at variance with his revealed will are in philosophical rather than biblical territory. To be evangelical means to affirm both the invincibility and the universal outreach of God's love. Indeed, the heart of the gospel message is that God loved the whole world, that he justified the ungodly even while they were yet in their sins (cf. John 3:16; Rom. 4:5; 5:6).

Finally, evangelicals have a high view of man. We were given dominion over the animals and made a little lower than the angels (Ps. 8:5–8 KJV). We were created in the image of God and elected for salvation by God. We were even chosen to be covenant partners with God. Yet evangelical theology does not have an exaggerated view of humanity. There is no identity with God even in the exalted state of mystical union. Nor is there deification if this means being transformed into divinity.

Evangelicals are pessimistic with regard to what human beings can do on their own but optimistic about what God can accomplish in and through them. Grace does not reduce man to nothingness but instead raises him to fellowship with his Creator. Irenaeus put it succinctly: "The glory of God is man fully alive." Amandus Polanus, sixteenth-century Basel professor and Reformer, stated the complementary truth: "The glory of man is the living God." In other words, the glory of man lies outside himself in Jesus Christ.

While recognizing the myriad possibilities given to humanity in creation and the new powers of faith, hope and love given in redemption, evangelical theology is agonizingly aware of the lostness and despair of humanity as well. It fully accepts the biblical testimony that sin has penetrated into every area of human existence, thereby distorting and corrupting the creative accomplishments of humankind (Ps. 14:1–3; 36:1–4; 53:1–3; Isa. 64:6; Jer. 17:9; Rom. 3:9–12, 23; 7:18; Eph. 2:3; 4:18). It is not averse to speaking of the bondage of the will, the incapacity of sinful human beings to come to God or to do the good that God demands. Although fallen humanity is still free in the things below, it is not free in the things above—in the area of morality and salvation. As sinners we still have free choice, the freedom to do what we please, but it is only by grace that we receive the liberty of the children of God, the freedom to do what pleases God.

EVANGELICALISM, ORTHODOXY AND FUNDAMENTALISM

From this list of theological distinctives, it might be inferred that evangelicalism is merely a form of traditionalism or what might be called orthodoxism. Such is far from the case. Evangelicalism seeks to be orthodox, but it places its orthodoxy under the judgment of the Word of God. The ruling norm for faith is not the creeds and confessions of the church, nor the consensus of the church fathers, nor the affirmations of the Reformers (though all of these may function as subordinate norms). Instead, the infallible standard is the biblical Christ whose word is communicated through and attested in Holy Scripture. Church tradition also serves as a vehicle and witness of the living Word of God, but as a secondary, not a primary witness (unlike Holy Scripture).

Evangelical theology holds that what Christ says today does not contradict what his witnesses say in Scripture but may go beyond it, as the Spirit of Christ clarifies and makes explicit what may be only implicit in the text. Against an orthodoxy that is content to live in the past and does not seek a fresh word from God in Scripture, evangelical theology shares the confidence of the Puritan divine John

Robinson that "the Lord has more light and truth yet to break forth out of his holy Word."

At the same time, evangelicals vigorously object to the current tendency in neo-Protestantism to draw a cleavage between God's self-revelation in Christ and the biblical testimony. We have this revelation only in the earthen vessel of the prophetic and apostolic witness in the Bible. To bypass this witness or to seek a Word that in effect supersedes this witness is to veer either toward rationalism, in which we interpret the Bible through the eyes of a secular philosophy, or toward mysticism, in which we try to get beyond words and concepts altogether. Neo-Protestants following Schleiermacher and Hegel often appeal to the Spirit over the Bible. But the Spirit does not overthrow God's inspired Word, but instead enables us to hear it anew, to understand it rightly, and to apply it to our lives.

Doctrinal orthodoxy will always rank high on the agenda in authentic evangelicalism, but orthodoxy in thought is never enough: We must also have orthodoxy in life, orthopractice. Christian practice is as necessary as Christian doctrine, though in some periods of history one of these will probably have to be stressed more than the other. The evangelical seeks to be not only a herald of the true gospel but also a servant of the One who has embodied this truth.

Just as evangelicalism is not to be identified with an orthodoxy oriented to the past or divorced from life, so it must not be confused with fundamentalism. Fundamentalism as a folk religion elevates human traditions to practically the same level as God's self-revelation in Christ, attaching inordinate importance to such things as the pre-tribulation rapture, the seven dispensations, Sabbatarianism, and the various taboos on liquor, tobacco, dancing, the theater, etc.

The preaching of the gospel, it might be supposed, would be central in worship services of fundamentalist churches. The sad but irrefutable fact is that in many cases the sermons consist largely of reductionist Bible studies (in which the biblical passage is reduced to a topic of current interest) instead of the proclamation of the good news of God's act of reconciliation in Jesus Christ.[22] In some of these so-called biblical sermons, the grace of Christ is barely mentioned, and what we then have is the preaching of law rather than gospel. Equally disturbing is the frequency with which sectarian themes form the content of the sermonic witness rather than God's saving work in Jesus Christ. Or the preacher begins sharing his own personal experiences, and the gospel is then in danger of being confused with an interior state of subjective illumination.[23] Still another temptation is to politicize the gospel, to show how faith in God undergirds the American Way of Life. Here as elsewhere an affinity can be discerned between cultural fundamentalism and an accommodationist religious liberalism.[24]

Evangelicalism unashamedly stands for the fundamentals of the historic faith, but as a movement it transcends and corrects the defensive, sectarian mentality commonly associated with fundamentalism. Though many, perhaps most, fundamentalists are evangelicals, evangelical Christianity is wider and deeper than fundamentalism, which is basically a movement of reaction in the churches in this period of history. Evangelicalism in the classical sense fulfills the basic goals and aspirations of fundamentalism but rejects the ways in which these goals are realized.

III

The New Conservatism

We do not belong to our Lord Jesus Christ, nor can we be of God's church, except it be by following the pure doctrine of the law and the gospel.

JOHN CALVIN

Orthodoxy is a willingness to fight and, if necessary, die for the continuity and authenticity of the tradition.

THOMAS ODEN

So carnal is the body of Christians which composes the conservative wing of the Church, so shockingly irreverent are our public services in some quarters, so degraded are our religious tastes in still others, that the need for [sanctifying] power could scarcely have been greater at any time in history.

A. W. TOZER

He who boasts of orthodoxy . . . sins against Justification by Christ alone, for he justifies himself by appeal to his own beliefs or his own formulations of belief and thereby does despite to the Truth and Grace of Christ. Once a Church begins to boast of its "orthodoxy" it begins to fall from Grace.

THOMAS TORRANCE

THEOLOGICALLY CONSIDERED, the new conservatism is by no means a monolithic movement. It includes a wide variety of people from the far right to the right of center on the theological spectrum. Depending on one's perspective, it even embraces some who could properly be classified as centrist and yet who are especially intent on preserving the abiding values and essential doctrines of the historic faith. All of the various strands in the new conservatism would gladly accept the term "evangelical" with very few exceptions (mainly on the far right). Even pastors and theologians who stand in the theological tradition of Karl Barth and Emil Brunner have no compunction in identifying themselves as evangelical, though the left wing of the neo-orthodox movement might feel uncomfortable with this designation.[1]

In this chapter I shall delineate the various movements that are part of the new theological conservatism and name persons and churches associated with each one. I shall be frank in stating my own allegiance and showing where the future of a vital evangelical Christianity lies.

FUNDAMENTALISM

Fundamentalism represents the right wing of the evangelical movement, though it contains thrusts and ideas that signify a divergence from classical Protestant orthodoxy. Essentially, fundamentalism is a phenomenon of the late nineteenth century and the twentieth century. It arose specifically to counter the growing modernism in the churches, evidenced in the often uncritical acceptance of the theory of evolution and the historical-critical method in biblical interpretation. Fundamentalism has thus for the most part been a defensive movement designed to safeguard the supernatural elements in the faith.

The movement derived its name from twelve pamphlets entitled *The Fundamentals: A Testimony to the Truth*, published from 1910 to 1915.[2] It took on a more organized form in May of 1919, which saw the convening of the World Conference on Christian Fundamentals in Philadelphia. Among the doctrines affirmed were the divine inspiration of Scripture, the deity of Christ, the substitutionary atonement, the creation and fall of man and the personal and imminent return of Christ. On the whole, fundamentalism has stressed the plenary, verbal inspiration of Scripture, and only in its later development has special emphasis been placed on biblical inerrancy.[3]

One of the hallmarks of fundamentalism is the inordinate attention given to eschatology. Besides the visible, imminent return of Christ, it has generally upheld the millennial reign of Christ on earth before the final consummation of all things in the kingdom of God. This premillennial doctrine differentiates fundamentalism from the theology of the Reformation (which was basically amillennial) and from the Puritans and Pietists (who were generally postmillennial).[4] One strand of fundamentalism has adopted the dispensational form of premillennialism in which history is said to be divided into seven dispensations, the last of which will be the millennial reign of Christ from an earthly Jerusalem. Dispensationalism makes a sharp distinction between the church and the messianic kingdom of Christ and speaks of the rapture of the saints into glory before the great tribulation that immediately precedes the premillennial coming of Christ. Dispensationalism was given special promotion in the widely circulated *Scofield Reference Bible.*

Another hallmark of fundamentalism is its separatism. This is most prominent among the dispensationalists, who dwell on the twilight of the church in the end times and the need to separate from the apostate (mainline) churches. Fundamentalists like to appeal to Paul's warning against fellowship between the children of light and the children of darkness (II Cor. 6:14). The hard core of the fundamentalist movement has expressed its displeasure with Billy Graham because of his willingness to cooperate with nonfundamentalist Christians in his evangelistic crusades. Graham's participation in a Russian Orthodox-sponsored peace conference in Moscow (May, 1982), in which he acknowledged a certain degree of religious freedom in the Soviet Union, has further riled the evangelical right wing.

In the area of epistemology, fundamentalism represents a kind of evangelical rationalism, since it identifies the revelation of God with the propositions of Scripture. Its approach is either deductive, by which we deduce logical conclusions from metaphysical first principles (as with Gordon Clark) or inductive, by which we reason from particular facts to general conclusions (as with Charles Hodge). Being a defensive movement, fundamentalism gravitates toward an apologetic theology which seeks to justify the tenets of the faith at the bar of reason. Any conflict between reason and revelation is due either to faulty logic or to a misleading use of Scripture. One of their critics contends that for fundamentalists "saving faith" is indistinguishable from "warranted belief," belief validated by the canons of scientific rationality.[5] Not all fundamentalists elevate reason over faith, but even a theologian like Cornelius Van Til, who argues that one must begin with faith presuppositions, calls Christianity "an absolute rationalism."

Fundamentalism is also noted for its emphasis on individual salvation and the church's spiritual mission. Needless to say, it has been conspicuously deficient in the areas of ecclesiology and social ethics. This is not to suggest, however, that it is without a social vision. The early fundamentalists were one of the main forces behind the prohibition movement, and their spiritual descendants are active in the right-to-life and antipornography movements. Yet its social message can be criticized for focusing on curtailing wayward human passions while neglecting the plight of the economically deprived and the politically oppressed (including racial and ethnic minorities).

What has prevented fundamentalism from being in the foreground in the battle against social injustice is its tacit and sometimes open alliance with capitalism.[6] It is common in these circles to identify Christian values and the American Way of Life, and to regard economic prosperity as a providential sign of sanctity.

Fundamentalism as a religious movement is a complex phenomenon, and there is some disagreement in scholarly circles on how it should be defined. Ernest Sandeen sees the roots of fundamentalism in the coalescing of the eschatological views of the Plymouth Brethren and the late scholastic orthodoxy of the so-called Princeton School of Theology (Charles Hodge, A. A. Hodge, Benjamin Warfield).[7] George Marsden regards fundamentalism as a broader movement, including a large part of the revival tradition, and argues that it is the direct heir of nineteenth-century evangelicalism.[8] In my estimation, fundamentalism is a distinctly modern expression of historic evangelicalism, reflecting as well as obscuring significant motifs and emphases of the evangelical heritage.

One strand of fundamentalism has its roots in evangelical Pietism. The spirituality of this group is manifested in the Bible and missionary conferences that still continue across the nation and in other countries. The other strand is closer to confessional or scholastic orthodoxy. Its conferences are inclined to be of a more intellectual nature, with an emphasis on points of doctrinal precision. The Philadelphia Conference on Reformed Theology is an heir to this particular tradition, though the sponsors of the conference have moved from a rigid fundamentalist posture and are better classified as neofundamentalist or neoevangelical.[9]

Fundamentalism has made special inroads in the Presbyterian and Baptist churches. Pockets of fundamentalism remain in the Presbyterian Church (U.S.A.), the Reformed Church in America, the American Lutheran Church, the Lutheran Church in America, the American Baptist Churches in the U.S.A., and the Southern Baptist Convention.

Churches today that stand more or less in the tradition of separatistic fundamentalism are the following: the General Association of Regular Baptist Churches, the Conservative Baptist Association of America, the Independent Fundamental Churches of America, the Independent Fundamental Bible Churches, the Baptist Bible Fellowship, the Fundamental Baptist Fellowship, the Bible Presbyterian Church, the Missionary Church, the Christian (Plymouth) Brethren, the Fellowship of Grace Brethren Churches, the Fellowship of Independent Evangelical Churches and Grace Gospel Fellowship. There are some other denominations that have been noticeably influenced by fundamentalism, but their ethnic or confessional particularity differentiates them from the wider fundamentalist movement. They include the Lutheran Church–Missouri Synod; the Wisconsin Evangelical Lutheran Synod; the Churches of Christ; and the Reformed Episcopal Church. Parachurch movements that can be categorized as fundamentalist are the American Council of Churches, the International Council of Churches, the World Fundamentalist Fellowship, Word of Life, Youth for Christ, Operation Mobilization and Campus Crusade for Christ.

Theological schools reflecting the fundamentalist mentality include Dallas Theological Seminary, School of Religion of Bob Jones University, Grace Theological Seminary, Capital Bible Seminary, Western Conservative Baptist Seminary, Liberty Baptist College and Seminary, Luther Rice Theological Seminary, and Faith Evangelical Lutheran Seminary. One could add to this list a large number of Bible schools, for example the Criswell Bible Institute, the Moody Bible Institute, Northeastern Bible College, the Multnomah School of the Bible, Washington Bible College, the Philadelphia College of the Bible and the Prairie Bible Institute. Some of these institutions (such as Dallas Seminary and the Moody Bible Institute) represent a more open fundamentalism, not averse to cooperating with other evangelical Christians. Others (such as Bob Jones University) typify a closed fundamentalism, which anathematizes those who engage in fellowship with Christians regarded as heterodox.

A number of publishing houses are committed to advancing the fundamentalist cause: the Moody Press, Vision House, Victor Books (Scripture Press), Regal Books, and Loizeaux Brothers. Some of these also publish books from authors whose spiritual affinities are closer to neofundamentalism and neoevangelicalism.

Magazines that mirror the fundamentalist ethos are the *Fundamentalist Journal*, publishing arm of Jerry Falwell's ministry; the *Southern Baptist Journal*; the *Baptist Bible Tribune*; *Christian News*; *Sword of the Lord*; *Christian Beacon*; *Bibliotheca Sacra*, a high-powered theological journal based at Dallas Seminary; *Voice*, published by the Independent Fundamental Churches of America; *Moody Monthly*; and *Lutherans Alert*.

Among the spiritual leaders and philosophical lights of the fundamentalist movement in its early days were William B. Riley, Arthur T. Pierson, Charles R. Erdman, J. Frank Norris, Clarence E. Macartney, Arno C. Gaebelein, T. T. Shields and R. A. Torrey. More recent on the scene are John R. Rice, Carl McIntire, Ian Paisley, J. Oliver Buswell, Cornelius Van Til, Gordon Clark, John F. Walvoord, Robert Lightner,[10] René Pache, Hal Lindsey, James Robison and Jerry Falwell.[11] Princeton Theological Seminary professors Benjamin Warfield and A. A. Hodge, whose roots lay in the older scholastic Calvinist orthodoxy, prepared the way for fundamentalism by contending that Scripture is without error in matters of science and history as well as faith and morals.[12] Norman Geisler, professor of systematic theology at Dallas Seminary seeks to combine Thomism and dispensationalism. His empathies are with an open fundamentalism that is willing to engage in dialogue with opposing views.[13] J. Gresham Machen, one of the founders of Westminster Theological Seminary, rejected the fundamentalist label and preferred to be known simply as "orthodox."

In recent years political movements such as Jerry Falwell's Moral Majority, Christian Voice and Religious Roundtable indicate that a resurgent fundamentalism is breaking away from privatism and individualism. Among characteristic themes of these movements are the right to life, a strong military defense, the integrity of the family, the evil of forced busing, prayer in the public schools and free enterprise. Their strength belies the ever recurring rumor that fundamentalism is in eclipse.[14]

Fundamentalism at its best has preserved the supernatural dimension of the faith in an age when the mainline churches and seminaries have too readily accepted the naturalistic presuppositions of the higher critics. It has also maintained a needed critical stance toward the theory of evolution, whose scientific basis is still very much in question.[15] Again, it has fostered personal fellowships of faith where the innermost needs and concerns of its people are satisfied, where the koinonia (fellowship of love) is very much in evidence. The recent involvement of fundamentalism in politics is not altogether to be deplored. Though it is inclined to oversimplify and take an absolutist position against abortion, its advocacy of the rights of the unborn child is consistent with the historic Christian witness on this question. Fundamentalism, moreover, has continued the strong missionary emphasis that certainly belongs to a vital evangelical Christianity.

At its worst, fundamentalism has promoted divisiveness in the church by elevating sectarian tenets (such as the pretribulation rapture) into doctrinal essentials. It has also been guilty of maintaining a docetic view of Scripture which in fact denies the true humanity of Scripture. By refusing to deal with the question of historical and cultural conditioning in the writing of Scripture and by insisting on the literal facticity of practically everything reported in Scripture, it encourages obscurantism and thereby sets up false stumbling blocks to faith. Finally, in the area of interpersonal relationships, fundamentalism can be justly accused of promoting a rigid patriarchalism which has denied to women their rightful role in the ministry of the church.

NEOEVANGELICALISM

Since the end of the Second World War, there has been a significant shift in the attitudes and concerns of many of those who have come out of fundamentalism. While the doctrinal basis is still more or less intact, the emphasis has changed, and it is therefore appropriate to speak of a "neoevangelical" movement. This is one of the principal strands in the emerging new evangelicalism, which is broader and deeper than any one movement or school. Neoevangelicalism seeks to relate the historic evangelical faith to current needs and problems in the church and in the wider society.

Within neoevangelicalism, moreover, two distinct strands can be detected. The first signifies a cautious opening to modern trends which might best be described as neofundamentalism. The second is a more progressive evangelicalism which seeks to move beyond a rigid position on biblical inerrancy. Both these movements wish to be known as evangelical rather than fundamentalist, but only the second is inclined to reject the fundamentalist label.

While the right wing of the neoevangelical movement is particularly insistent on the inerrancy of Scripture, the moderate and left wings prefer to speak of the infallibility of Scripture.[16] Following Hodge and Warfield, the right-wing evangelicals nonetheless qualify inerrancy, claiming that only the original manuscripts or autographs (which are no longer available) are without error. This allows for critical textual work on the various copies and translations. When moderate neoevangelicals employ the term "inerrancy" in reference to Scripture, they generally have in mind its teaching or doctrine.

A rationalistic apologetics is still very much in evidence among neoevangelicals; at the same time, there is an attempt to dialogue with antirationalistic modern philosophies and learn from them. As in the older fundamentalism, there is a special interest in the rise of the cults and the need to meet this challenge. The task of reconciling the conflicting claims of science and religion is also a major preoccupation.[17] Among the moderate and left-wing evangelicals, there is a marked openness to theistic evolution, the idea that God is at work in the process of evolution.[18] C. S. Lewis is held in high esteem by almost all neoevangelicals and is considered a model in the apologetic task.

In contrast to the older fundamentalism, neoevangelicals have not hesitated to speak out on the problems of race, poverty and war. Carl Henry's *The Uneasy Conscience of Modern Fundamentalism* was a harbinger of an awakened evangelical social consciousness.[19] Neoevangelicals have also become involved in the right-to-life movement, but they generally maintain a critical stance toward the political new right.

An openness to Christians of other traditions is another salient feature of neoevangelicalism, marking a definite break with the separatistic mentality of the older fundamentalism. The emphasis is no longer on *separation* from the mainline denominations but rather on the *infiltration* of these denominations. Many people who can be categorized as neoevangelical cooperated in the ecumenical evangelistic campaign known as Key '73, and nearly all identify with the Billy Graham crusades, which sometimes even have Catholic sponsorship. The anti-Catholicism that has so often tainted fundamentalism is not nearly so evident in neoevangelicalism; yet there is a continued resistance to many of the emphases and practices within Catholicism.

Among neoevangelicals, premillennialism recedes into the background, though this is still the dominant position of those on the right. Many moderate and left-wing evangelicals are moving toward amillennialism and some even toward postmillennialism.[20] All neoevangelicals are united with their fundamentalist brethren in affirming the second advent of Christ and seeing it as a cataclysmic intervention into human history.

Whereas fundamentalists of the dispensational variety look to late nineteenth-century revivalism and those of the Reformed variety appeal to the Calvinistic Reformation and Protestant orthodoxy, neoevangelicals are ready to include among their spiritual forbears not only the Reformers and their orthodox interpreters but also the Pietists and Puritans. The Puritans in particular are being increasingly appreciated, especially in the neo-Reformed strand of neoevangelicalism.

In the area of biblical interpretation, we find a growing diversity in the ranks of neoevangelicalism. In the right wing, there is a general acceptance of textual or lower criticism but still a profound distrust of higher or historical-literary criticism. The moderate and left-wing neoevangelicals have no difficulty in accepting historical investigation of Scripture, including even form and redaction criticism, but they are emphatic that such investigation must be separated from the naturalistic presuppositions that have dominated this kind of study in the past.[21] Moderate evangelicals now stress the need to discover the intention of the author in the hermeneutical task. Those in the neofundamentalist camp continue to hold to the Mosaic authorship of the Pentateuch, the single authorship of Isaiah, the early date for Daniel, and the first eleven chapters of Genesis as literal history. A growing number of evangelical scholars, however, are willing to entertain other positions.

Neoevangelicals generally hold to propositional revelation, but not all are willing to equate revelation with the very words of Scripture. While recognizing that revelation may take propositional form, they are acutely aware that it contains a personal and historical dimension as well. Bernard Ramm prefers "conceptual revelation" to "propositional revelation," since the latter term tends to reduce faith to mental assent and pictures God as "dictating Euclidean theological statements to the prophets and apostles."[22] For Carl Henry, on the other hand, revelation, even though mediated through history and personality, is essentially ideational and propositional.[23]

The left wing of the new evangelical movement sees as the main theological issue not the inerrancy of Scripture (as in the right wing) nor biblical hermeneutics (as in the moderate wing) but the authenticity of a gospel existence. It is not right doctrine nor methods of biblical interpretation but faithfulness in vocation that should be given top priority. Some of the new breed of evangelicals sense an affinity to liberation theology, but they generally eschew violence as a means of accomplishing social justice, and they are not hesitant to subject the Marxist analysis of society to the scrutiny of Scripture. One part of the evangelical left is also involved in the feminist movement, though it repudiates the call of radical feminists for a new religion. Paul Jewett takes issue with many evangelical feminists in resisting their demand for a new inclusive gender language regarding God and Christ.[24]

Evangelical theologians who still move within the thought patterns of fundamentalism but try to engage in dialogue with the modern world include Francis Schaeffer, R. C. Sproul, James Boice, James Packer, Harold O. J. Brown, John Gerstner, John Warwick Montgomery and Harold Lindsell. Scholars noted for their ecumenical openness and innovative spirit but who generally remain within the framework of the Hodge-Warfield position on biblical authority and inerrancy are Carl Henry, Roger Nicole, John R. W. Stott, Morris Inch, Vernon Grounds, Ronald Nash and Kenneth Kantzer. Other scholars have questioned the emphasis on inerrancy but still see the Bible as the infallible standard for faith and practice. Among these are Clark Pinnock, F. F. Bruce, Bernard Ramm, H. M. Kuitert, Ray S. Anderson, Stephen Davis, Bruce Metzger, George Eldon Ladd, Kenneth Grider, Robert Johnston, Richard Coleman, Jack Rogers, Richard Mouw, James Daane, Ward Gasque, Paul Jewett, Lewis Smedes, M. Eugene Osterhaven and Timothy L. Smith. Not all these theologians would jettison the term "inerrancy," but they would reinterpret it in order to do justice to the true humanity of Scripture. The Lausanne Covenant, which declares that the Bible is "without error in all that it affirms," reflects the viewpoint of the dominant stream in neoevangelicalism today.[25]

Magazines that mirror the new mood in evangelicalism include *Eternity, Christian Scholar's Review, United Evangelical Action, Crux, The Evangelical Quarterly, Evangel* and *Evangelical Newsletter*. Concerns of the evangelical right find expression in the *Journal of the Evangelical Theological Society, The Westminster Theological Journal* and *Trinity Journal.* The influential *Christianity Today*, which reaches a wide and ever-growing audience, seeks to speak for both the evangelical right and center. *The Presbyterian Journal* has a similar orientation except that its clientele is mainly Reformed and Presbyterian. More avant-garde are *TSF Bulletin* (edited by Mark Branson) and *Themelios*, both reflecting concerns of the Theological Students Fellowship (the seminary branch of InterVarsity Christian Fellowship). Representing the evangelical left are *Sojourners, The Other Side, Radix, Katallagete* and the *Wittenburg Door.* The first freely acknowledges its indebtedness to the Anabaptists.

Neoevangelicalism has also made an impact among publishing companies. Those addressing themselves to neoevangelical concerns but still seeking to retain their fundamentalist constituency include Zondervan Publishing House, Thomas Nelson, Baker Book House, Tyndale House Publishers and Banner of Truth Publishing Company. More receptive to new trends in theology and the church but still unreservedly evangelical are the William B. Eerdmans Publishing Company, InterVarsity Press, Fleming H. Revell, Word Books and Paternoster Press.

Seminaries that are open to the new mood but retain distinctives associated with fundamentalism (such as premillennialism and biblical inerrancy) are Trinity Evangelical Divinity School, Denver

Theological Seminary, Covenant Theological Seminary and Talbot Theological Seminary (the last can also be placed in the category of open fundamentalism). Some other schools have moved further from fundamentalism but still preserve the evangelical heritage: Fuller Theological Seminary, Gordon-Conwell Seminary, Anderson School of Theology, Bethel Theological Seminary, Regent College, Eastern Mennonite Seminary, Eastern Baptist Theological Seminary, North Park Theological Seminary, Southwestern Baptist Theological Seminary at Fort Worth, Asbury Theological Seminary, Nazarene Theological Seminary and Trinity Episcopal School for Ministry in Ambridge, Pennsylvania.

Churches where neoevangelicalism has made a significant impact include the Evangelical Free Church, the General Conference Baptists, the Conservative Baptist Association of America, the Evangelical Covenant Church, the Salvation Army, the Evangelical Church of North America, the Wesleyan Church, the Church of the Nazarene, the Church of God (Anderson, Indiana), the Christian and Missionary Alliance, the American Baptist Churches in the U.S.A., the Southern Baptist Convention and nearly all the Presbyterian communions.

In the mainline denominations, various evangelical renewal fellowships seek to reform the church from within: the Lutheran Evangelical Movement (in the American Lutheran Church), Presbyterians United for Biblical Concerns (in the Presbyterian Church [U.S.A.]), the Presbyterian Lay Committee (in the PCUSA), the Covenant Fellowship of Presbyterians (in the PCUSA), the Fellowship of Witness (in the Episcopal Church), United Church People for Biblical Witness (in the United Church of Christ), the American Baptist Fellowship (in the American Baptist Church), the Brethren Revival Fellowship (in the Church of the Brethren), the National Evangelistic Association (in the Disciples of Christ), the United Church Renewal Fellowship (in the United Church of Canada) and the Good News movement (in the United Methodist Church).

Other parachurch movements reflecting an ecumenical kind of evangelicalism are the National Association of Evangelicals, the Evangelical Theological Society, World Vision, the Inter-Varsity Christian Fellowship, the International Fellowship of Evangelical Students, Young Life and the World Evangelical Fellowship.

What is important to recognize is that every person and fellowship mentioned in this section, as in the rest of the chapter, is moving. While some may be neoevangelical or neofundamentalist in this period, in another few years they may belong more properly in another category. Some neoevangelicals are returning to fundamentalism, whereas others are breaking through to a catholic vision of the church.

It should also be borne in mind that the various persons and groups mentioned have more in common than might be supposed. Evangelicals of all varieties sense an affinity to one another that simply does not exist, for example, between evangelicals and ideological liberals. Evangelicals, unlike Catholics and liberals, steadfastly affirm the divine authority and primacy of Holy Scripture over the church and religious experience. The tragedy is that they have frequently given more attention to those things that divide rather than unite them.

CONFESSIONALIST EVANGELICALISM

Besides the evangelicals coming out of Protestant fundamentalism, where the revival tradition plays a major role, many of those who call themselves both conservative and evangelical stand in the tradition of Protestant confessionalism. All evangelicals are confessional in the sense of confessing Christ as Lord and Savior, but I am thinking here of statements of faith that function together with the Bible as standards for faith and conduct. While the confession of faith is never placed on the same level as Scripture, it frequently carries the force of a divine mandate. Those who are confessional in this sense include the old Lutherans and the old Reformed, those who pride themselves on being Lutheran or Calvinist.

Confessionalist evangelicals seek to preserve continuity with the Protestant Reformation, and especially with the confessions of the Reformation or those that are in accord with Reformation faith. Conservative Lutherans are inclined to uphold both the Augsburg Confession and the Formula of Concord. Reformed Christians of continental lineage are particularly fond of the Heidelberg Catechism, the Belgic Confession and the Canons of the Synod of Dort. Anglo-Saxon Reformed Christians generally adhere to the Westminster Confession of Faith.

Confessionalist evangelicals distinguish themselves from fundamentalists by the important role they assign to the teaching authority of the church. While the church is always under Scripture, the Spirit of God, they believe, guides the church in its interpretation of Scripture. The church's interpretation must itself be subjected to the scrutiny of Scripture, but in fact they often read Scripture through the eyes of the confession rather than vice versa.

Among confessionalist evangelicals there is a growing social awareness as well as an increasing openness to critical biblical study. Horace Hummel's *The Word Becoming Flesh* demonstrates how a respected Missouri Synod Lutheran scholar using the tools of historical-literary investigation understands the formation of the Pentateuch and other Old Testament writings.[26] While adhering to the tradition of Mosaic authorship, he contends that much of the original material was amplified and supplemented by redactors.

Theologians in recent times who would identify themselves as confessionalist evangelicals include Fred Klooster, Horace Hummel, Anthony Hoekema, Cornelius Van Til, Martin Scharlemann, Edmund Schlink, Robert Preus, David Scaer, Paul Althaus, Ford Lewis Battles, G. C. Berkouwer, Peter Beyerhaus, Gerhard Maier and Walter Künneth. The last three have been active in the No Other Gospel movement (*Kein Anderes Evangelium*) in Germany. A much more irenic spirit is present in G. C. Berkouwer, who has been a source of inspiration to many neoevangelicals, especially to those of Presbyterian and Reformed backgrounds.

Theological schools that seek to be evangelical within a confessionalist context are Concordia Seminary (St. Louis), Concordia Theological Seminary (Fort Wayne, Indiana), Calvin Theological Seminary, Wisconsin Lutheran Seminary and Reformed Theological Seminary (Jackson, Mississippi). The last school, as well as Westminster Theological Seminary, contains both confessionalist and neoevangelical strands. Western Theological Seminary in Holland, Michigan, an institution of the Reformed Church in America, is confessionalist in its background, but it now has a neo-orthodox slant.

In the publishing world Concordia Publishing House, Northwestern Publishing House, Presbyterian & Reformed Publishing Company and Verdict Publications tend to maintain a confessionalist evangelical stance. The last is perhaps more neo-Reformational than confessionalist, but it has had a high regard for such confessions as the Lutheran Formula of Concord.

Verdict Ministries is of special significance, since it was founded by ex-Seventh-Day Adventists who rediscovered the message of the Reformation, particularly salvation by the righteousness of God apprehended by faith alone. Like the old Lutherans, Robert Brinsmead, editor of *Verdict* magazine, contends for a forensic, extrinsic justification, the kind portrayed in the Formula of Concord. At the same time, Brinsmead is adamant that the gospel alone is the final criterion and that it takes priority over every creedal or doctrinal formula. Verdict Ministries is steadily becoming more critical of classical Protestantism.

A number of magazines consciously promote a confessionalist evangelicalism: *Concordia Monthly; The Banner; Calvin Theological Journal; The Journal of Theology,* representing the Church of the Lutheran Confession; and the *Wisconsin Lutheran Quarterly. Lutherans Alert* is both confessionalist and neofundamentalist. *The Reformed Journal* brings together motifs drawn from both confessional Reformed theology and neo-orthodoxy.

Churches that can be called confessionalist evangelical are the American Lutheran Church; the Lutheran Church–Missouri Synod; Association of Evangelical Lutheran Congregations; the Wisconsin Evangelical Lutheran Synod; the Christian Reformed Church; the Reformed Church in America; the Protestant Reformed Churches in America; the Church of the Lutheran Confession; the Orthodox Presbyterian Church; and the Presbyterian Church in America. The new Presbyterian Church (U.S.A.) does not have any one guiding confession of faith but a book of confessions, which provides some kind of normativeness in the area of doctrine and conduct but which is frequently treated historically rather than juridically, as comprising statements that command allegiance. The confessional basis of the old United Presbyterian Church (now part of the PCUSA) was strengthened at its General Assembly in 1981 in that ordinands were required to "sincerely adhere" to the Book of Confessions. Not surprisingly, there was massive resistance to this proposed change.

The strength of confessionalist evangelicalism lies in its recognition that God is at work in the history of the church as well as in the history of biblical times, that the message of the gospel has been rediscovered and interpreted anew in certain periods of ecclesiastical history. Its weakness is that by emphasizing the merits of the creeds and confessions of the Reformation, it tends to underplay the working of the Spirit in the ecclesiastical history prior to the Reformation. There is also the temptation to absolutize the position of the Reformation so that confessional statements are seen no longer as broken symbols needing to be fulfilled in new interpretations but as sacrosanct symbols having eternal validity. The way is then open to a creedal idolatry, which confessionalist evangelicalism at its best rightly abhors.

CHARISMATIC RELIGION

Still another branch of the new conservatism is the movement of the charismatic or latter rain revival. I am here including traditional Pentecostalism as well as neo-Pentecostalism, the charismatic renewal within the mainline churches. Pentecostalism began at the turn of the century with the manifestation of glossolalia in a Holiness prayer meeting at Bethel Bible College in Topeka, Kansas. Charles Parham, founder of the college, and William Seymour, a black Holiness preacher and pastor of the famed Azusa Street Mission in Los Angeles, were the two men most prominent in the beginnings of modern Pentecostalism. Neo-Pentecostalism dates back to 1960, when a rediscovery of the charismatic gifts (especially the charism of tongues) described in I Corinthians 12–14 took place at St. Mark's Episcopal Church in Van Nuys, California, under the ministry of Dennis Bennett. The Catholic charismatic movement was born in Duquesne University in Pittsburgh in 1966.

Out of Pentecostalism and neo-Pentecostalism have emerged various charismatic theologies which seek to articulate the experience of the baptism of the Holy Spirit with its accompanying gifts, notably speaking in tongues. Originally the gift of tongues was thought to be the empirical evidence of having received the Holy Spirit, but in Pentecostal and neo-Pentecostal bodies today there is great diversity in this as in other areas. Some charismatic theologians regard speaking in tongues as only one of the evidences of the baptism of the Spirit.[27] Others virtually equate the baptism of the Spirit and the new birth, though most view Spirit baptism as an experience subsequent to conversion.

Where charismatic theology differs from mainstream evangelical theology is in its emphasis on the gifts of the Spirit and the present work of the Spirit in addition to biblical fidelity. Special attention is given to healing, the discernment of spirits, miracles, the word of knowledge, prophecy, speaking in tongues and the interpretation of tongues.

While classical evangelicalism has underscored the need to walk by faith alone, charismatic theologians contend that signs and wonders will follow the preaching of the Word. Frequently appealing to Hebrews 2:4 and Mark 16:17, 18, they believe that these signs are given to induce faith and confirm faith.

Whereas church tradition, both Catholic and Protestant, has generally perceived the Holy Spirit as an invisible and transcendent reality, charismatics regard the Holy Spirit as a demonstrable, empirical reality. God is not the Wholly Other of Barthianism nor is he the undifferentiated unity of mysticism. Instead, he is the power of creative transformation that revitalizes the believer from within, and this power can be felt and experienced.

A dualistic perspective is another hallmark of charismatic theology. In historic evangelicalism, the human predicament is believed to be rooted in an inherited spiritual affliction (original sin); for charismatic evangelicalism, on the other hand, the key to human misery is being held captive by a foreign power (the devil). While traditional faith stresses human bondage to sin, charismatic religion speaks of being victimized by the devil. Though not denying that sin and death are also major problems confronting the human race, it focuses primarily on the need to combat the demonic adversary to God and man called Satan, Lucifer or the devil.

In addition to the devil, charismatic theology also warns against demons which are sometimes but not always connected with the devil.[28] For the most part, demons are conceived in animistic terms, as disembodied spirits coming out of the nether world of darkness in search of bodies to inhabit. Demon possession is often regarded as a result of misfortune rather than of sin.

With such a strong emphasis on the devil and demons, it is not surprising that charismatics give much attention to the deliverance ministry. The exorcism of unclean spirits, which has only survived as a little-practiced ritual in the Catholic branches of mainline Christianity, is a major ingredient in the ministry of the charismatic or Pentecostal churches.

Where Pentecostalism (both classical and new) deserves special acclaim from the mainline churches is in its remarkable success in giving tangible expression to the priesthood of all believers. In stark contrast to the prevailing pattern in Reformed and Lutheran churches, where the pastor alone is seen as the minister in a congregation, Pentecostalism makes a place for many types of ministry including evangelism, prophecy, healing, deliverance and spiritual counsel. Moreover, it has given due recognition to the role of women in ministry. Half the staff of the Azusa Street Mission in 1906 were women. Aimee Semple McPherson was the celebrated founder and leader of the International Church of the Foursquare Gospel. Women leaders in the neo-Pentecostal movement include Agnes Sanford; Jean Stone, founder of the now defunct Blessed Trinity Society; Kathryn Kuhlman, whose ministry of healing extended throughout the world; Jean Darnall in England; and Catherine Marshall, Presbyterian laywoman and novelist.

Another area where charismatics have pioneered is in their surmounting of age-old barriers between churches. The ecumenical dimension is much more noticeable in neo-Pentecostalism than in classical Pentecostalism. The former movement is for the most part reformist, not separatist. At many charismatic gatherings, Catholics and Protestants have come together in a display of ecumenical fellowship that is rarely equaled in establishment Christianity. On some occasions there has even been sacramental intercommunion. Michael Harper, an Anglican charismatic, asserts that "this movement is the most unifying in Christendom today . . . *for only in this movement are all streams uniting, and all ministries being accepted and practiced.*"[20] Even Pentecostals who have been influenced by the separatism of dispensational fundamentalism often display an ecumenical openness not found in non-Pentecostal dispensationalism.

Less commendable, however, is the way in which many Pentecostals have embraced the prosperity doctrine, originating in New Thought and other varieties of neotranscendentalism. According to this doctrine, a sure indication of being in the favor of God is good health and financial prosperity. When we place our trust in God, it is said, we shall be given the desires of our heart (an appeal is often made to Psalm 37:4). We need only ask in faith, and we shall then receive. Indeed, we should claim what we ask for, since faith entails such bold presumption. Also fostered in these circles is the closely related idea of "seed faith," which means that to get wealth one must give wealth. Therefore, financial sacrifice may be viewed as a means to prosperity or as a test of obedience and faith. Not surprisingly, the prosperity doctrine is being repudiated by an increasing number of theologians in both Pentecostalism and neo-Pentecostalism.[30]

Pentecostalism in its widest sense has affinities to Montanism, radical Pietism and Christian mysticism. Its immediate precursor was the Holiness movement, in which Wesleyan theology was united with a kind of biblicistic fundamentalism. Most Pentecostals of the classical type are premillennial and some are dispensational. Neo-Pentecostalism is characterized by a deeper appreciation of the tradition of the whole church, including the church fathers.

Among the thriving Pentecostal churches in this country are the Assemblies of God;[31] the Church of God in Christ; the United Pentecostal Church International (which holds to a unitarianism of the second person); the Pentecostal Holiness Church; the Pentecostal Assemblies of the World; the Apostolic Faith Mission; the Elim Fellowship; the International Church of the Foursquare Gospel; the Open Bible Standard Churches; and the Church of God of Prophecy. Communions somewhat different from historical Pentecostalism in their general orientation but nonetheless making a real place for the gifts of the Spirit and various other Pentecostal emphases include the Catholic Apostolic Church and the New Apostolic Church.

Paraparochial movements associated with either classical or neo-Pentecostalism are Fountain Trust in England, the Full Gospel Business Men's Fellowship, the PTL Club, the 700 Club, Teen Challenge and the Blessed Trinity Society (now defunct). Religious communities where Catholic and Protestant charismatics have come together for the purpose of fellowship and mission include the Word of God community in Ann Arbor, Michigan; the People of Joy community in Phoenix, Arizona; the People of Praise community in South Bend, Indiana; and the People of Hope community in Newark, New Jersey.

Seminaries and Bible colleges that promulgate charismatic theology are the following: Melodyland School of Theology in Anaheim, California; Whole Word Theological Seminary in Oakton, Virginia;

Oral Roberts School of Theology in Tulsa, Oklahoma; Evangel College in Springfield, Missouri; Assemblies of God Graduate School, also in Springfield, Missouri; Faith Bible Institute in Oklahoma City, Oklahoma; Liberty Bible College in Pensacola, Florida; Berea Bible Institute in E. Montreal, Quebec; and Eastern Pentecostal Bible College in Peterborough, Ontario.

Magazines that carry the Pentecostal message should also be noted: *New Wine; New Covenant,* the voice of Catholic Pentecostalism; *The Logos* (Eastern Orthodox); *Theosis* (Eastern Orthodox); *Logos Journal; Renewal,* the magazine of Fountain Trust; *Full Gospel Business Men's Voice; Pastoral Renewal; Charisma; Charisma Digest;* the *Pentecostal Evangel;* and *Agora,* with roots in classical Pentecostalism and a reputation for the avant-garde. Some of these journals have in recent years become more consciously evangelical and less distinctively Pentecostal.

Among theologians who can be called Pentecostal or neo-Pentecostal are J. Rodman Williams;[32] Gordon Fee; Robert E. Cooley, president of Gordon-Conwell Seminary; Pat Robertson, founder of the 700 Club; Larry Christenson, a spark plug in the charismatic revival movement in the American Lutheran Church; Thomas Smail;[33] Michael Harper; Derek Prince; Arnold Bittlinger, prominent in renewal circles in German Protestantism; and Tormod Engelsviken, a pioneer in the charismatic renewal in Norwegian Lutheranism. Various Roman Catholic scholars, too, have been active in the charismatic movement: Edward O'Connor, Simon Tugwell, Donald Gelpi, Cardinal Léon Suenens, Josephine Massingberd Ford, Kevin Ranaghan, Stephen Clark and Ralph Martin (the last two from the Word of God community). Eusebius Stephanou, Gregory Gavrilides, Gerrald Munk and Angelo Hoty are representative of the charismatic renewal in Eastern Orthodoxy.

Pentecostalism and neo-Pentecostalism are to be included as part of the new conservatism, because their emphasis is on the restoration of biblical faith in all of its purity and power. In Catholic Pentecostalism this is united with an appreciation of Catholic tradition and a reaffirmation of the Marian doctrines and the papacy. Yet evangelical motifs are prominent among Catholic Pentecostals, and a few are even willing to critique church practice and doctrine in the light of Holy Scripture.[34]

Some may question whether neo-orthodoxy really forms a part of the new conservatism, but any serious reading of the writings of Karl Barth and Emil Brunner, for example, will show that their aim was the recovery of true orthodoxy. Their attack was leveled at both liberal theology and a dead or scholastic orthodoxy. Their hope was for the emergence of a living, dynamic orthodoxy that would be related to the contemporary situation. Their concern, moreover, was not only the renewal of theology but also the renewal of the church.

Neo-orthodoxy has been in partial eclipse in the past decade and a half. In 1974 Diogenes Allen of Princeton Seminary commented that the "most significant event [in recent years] has been the collapse of the middle ground between liberalism and fundamentalism." By the middle ground he had in mind the neo-orthodoxy of Barth, Brunner, the Niebuhrs and Tillich.[35]

Neo-orthodoxy emerged in the 1920s after the First World War and was sparked by Barth's *The Epistle to the Romans* (1918), which went into six editions. Originally known as the dialectical theology and in this country as the theology of crisis,[36] the new movement enlisted the support of many disillusioned liberals whose faith in the natural goodness of man and the dogma of progress had been irrevocably shattered. It also attracted some of those who had been identified with the old orthodoxy, such as John Mackay and Frederick Bronkema.

In its earlier phase neo-orthodox theology was largely shaped by Karl Barth, Emil Brunner, Eduard Thurneysen, Friedrich Gogarten and Rudolf Bultmann, though the last two began moving in another direction in the later 1920s. Hendrik Kraemer in the Netherlands; Dietrich Bonhoeffer, Otto Weber and Wilhelm Vischer in Germany; Daniel Jenkins in England; and Thomas Torrance in Scotland were also attracted to this movement. In Sweden Gustaf Aulén and Anders Nygren spearheaded a parallel movement, which might be considered a type of neo-Lutheranism.[37] The American contingent was best represented by Reinhold Niebuhr, who increasingly moved from an existentialist orientation toward classical orthodoxy.[38]

Conservative evangelicals have generally not been happy with neo-orthodoxy, mainly because of its openness to historical and literary criticism in biblical studies and its candid recognition of the element of myth in the Scriptures. Cornelius Van Til has denounced the neo-orthodox movement as a "new modernism," regarding it as a greater threat than the old liberalism. Charles Ryrie contends that "neo-orthodoxy is a theological hoax. It attempts to preserve the message of the Bible while denying the facts of the Bible."[39] On the other hand, Bernard Ramm believes that liberalism was not successfully countered until the rise of neo-orthodoxy.[40]

A particular distinctive of neo-orthodoxy is its stress on the uniqueness of the biblical revelation. This was already evident in the early writings of Karl Barth, where revelation was depicted in Kierkegaardian terms as "the Moment" when Eternity entered into time. The Bible itself was not seen as the revelation but as the original witness to the one and final revelation, Jesus Christ. God revealed himself fully and definitively once for all times (*Einmaligkeit*) in the person and work of his only begotten Son, Jesus Christ.

Revelation was said to have a dynamic character. It was not simply propositional truth but the reality of the living presence of God that could only faintly be grasped through propositions and concepts. Revelation was described in terms of "events" rather than "ideas," though the cognitive quality of revelation was never seriously disputed. Barth has been accused by some of his critics of "actualism," imposing a philosophical principle of truth as act upon the Scriptures.

A disjunction was also drawn between revelation and religion. Barth described revelation as the abolition of religion, and yet he acknowledged the possibility of a true religion, a religion purified of egocentricity, one that could serve as a vehicle of revelation. Just as revelation has its source in God's search for man, so religion is rooted in man's quest for God. Even empirical Christianity, it was said, must be judged in the light of God's self-revelation in Jesus Christ attested to in the Bible.

Neo-orthodox theologians have also been noted for their strictures on natural theology. Even Emil Brunner, who consistently affirmed the reality of a natural knowledge of God, nonetheless held that this knowledge always results in a misunderstanding because of human sin. Theology therefore cannot be built on an erroneous understanding of God but can only be based on the revelation of God in Jesus Christ, which brings people a true understanding of God's will and purpose for the world. Conservative evangelicals have been quick to fault neo-orthodoxy for downplaying or ignoring the general revelation of God in nature.[41]

An emphasis on the utter transcendence of God has also been characteristic of neo-orthodoxy. Barth in his earlier phase frequently referred to God as the Wholly Other (*totaliter aliter*), steadfastly affirming Kierkegaard's principle of the "infinite qualitative difference between God and man." In the early and later (as opposed to the middle) phases of his theology, Barth regarded the Bible and the church as only pointers to the Word of God, not as means by which we come to receive the Word of God. Here we see a disjunction or separation between the divine Word and the human words of the Bible. A continuing theme in neo-orthodoxy has been the "Word behind the words" in contradistinction to the "Word within the words" or the "Word becoming words." Unlike neo-evangelicalism, neo-orthodoxy has difficulty with the historic Christian affirmation that the Bible *is* the Word of God.[42]

The historic Christian conception of the sacraments is also called into question. No longer means of grace or salvific signs by which we receive the remission of sins and the power of the new life in Christ, they are often reduced to "vivid illustrations of the Word." Barth came to view baptism and the Lord's Supper as ethical ordinances affording us an opportunity to dedicate ourselves to the way of the cross. In his mind, only Jesus Christ can legitimately be referred to as a sacrament, a visible sign of an invisible grace. Joseph Haroutunian saw the means of grace as neither the sermon nor the sacraments as such but as interpersonal relations.[43]

Having inherited the Ritschlian suspicion of metaphysics, neo-orthodoxy placed the emphasis on ethics. The gospel was seen as a report of the saving deeds of God rather than a view of life and the world that competed with secular world views. This was more true of Barth than of either Brunner or Reinhold Niebuhr.

In the area of apologetics, neo-orthodox theologians unanimously criticized efforts to harmonize biblical and philosophical themes. The biblical-classical synthesis of the early church in which biblical doctrines were virtually Hellenized was laid at the door of apologetics. Yet neo-orthodox scholars have generally made a place for "eristics," the attack upon the cultural and philosophical presuppositions of secular man. Barth, as opposed to Brunner and Niebuhr, questioned the validity of the whole apologetic enterprise because of the almost irresistible temptation to compromise with secular thought. According to Tillich, Barth's theology is kerygmatic rather than apologetic, based on the conviction that the only way to reach secular man is through the power of the proclamation of the gospel itself. There nevertheless persists an apologetic element in Barth's *Church Dogmatics* in that he gives a biblical critique of non-Christian systems of thought. At the same time, he seeks to speak to the church and not to the world as such, though always with the hope that the world, too, might listen.

Finally, we should take note of the downplaying of sanctification by neo-orthodox theologians. Niebuhr concentrated on the sin of man rather than on the renovation of man through grace. He could even say that we are saved "in principle, but not in fact." Humility in the face of the awesome presence of God was more important for him than the victorious life in Jesus Christ. Barth made a real place for sanctification in his later writing, but even then he remained suspicious of human virtue. His emphasis was on the call to discipleship, never on the call to sainthood. His concern was not so much purity of life as ethical obedience to the social imperatives of the faith. The focus of neo-orthodoxy remained on God's invasion into history rather than on man's ascent to God. This explains in part neo-orthodoxy's aversion to Pietism and mysticism (here again we see an affinity with Ritschlian theology).

Additional neo-orthodox themes include the portrayal of sin as willful revolt against God and idolatrous pride (as opposed to ignorance and weakness);[44] a fascination with messianic socialism but stopping short of confusing a socialist utopia with the kingdom of God; a futuristic over a realized eschatology; and a tendency to see the kingdom of Christ as more inclusive than the empirical church.

The following theologians have continued to maintain the salient emphases of neo-orthodoxy: Helmut Gollwitzer, Rudolf Ehrlich, Jacques Ellul, Markus Barth, William Hordern, Arthur Cochrane, Werner Koch, Joseph Haroutunian, Ronald Goetz, David Demson, Paul Lehmann, W. A. Whitehouse, John Leith, Paul and Elizabeth Achtemeier and to a lesser extent Paul Holmer. Donald Dayton seeks to unite both a Wesleyan holiness tradition and an Evangelical Left orientation with Barthian theology. Philip Watson has tried to forge a synthesis between classical Wesleyanism and the Lundensian theology. Neo-orthodoxy has also proved to be a formative influence on Brevard Childs, Yale Old Testament scholar.

Churches in this country that have been heavily influenced by neo-orthodoxy are the old Evangelical and Reformed Church (now part of the United Church of Christ), the Reformed Church in America, the Lutheran Church in America, the former United Presbyterian Church in the U.S.A. and the former Presbyterian Church in the U.S. These last two denominations have recently merged to form the Presbyterian Church (U.S.A.). Among seminaries where neo-orthodoxy has made an impact are Princeton Theological Seminary, Lancaster Theological Seminary, Eden Theological Seminary, Union Theological Seminary (New York), McCormick Theological Seminary, Western Theological Seminary and the University of Dubuque Theological Seminary. Only the last two schools continue to reflect, at least in part, motifs associated with neo-orthodoxy.[45]

Periodicals that generally maintain a neo-orthodox slant are *Scottish Journal of Theology, Reformed Review, Interpretation* and to a lesser degree *The Reformed Journal.* The now defunct *Theology and Life* was neo-orthodox, with a pronounced ecumenical orientation. *Theology Today,* though at one time predominantly neo-orthodox, has become more pluralistic. The William B. Eerdmans Company is one of the few publishing concerns today that tend to promote neo-orthodox (especially Barthian) theology. The Westminster Press, an organ of the Presbyterian Church (U.S.A.), though once known as the voice of neo-orthodoxy, now stands closer to neoliberalism.

The question has been raised: Can one be evangelical and neo-orthodox at the same time? It is well to remember in this connection that Karl Barth attacked Emil Brunner for compromising the doctrine of *sola gratia,* which is probably the principal evangelical distinctive. Markus Barth has criticized both the sermons and the theology of Reinhold Niebuhr for taking as their point of departure not the gospel but the human predicament. Karl Barth himself has been indicted by conservative evangelicals for a universalistic thrust and for underplaying the decision of faith.

Yet it should be borne in mind that the leading spokesmen of neo-orthodoxy in both the recent past and the present definitely regard themselves as evangelical.[46] It can be shown, moreover, that neo-orthodoxy has generally endorsed the basic affirmations of the Ref-

ormation including *sola scriptura, sola gratia* and *sola fide.* Its view
of revelation has much more in common with the original Reformers
than its conservative critics care to acknowledge. Where neo-
orthodoxy can be described as deficiently evangelical is in its tendency to speak of the inspiration only of the writers of Scripture and
not also of the words, its emphasis on the objective atonement to the
detriment of subjective decision (this is not true of either Brunner or
Niebuhr), its stress on justification over sanctification (the later
Barth is here more balanced than either Brunner or Niebuhr) and
its reluctance to see the mission of the church in terms of the conversion of souls.

What are the prospects for neo-orthodoxy? While it is true that
both Emil Brunner and Reinhold Niebuhr are in partial eclipse, it is
also true that the 1980s are experiencing a Barthian renaissance (in
both America and Germany). The Karl Barth Society of North
America has been holding well-attended meetings for several years,
and books on Karl Barth are beginning to appear once again, especially in evangelical circles.[47] Barth is also being rediscovered by
some liberation theologians, who can identify with his call to ethical
obedience. It is interesting to note that while the political right
(Michael Novak and Jeffrey Hart) is beginning to draw upon Reinhold Niebuhr, so the political left sees in Barth a source of support.

In my opinion, neo-orthodoxy can be faulted not only for its neglect of the call to sainthood and the life of holiness but also for not
giving sufficient attention to the doctrine of the church and the sacraments. It sparked a renewal in theology but not a renewal of the
church, though this was its intention.[48] Neo-orthodoxy failed to realize that the Protestant principle needs to be united with catholic
substance if the church is to be revitalized and restored as the vehicle of the kingdom of Christ.

CATHOLIC EVANGELICALISM

The last category that I shall deal with is catholic evangelicalism,
a movement embracing not only mainliners who are seeking renewal within their respective denominations but also many who
have come out of a restrictive fundamentalism and have grown
weary of battles over nonessentials. Unlike restorationists, who simply wish to return to New Testament Christianity,[49] they are con-

cerned to maintain continuity with the tradition of the whole church. At the same time, they generally see the Bible as having priority over tradition. There is in this camp a stress on evangelical essentials but within the context of catholic faith. A serious attempt is made to uphold the inspiration and infallibility of Scripture but without getting bogged down in interminable warfare over inerrancy or the millennium.

Catholic evangelicals not only draw on the Reformation and the post-Reformation purification movements of Pietism and Puritanism, but they also encourage a renewed appreciation for pre-Reformation evangelicalism. In striving for a revitalized church in our time, they seek to enlist the support not only of the Reformers but also of the church fathers and doctors of the medieval church. Whereas fundamentalists and many Pentecostals look to separatist, nonconformist groups like the Donatists, the Montanists, the Novatians and the Waldensians,[50] catholic evangelicals appeal to the mainstream of the church, particularly to the early fathers.

In marked contrast to popular evangelical conservatism today, catholic evangelicalism is profoundly disturbed by the mindless activism that pervades the evangelical and indeed the wider Christian community. It sees the fascination with communication skills over sound theology and the concentration on church growth techniques over purity of worship as a sign of capitulation to the technological materialism of our age. Acutely aware of the need for training in discipleship, catholic evangelicals emphasize evangelism *and* nurture. While acknowledging the crucial role of evangelism in any vital Christianity, they are insistent that evangelism can never take the place of worship. Nor can social service preempt our obligations to draw near to God in prayer and adoration. In line with the catholic tradition at its best, catholic evangelicals stress being before doing, faith before works, contemplation before action.

At the same time, works whether of mercy or piety are by no means neglected. Indeed, a hallmark of the movement for catholic evangelical renewal is the attempt to hold justification and sanctification in balance. The Reformation emphasis on the justification of the ungodly must be united with the Catholic and Wesleyan concern for the sanctification of the godly. The call to repentance must be supplemented by the call to sainthood. Growth in faith is almost as important as the decision of faith.

Like classical Calvinism, this new kind of evangelicalism sees the church as always being reformed (*ecclesia semper reformanda*). The Reformation must continue, and this means that theological formulations as well as confessional statements need always to be further refined, amplified and even corrected.

A catholic evangelical church will be confessional in the sense that it will seek to confess the historic faith anew but in the language of our own age. Such a confession may well take the form of a confessional statement of faith, but this statement will always be seen as a broken symbol that allows for further amplification and even reformulation. The confession, moreover, will never have equal validity with the Bible but will always be under the Bible.

In contrast to the sectarianism that afflicts the ideological right wing of the evangelical movement, catholic evangelicals desire church unity. They are not content with spiritual unity but press on to the ideal of visible unity. This does not necessarily mean a super-church, but it does surely entail altar and pulpit fellowship between all the branches of Christendom. These people are also not satisfied with a panevangelicalism but entertain the hope of Evangelical-Catholic unity. At the same time, with confessionalist evangelicals, they have serious reservations about "unionism," the attempt to merge denominations for the purpose of greater efficiency. In unionism truth is invariably sacrificed to "love."

At the Chicago Call conference in 1977, two divisions became readily apparent in the catholic evangelical movement.[51] First, there were those who sought to underline Catholic concerns and subordinate Reformation emphases to a more inclusive thrust. The appeal was not to the Protestant Reformation of the sixteenth century but to the undivided church of the first five centuries. Persons identified with the New Covenant Apostolic Order (now the Evangelical Orthodox Church) and the new Oxford movement within Anglicanism could be included in this first strand within catholic evangelicalism.

The second strand was composed of persons who did not wish to bypass the Reformation but who believed that the coming great church must incorporate the valid and enduring contributions of the Reformation. For them, the path to renewal lies not in returning to a pre-Reformation golden age of the church but in identifying with the battle that the Reformation waged on behalf of purity in worship and doctrine. At the same time, unlike many confessionalist evangelicals, this segment of catholic evangelicalism does not accept the Reformation uncritically. With Jaroslav Pelikan, it regards the Reformation as a tragic necessity.[52] It was tragic because it sundered the unity of the Western church. It was necessary because the Church of Rome was not open to basic reform in doctrine, though it was amenable to various reforms in practice.

A third branch of catholic evangelicalism was also evident at the Chicago Call conference, and since then it has become more visible. This position, with which I identify, appeals not only to the Reform but also to the Revival. It sees the evangelical awakenings for all their excesses as something positive, and here the differences from neo-orthodoxy, the new Oxford movement and liberal Christianity become apparent. It believes that it is better to err on the side of enthusiasm than on the side of formalism. At the same time, it acknowledges the need for cultus as well as charism, for sacraments as well as inward spiritual experience. It shares the concern in the wider catholic evangelical movement for appreciation of the church fathers and medieval reformers, but it insists that the Roman and Eastern Orthodox traditions (as well as the Reformation tradition) must be purified of unbiblical practices and ideas before any kind of church unity can become a practical reality.

The catholic evangelicalism that I uphold seeks always to distinguish a vital Christianity from formalistic orthodoxy or ecclesiasticism. Even though it makes an important place for sacraments and an ordained ministry, it eschews sacramentalism and sacerdotalism. Like the Puritans, it also objects to unnecessary or overelaborate symbolism in the church and to a concern for vestments and liturgy over inward faith and experience. Nonetheless, with Calvin and other mainline Reformers, it also regards with disapproval an unstructured or totally free service of worship. It favors a liturgy of the Word and the sacrament, but with the sacrament subordinated to the Word.[53] Its objections to Roman Catholicism arise, at least partly, out of the conviction that catholicity is unnecessarily confined to one particular tradition in the church; therefore, the Church of Rome is not catholic enough. This criticism is shared by other strands of catholic evangelicalism, though the new Oxford movement, for example, is anxious to maintain a conciliatory stance toward Rome.

Among the luminaries in the past with whom I can identify in this connection are Richard Sibbes,[54] Philip Spener, Count Nikolaus von Zinzendorf, P. T. Forsyth, Philip Schaff,[55] Friedrich Heiler and Nathan Söderblom.[56] It was Söderblom who brought the term "evangelical catholicity" into prominence in the twentieth century.

People in our day who might be included in the catholic evangelical movement in its wider sense are Daniel Jenkins, Michael Green, Thomas Torrance, G. W. Bromiley, J. J. Von Allmen, J. L. Leuba, Max Thurian,[57] A. W. Tozer,[58] Klara Schlink,[59] Max Lackmann,[60] Howard Hageman, Richard Lovelace,[61] John Hesselink, Robert Webber,[62] Bela Vassady,[63] John Weborg, Robert Paul, Peter Gillquist[64] and Thomas Howard. Roman Catholic scholars who are striving for an Evangelical-Catholic rapprochement include Kevin Perrotta, Stephen Clark, Ralph Martin[65] and Kerry Koller (all related to ecumenical charismatic communities).

Publications that reflect this new mood are *Living Faith* and *"No Other Foundation,"* renewal magazines in the United Church of Christ; *New Oxford Review*, which seeks to bring together evangelicals and Anglo-Catholics; *Christian Challenge; New Heaven/New Earth; Again,* the voice of the Evangelical Orthodox Church; *Commonlife;*[66] and *Pastoral Renewal.* Publishing companies supportive of this kind of orientation include the Augsburg Publishing House, William B. Eerdmans Publishing Company, Servant Publications and Crossway Books (a branch of Good News Publishers). The last, whose editors are Jan and Lane Dennis, both conveners of the Chicago Call conference, seeks to voice the concerns of that brand of conservative evangelicalism associated with Francis Schaeffer and the L'Abri Fellowship and that kind of catholic evangelicalism associated with the new Oxford movement.

THE ROAD AHEAD

It should be kept in mind that the categories presented in this chapter are ideal types. No one theologian or spiritual leader fits completely into any one type, and most have associations with various types.[67] Both Luther and Calvin, for example, can be claimed by fundamentalists, neoevangelicals, confessionalist evangelicals and catholic evangelicals.[68] At the same time, because modern evangelicalism is so diverse, it is important to make distinctions for the purpose of showing who we are and where we are going.

Evangelicalism today is open and fluid, and this accounts for its strengths as well as its weaknesses (e.g., its surprising susceptibility to heterodoxy). A growing number of fundamentalists are moving toward neofundamentalism and neoevangelicalism. Pentecostals, even those in sectarian churches, are increasingly willing to identify with the larger evangelical community. Many neoevangelicals are moving toward what I have called a catholic evangelicalism. Some of the new evangelicals are discovering that they have much more in common with liberalism than was first supposed (e.g., various evangelical feminists). Others are finding the key to evangelical renewal in the theology of Karl Barth.[69] Still others are moving back into neofundamentalism and fundamentalism. We are witnessing today signs of growing retrenchment as well as new openness.

Richard Quebedeaux, always an astute observer of the evangelical scene, sees the principal cleavage today as between establishment evangelicals and young evangelicals. Without denying what is valid in his perception, I regard the new cleavage as between a sectarian evangelicalism united with the new right and an ecumenical evangelicalism that is concerned to bind the wounds that divide the churches today.

The new stirrings of evangelical sentiment within the mainline denominations[70] are a sign that all is not lost and that many evangelicals are splitting from their parent bodies prematurely. My advice is for evangelicals to remain within their respective denominations as long as they can, indeed, until they are practically forced to leave. Both Calvin and Luther, it should be remembered, did not wish to leave the Roman Catholic Church but were thrown out because they persisted in adhering to Reformation doctrine. Dispensationalists call their fellow evangelicals out of churches that they regard as apostate. But we should bear in mind that there are heresies on the right as well as the left, and dispensationalism itself is already a kind of heterodoxy.

It is important that the new conservatism not become allied with any ideology—either of the right or the left. Ron Sider, head of Evangelicals for Social Action, has tried to break through the ideological cleavage, as can be seen in his forthright stand against both abortion on demand and militarism.[71]

While there is much diversity in the evangelical fold, I believe that evangelicals of all varieties have more in common with each other than with liberalism or modernism. J. Gresham Machen was not far from the truth when he contended that evangelical Christianity and Protestant liberalism represent two different religions.[72] Yet this does not mean that many of our liberal colleagues and friends are necessarily non-Christian. While their interpretations of the faith can be questioned, it is undeniable that many of them continue to maintain a personal relationship with the living Christ that often conflicts with their theological formulations. Karl Barth kept a portrait of Schleiermacher near his desk and would sometimes point some of his ultraorthodox friends and students to this portrait with the words, "He too is a Christian." Evangelicals need to be charitable without being compromising. We, too, stand under the judgment of the Word of God, and if we persist in living in the past and closing our eyes to the real spiritual and moral issues of our time, then we will be judged more severely than the others (cf. James 3:1).

IV

Evangelical Disunity

Have nothing to do with stupid, senseless controversies; you know that they breed quarrels.

II Timothy 2:23 RSV

He will also judge those who cause divisions. Void of the love of God, they look to their own advantage and not to the unity of the church: for small and trifling reasons they rend the great and glorious body of Christ into pieces.

IRENAEUS

Union among Christians is becoming more and more an imperative necessity if they are to conquer in the great conflict with infidelity and anti-Christ.

PHILIP SCHAFF

You Christians must show me that you are redeemed before I will believe in your Redeemer.

FRIEDRICH NIETZSCHE

WITH SUCH A DIVERSITY OF STRANDS, it is scarcely surprising that the evangelical fabric is showing signs of strain. Membership is growing and giving increases; yet there are widening cracks in the citadel of evangelicalism. Carl Henry voices the new mood of uneasiness: "Despite its far-reaching theological agreement, the evangelical body lacks a sense of comprehensive family identity and loyalty."[1] Even this supposed theological agreement is open to question: there is ample reason to believe that the growing dissension in evangelical ranks has a theological as well as a sociological or cultural basis. To be sure, an inner bond of unity persists in the evangelical community, but how long this can be maintained in the midst of polemical strife is debatable.

Old divisions in the evangelical family are reappearing. One of these is Calvinism versus Arminianism. While Calvinists or Reformed Christians champion predestination, those whose theological heritage goes back to Arminius and Wesley stress the need for personal decision and obedience. Calvinists complain that Arminians sacrifice the sovereignty of grace for human potentiality. Arminians retort that Calvinists compromise human responsibility by an exaggerated emphasis on divine grace, which finally leads to philosophical determinism. It is becoming commonplace today to hear both Reformed and Lutheran theologians criticize "decisionism," which, in their view, is the latest variety of Pelagianism.

Another relatively ancient schism that is resurfacing is that between Calvinism and Lutheranism. Many neo-Lutherans are noted for their questioning of the third use of the law, the law as a guide for the Christian life, whereas Calvinists faithful to their tradition insist that the third use is the principal one. Calvinists accuse Lutherans of downplaying sanctification; Lutherans express an ever-recurring and sometimes justified fear that a rigid Calvinism ends in legalism.

Then there is the perennial battle between Baptists and those in the mainstream Reformation tradition over the meaning and mode of baptism. Baptists vigorously contend that the practice of infant baptism smacks of magic, especially where baptismal regeneration is affirmed. Reformed theologians argue that the promises of the covenant extend to the children as well as to the parents (cf. Acts 2:39), and therefore baptism as the sign and seal of these promises can legitimately be offered to infants.[2]

Lutherans generally hold that grace is imparted through the sacramental signs irrespective of whether the recipient has faith. The hope is that the infant when reaching the age of reason will discover and dedicate himself to the faith into which he was baptized. Whatever the case, regeneration has already occurred if there has been a valid baptism. One must struggle to remain true to one's baptism, but, Lutherans insist, to suppose that regeneration is withheld until one makes a personal commitment of faith smacks of the decisionist heresy.

Karl Barth has added fuel to the fire by withdrawing his support from infant baptism and concluding that believer baptism is the only practice that has biblical and theological sanction.[3] He sees baptism as an ethical ordinance of the church whereby the believer pledges to follow Christ in a daily walk of obedience. At the same time, it is a sign of God's incomparable grace poured out in Jesus Christ for all people. This grace is for us and with us before our decision, but not until we take up the cross and follow Christ in daily obedience is it manifested to the world.

Finally, it should come as no surprise that the conflict between amillennialists, postmillennialists and premillennialists is becoming more acrimonious after a decade of relative peace on this issue. What is surprising is that evangelical adherents of postmillennialism are beginning to express themselves. Support of what had seemed to be a discredited theory is coming from such Reformed bastions as Westminster Theological Seminary and the Christian Reconstructionist movement.[4] Within the ranks of premillennialism, debate is sharpening between the classical premillennialists, represented by George Eldon Ladd, and the dispensationalists, who hold that the church will be raptured into heaven seven years before the inbreaking of the millennial kingdom.[5]

In addition to these simmering historical conflicts, new divisions are beginning to appear in the evangelical movement. One of these concerns the charismatic renewal within the churches, which is welcomed by some evangelicals but castigated by others. This contro-

versy corresponds in part to that between the New Lights and the
Old Lights in eighteenth-century Congregationalism and in nineteenth-century Presbyterianism in America. It also has parallels to
the dispute between the Pietists and the Established churches in
Norway and Sweden in the late nineteenth and early twentieth centuries.

Charismatics urge their fellow Christians to seek a still higher experience, the baptism of the Holy Spirit, which brings power for
witnessing and a deeper degree of holiness. They insist, moreover,
that speaking in tongues is *the* sign or one of the principal signs of
having received this baptism of fire. Traditional evangelicals assert
that there is only one work of grace but with a twofold aspect—
justification and sanctification. To seek for a higher salvation de-
tracts not only from justification but also from faith and baptism.

Another salient indication of growing polarization in evangelical
ranks is the conflict between the so-called pietists and social activists.[6] Salvation, the pietists say, is an inward experience, with outward manifestations to be sure, but basically a matter of one's personal relationship with God. The social activists argue that salvation
is realized in the ongoing struggle on behalf of the poor and the
oppressed. Thus, the evangelical left tends to be politically activist,
whereas the evangelical right focuses much more attention on cultivating personal piety.[7]

There is also mounting tension between rationalists and fideists.
On the evangelical right, it is fashionable to express this dichotomy
in terms of confessionalists versus evidentialists.[8] Not all rationalists,
however, are evidentialists (Gordon Clark certainly is not), though
most, but not all, confessionalists tend toward fideism. The rationalists accuse the fideists of portraying faith as a blind leap in the
dark and thus disregarding the confirmatory evidence which history
and archaeology provide concerning the extraordinary events in biblical history. The fideists charge the rationalists with underplaying,
even ignoring the noetic effects of sin and making faith conditional
on historical and rational proofs for God's self-revelation in Christ
and the full reliability of Scripture. While the first position sees a
creative role for reason in preparing the way for faith, the second
stresses understanding proceeding out of faith.

Those closer to fideism generally appeal to the Pietist tradition
and the Reformation; those assigning a greater role to reason are

likely to hold Augustine and, even more, Thomas Aquinas in high esteem.[9] The second group is also at home in the thought world of Protestant orthodoxy (both Lutheran and Reformed), which brought back Aristotle in the elucidation and defense of the faith.[10] Fideists find some support in the Dutch theological tradition emanating from Abraham Kuyper.[11]

Francis Schaeffer reveals his affinity to the scholastic tradition of Protestant orthodoxy in his well-known and ground-breaking work *Escape From Reason*.[12] For Schaeffer, the malady of modern civilization is a flight from reason into the irrational. He cites various existentialist writers to illustrate the modern contempt for logic and reason. While presenting some substantiation for his thesis, Schaeffer does not fully consider that behind the flight from reason there is a flight from faith itself and that the former is only a symptom of the latter. He also tends to ignore the other side of the flight from faith—the enthronement of reason, which is present in educational and analytic philosophies as well as conservative theology.

Among those in the evangelical camp who seek to retain a determinative role for reason in preparing the way for faith are Carl Henry, Gordon Clark, Bruce Demarest, Paul Feinberg, Francis Schaeffer, Kenneth Kantzer, Gordon Lewis, Norman Geisler and Clark Pinnock. Those who stress the priority of faith over reason include G. W. Berkouwer, Jack Rogers, Mark Noll, David Wells, Donald McKim, Lewis Smedes, James Daane, Arthur Cochrane and this author.

The sacraments also signify an area of recurring tension within evangelicalism. I have already touched on the conflict over baptism, but the whole question of sacraments is becoming an issue today. A large part of the evangelical community does not even regard baptism and the Lord's Supper as sacraments, i.e., means of grace; instead, they are reduced to mere ordinances whereby we pledge ourselves to the service of the kingdom. Two of the most influential Reformed theologians, Charles Hodge and Karl Barth, declared themselves against a sacramental view. Hodge went so far as to argue that Calvin was wrong in his interpretation of the Eucharist.[13] It should be borne in mind that having a high view of the sacraments (as the Reformers did) does not mean sacramentalism, in which the outward rite is regarded as efficacious for salvation simply by virtue of being performed (*ex opere operato*).[14] Significantly, even Baptist theologians are beginning to recognize the sacramental character of baptism and the Lord's Supper, though they are always careful to relate this to faith in Jesus Christ.[15]

Then we come to the debate between the inerrantists and infallibilists. The former, represented by the International Council on Biblical Inerrancy, hold that the Bible is without error in matters of science and history as well as faith and morals. They sometimes speak of total inerrancy, meaning that whatever Scripture "touches upon" is immune from error. Because God, the primary author of Scripture, is wholly truthful, Scripture itself cannot lie. For the infallibilists, who constitute the great majority of moderate evangelicals, Scripture is infallible in the sense that it unfailingly communicates the will and purpose of God for our salvation, but this does not mean that the writers were lifted out of their cultural and historical environments and exempted from cultural and historical limitations. The infallibilists, following Calvin, often speak of the accommodation of the Spirit to the world-view of the times, thereby acknowledging the element of historical and cultural contingency in Scripture. The Toronto Conference on Biblical Authority (June 1981), sponsored by Fuller Theological Seminary and the Institute for Christian Studies in Toronto, reflected the moderate evangelical consensus on this question. Among those who follow Warfield and A. A. Hodge in contending for total inerrancy[16] are R. C. Sproul, Harold Lindsell, James Boice, Norman Geisler and Carl Henry. Those who are prepared to qualify inerrancy in order to make room for cultural and historical factors in the writing of Scripture include Clark Pinnock, Jack Rogers, Daniel Fuller and James Daane.

No less heated than the inerrancy debate is the currently accelerating conflict between the solifidians (those who defend justification by faith alone) and the Holiness and Pentecostal movements, which insist that maintaining a Christian life is necessary for final salvation. This tension was already evident in the eighteenth century between John Wesley on the one hand and the Moravians and the hyper-Calvinists on the other. For Lutherans, Calvinists and Barthians, we do not procure our sanctification, though we can manifest and demonstrate it in a Christian life. But our final salvation is already assured because of our justification in Jesus Christ apprehended by faith, which is a completed act.

Verdict magazine, which celebrates the Protestant Reformation and regards the Holiness movement as a dangerous aberration,[17] argues that works of faith and love are necessary fruits of salvation but in no way contribute to the gaining of our salvation. Geoffrey Paxton, an Episcopal theologian from Australia and a longtime contributor to *Verdict,* is quick to attack the current emphasis on being born again as a perversion of the gospel.[18] In his view, the new birth is only an effect, not an integral part of the gospel. The gospel is an announcement of what has happened fully and definitively in the past history of Jesus Christ. Those who stand closer to the Pietist and Wesleyan traditions rightly object that this position underplays the outpouring of the Holy Spirit and indeed tends to separate the work of the Spirit from that of Christ.

In my lecture tours, the one issue that is almost invariably brought up is the running battle that has developed between feminists and patriarchalists. It is an issue with far-reaching practical consequences, which we are only beginning to see. Evangelical feminists object to the biblical principle of subordination on the grounds that it reflects the patriarchal ethos of the times and is in no way a part of revelation. From their perspective man and woman are equal at work and at home, and both should be granted positions of spiritual leadership in the church. Patriarchalists argue that the biblical teaching is that though men and women are equal heirs to salvation, only men are called to assume positions of leadership in church and family.[19] Some feminists seek an inclusive gender language in worship. Instead of addressing God as Father or Lord (symbols associated with a patriarchal culture), they prefer such substitutes as Father-Mother, Heavenly Parent, or even better, Spirit. Many of the recent splits in the Anglican and Presbyterian churches have been over the question of women's ordination to the ministry. In the Christian Reformed Church one of the burning issues is whether women should even be admitted as deacons, since that, too, is an office of spiritual leadership. Many conservatives see the traditional position on this question as the distinguishing mark between the true and the false church.

One of the promising signs in the evangelical renaissance today is the rebirth of social concern. This is true for the evangelical right as well as the left. Yet even in this area, and perhaps especially in this area, we see signs of disunity. *Sojourners* magazine upholds the Anabaptist ideal of renouncing coercive power in favor of the violence of love to bring in the new world order. *The Reformed Journal,* on the other hand, following Calvin, advocates the right use of power to fashion a holy community.

A large part of the evangelical community is involved in the right-to-life movement. Even *Sojourners* has taken an uncompromising stand against abortion on demand. Opposed to this movement are many of those evangelicals involved in women's liberation, who hold that abortion is a matter to be decided between the woman and her physician. While evangelical feminists generally repudiate pornography, they often tend to support gay liberation.[20] The evangelical right and center, on the contrary, are adamantly opposed to homosexual practices and are stout defenders of family solidarity.

A more recent issue which is beginning to split the evangelical world as well as the wider Christian community is that of nuclear weapons. There has always been a pacifist contingent in evangelical Protestantism, such as the Mennonites and Quakers, but now many of those who come out of the mainstream Reformation question whether the just-war theory can ever apply to a war that involves the use of weapons of mass extermination (nuclear and biochemical).[21] Ironically, many in the right-to-life movement are nonetheless hawkish concerning the need to maintain a strong military defense, and this includes for them a formidable nuclear deterrent. I am thinking here of such persons as Pat Robertson, Francis Schaeffer, Jerry Falwell and Harold O. J. Brown.[22]

Vernon Grounds of Denver Theological Seminary (Conservative Baptist) is one evangelical who is raising his voice against the enigmatic mind-set of many of his colleagues who decry abortion and yet remain silent in the face of the horrendous evil of nuclear war:

> What about the schizophrenia of people who cry out against the murder of embryonic babies yet refuse to cry out against wholesale murder by atomic bombs? For the use of nuclear weapons will indiscriminately kill millions of incalculably precious persons including, no doubt, at least a few million babies! In my judgment, consequently, the same logic which motivates the evangelical battle against abortion as an evil that destroys human life ought to motivate an impassioned anti-nuclear crusade. To denounce one evil while condoning the other is surely schizophrenic.[23]

Billy Graham, too, has become disturbed, if not alarmed, by the accelerating nuclear armaments race.[24] Graham does not call for unilateral disarmament, but he has urged the nation's leaders to take a few risks in curtailing our nuclear arsenal, advocating a freeze on the manufacture of nuclear weapons.

Matters such as these are of momentous significance, entailing grave and difficult ethical decisions. Much of the dissension in the evangelical world today, however, is to be attributed to the elevation of marginal matters into essentials. One of the divisive issues among conservative Baptists is whether the church will have to go through the tribulation before the millennium. In the Restoration movement a pivotal cause of schism has been the use of musical instruments in worship. The current debate on how inconsistencies in dates and numbers in the Bible can be reconciled also appears to be an example of majoring in minors. I think, too, of the preoccupation with behavioral requirements for evangelical clergy and faculty, such as total abstinence from liquor and the taboos on social dancing and card playing.[25]

On the other hand, the great questions of doctrine, including the authority and inspiration of Scripture, the sovereignty of divine grace, the centrality of the atonement, the necessity of a holy life, the meaning of the sacraments and the reality of the second advent of Christ, are indeed issues that the church of today (both liberal and conservative) must grapple with if it is to maintain its identity as the church of Jesus Christ. The role of women in ministry is also of major theological and social significance, and deserves the serious attention of evangelical scholars and leaders. Similarly, the pressing moral issues of our day—abortion, the population explosion, worldwide hunger, the growing disparity between rich and poor, persisting racial discrimination, and nuclear and chemical warfare—have to be included in any evangelical agenda that bears on the Christian life.

Division or polarization is not always a bad thing, because it is often only through vigorous debate that we can arrive at the truth that God wants us to hear. On the other hand, divisiveness or party spirit (Rom. 13:13; 14:19; Gal. 5:20; I Cor. 1:10–15) is always detrimental to the cause of Christ, for it signifies an unwillingness to listen to what our fellow believers are saying and a stubborn refusal to change, even when this may be the will of God. We should not hide from the great issues out of fear of causing a split in the church, but we should resolutely face these issues out of a real concern for the unity of the church. We should enter the debates of our time in a spirit of love and out of fidelity to the truth of the gospel. We should be strong in the confidence that the Spirit of God himself will lead us into all truth if we remain open to his guidance as given through the shared experiences of the believing community and preeminently through the Bible.

THE SCANDAL OF DISUNITY

The disunity of the Christian church today in the face of a resurgent paganism is indeed deplorable. But even more scandalous is the disunity that plagues the evangelical family, the very group within the wider church that stresses fidelity to the gospel and to the Bible. Christian disunity is a contradiction of Christ's prayer that his people be one (John 17:20–23). It also conflicts with Paul's declaration that there is only "one body and one Spirit . . . one Lord, one faith, one baptism" (Eph. 4:4, 5). Disunity on theological and even sociological grounds betrays an appalling ignorance of the nature of the church. Indeed, the classical marks of the church of Jesus Christ are oneness, holiness, apostolicity and catholicity. The last term denotes universal outreach and continuity with the tradition of the whole church.

It is incontestable that the church, and especially the evangelical church, has lost much of its credibility on the mission field because of the bitter infighting between missionary boards and churches. Some have conjectured that China's capitulation to Communism was due, at least to some extent, to the spiritual vacuum in China fostered partly by intra-Christian warfare which prevented the church from giving a consistent and united witness to the truth of the gospel. Some observers are of the opinion that evangelical Protestantism has not advanced in Peru because of "painful historic divisions."[26] The well-known missiologist Pierce Beaver has declared: "More and more I am convinced that exported divisiveness is the greatest hindrance to the spread of the gospel in the non-Christian world."[27]

The ecumenical ideal is not a deadening uniformity but a diversity within unity. The evangelical coat should be a coat of many colors. Yet it is not a coat in which the colors do not harmonize. There can be only one faith and one dogma, but much room for variation in liturgical practices, theological systems and modes of evangelism.

We need to ask: What is the nature of the unity that we should seek? Some evangelicals define this unity in terms of a particular approach to the Bible. The problem with this position is that it is possible to have a high view of Scripture and yet be off-center in both theology and spirituality. At the same time, the pathway to Christian unity certainly involves an acknowledgment of the Bible as the inspired Word of God, the infallible rule for faith and practice. Some contend that the key to unity lies in a common confession of Jesus as Lord. But we already have that, at least outwardly, and disunity is still a glaring reality in our midst.

In my view, there will never be real evangelical unity, let alone Christian unity, until there is an awakening to the reality of the oneness and catholicity of the church, and this will surely entail a confessional agreement on the essentials of the faith as well as an acceptance of the Reformation principle of the church always reforming itself in the light of the higher norm of the gospel as declared in Holy Scripture. With our technocratic mentality, it is painful for us to have to acknowledge that such an awakening will depend not on us (with our multifarious strategies and skills) but on a new outpouring of the Holy Spirit; this means that real unity, both visible and spiritual, will only come in God's own time and way. Yet we can pray and seek for this. We can prepare the way, but unity itself must finally come as a gift from God.

The growing worldliness of the church today perhaps accounts for the fact that so little progress toward church unity is being made. It is disconcerting to reflect that the early evangelicals were forces of *dissent,* but now, by and large, they have become forces of *consent.* Whereas once they were known as nonconformists, they are now for the most part defenders of the status quo, both political and religious.

The values of the technological society have penetrated the enclave of evangelicalism as much or nearly as much as they have the liberal establishment. Prayer is now seen as a technique for satisfying the desires of the heart. Salvation is interpreted as the fulfillment of the self in terms that society can understand and respect. God is portrayed as the unlimited possibility which we can tap into in order to gain security and happiness. Success is measured in terms of productive achievement. The Bible is evaluated according to how it functions in bringing people their desired goals in life.

The blight of modern liberalism since the Enlightenment has been latitudinarianism, the attitude that allows for a variety of ways to come to God. Today this is known as pluralism, which is considered an ideal in many liberal churches, such as the Disciples of Christ, the United Church of Christ, and the United Methodist Church. What liberals do not sufficiently grasp is that while there can be a certain pluralism in doctrinal formulation, there can never be a pluralism in dogma. For then the church ceases to be the church.

Paul Holmer astutely points to the baneful effects of the latitudinarian mentality:

> It certainly was one thing to have Lutherans, Calvinists, and Catholics contending; but at least there was a semblance of argument amid the acrimony. . . . But now there is seldom either acrimony or argument. Much of what we thought was standard and minimal, a kind of point of departure, is no longer quite that. There is hardly anything but the sight of theologians talking past one another.[28]

What evangelicals need to realize is that there is a creeping latitudinarianism in their own circles, especially among the so-called young evangelicals who are understandably trying to break loose from the theological and cultural rigidity and provincialism of their backgrounds. With the ebbing of confessionalism, the growth in mysticism and ethicism comes as no surprise. Mysticism connotes the spiritualizing of religion; ethicism signifies the moralizing of religion. The latter may also involve politicizing religion, a tendency discernible not only in liberal circles but also among some fundamentalists and evangelicals.

If evangelicalism abandons the quest for Christian unity and theological and social relevance, it is liable to become, in Carl Henry's words, "a wilderness sect." On the other hand, if it responds creatively to the challenges of the day by acknowledging its own deficiencies and by being willing to use contemporary rather than archaic philosophical tools to carry on the battle for the faith in our time, it may become the vanguard of a reborn Christianity. The great danger today is that evangelicalism may retreat into a religious ghetto characterized by biblical obscurantism and cultural isolationism. Evangelicalism must neither withdraw from the culture nor capitulate to it but confront it with the biblical gospel which alone can heal the wounds of division in both church and society by opening up a new horizon of meaning to an age afflicted by the anxiety of meaninglessness.

THE IDEOLOGICAL TEMPTATION

Nowhere is the church's capitulation to the culture more apparent than in ideological entanglements. One of the startling facts of the present time is the often tacit and sometimes open alliance of religion with economic and political interests. Perhaps this has always been the case in the history of religion, but we are more aware of this now, thanks to the rise of the science of the sociology of religion. The historical and cultural conditioning of religion is acknowledged not only by sociologists and historians of religion but by theologians as well, including Reinhold Niebuhr and Karl Barth.

Both evangelicals and liberals need to come to grips with the phenomenon of ideology, which has distorted the perception of both Christians and non-Christians and which in no small way accounts for the ruptures and schisms in the Christian world today. Drawing upon the insights of Karl Marx, Karl Mannheim[29] and Reinhold Niebuhr, we might define an ideology as a vision of society that serves to justify or rationalize the interests of a particular class or power structure in the social order. According to Langdon Gilkey, "Ideologies are views of the whole of reality, especially of historical and social reality, which are believed by a community, which claim to be the truth about the whole, but which actually represent a particular point of view or bias, and . . . which in that bias represent and further the interests of a certain class or group."[30] With Hans Küng, we need to recognize that an ideology "produces a distorted picture of the reality of the world, disguises real abuses and replaces rational arguments by an appeal to emotion."[31]

An ideology entails in addition to a theoretical system a definite sociopolitical program. Ideas are no longer abstract models of truth (as in pure philosophy) but now become tools in a program of social restructuring. Ideologies rely not on rational argument but on propaganda, which is truth twisted for political ends.

As Niebuhr astutely observes, there is an ideological taint to all human reasoning, but it is possible to transcend ideology by the humility which rises out of prophetic religion; such humility acknowledges that truth is both a matter of having and not having, that the final synthesis lies beyond the reach of human perception and conception.[32] Ideologists claim a premature possession of the truth and for the purpose of furthering vested interests. Theologians ideally see the truth as a possession of God and consider themselves servants rather than masters of the truth.

It is possible to be conservative or liberal, in both the theological and political sense, without necessarily being ideological. An ideologist regards politics as a matter of ultimate concern, whereas Christian faith relegates politics to the area of preliminary or penultimate concerns.

Evangelicalism is especially vulnerable to the lure of ideologies, because it is generally naive regarding the influences of historical and cultural factors on religious commitment. With disturbing frequency, it falls under the delusion that it is possible to arrive at a system of truth that is valid for all ages (à la Hegel). It sometimes makes the claim that the believer can attain a univocal (and not merely an analogical) knowledge of God that is exempt from the relativity of history (Gordon Clark, Carl Henry).

The impact of ideology can definitely be discerned on both the evangelical right and left. When Carl McIntire ventures to suggest that the New Testament church is being called today "to be a right-wing political organization,"[33] there is reason to believe that he has succumbed to the ideological temptation. Examples of sacrilege in Jerry Falwell's eyes are busing for racial integration, environmental protection laws, and social welfare and deficit spending. One can only conclude that he has not effectively resisted the ideology of conservatism (or classical liberalism). Similarly, Joseph Jackson, then president of the National Baptist Convention, reveals a not so subtle accommodation to conservative ideology: "We must support law and order, for there are no problems in American life that cannot be solved through commitment to the highest laws of our land and in obedience to the American philosophy and way of life."[34]

The shadow of ideology has also penetrated into Southern Baptist churches. Already in the spring of 1969 at a Christian Life Commission seminar at the University of Chicago, John Nichol, pastor of an integrated Southern Baptist church in Decatur, Georgia, lamented the ideological character of so many Southern Baptist churches reflected in "the absence of the cross in the call to discipleship" and "a commitment to secular standards of institutional success."[35]

Ideological coloration is present in the evangelical left as well. Vehement attacks on the injustices spawned by capitalism but the relative silence concerning the destruction of human liberties under socialism and communism are commonplace in left-wing circles, including parts of the evangelical left. A case can be made that as many younger evangelicals gravitate out of the lower middle class into the middle and upper middle classes, they often assume the cultural and political values of their peers. Hence their support for careerism for women, abortion rights and gay rights.[36]

Peter Berger has advanced the thesis that the principal ideological conflict today is between the business and farming communities that can only thrive apart from state regulation and control and the new class, the managerial and professional interests that depend upon state aid for carrying out their programs (such as ecological planning, the distribution of welfare benefits, the supervision of day-care centers, education for the underprivileged).[37] The evangelical right tends to be allied with the first, and the evangelical left with the second.

TYPES OF IDEOLOGY

In order to ascertain the extent of ideological bias in modern evangelicalism and how much it contributes to evangelical disunity, it is necessary to explore the various types of ideology that present particular threats on the American scene today. Much of what will be said here has relevance for the church in all countries forming part of Western civilization.

First, I shall consider what is commonly called conservative ideology, though in fact it represents the values and thought world of classical liberalism. This is the ideology that upholds private initiative and industry, what we have come to call free enterprise.[38] It sees a centralized government as the main threat to individual liberties and consequently supports governmental decentralization. Reflecting continuity with the liberal ideology of the Enlightenment, it regards property rights as practically on a par with human rights. In its rhetoric it champions individualism over statism, though its support of corporate expansion and its insistence on a strong national defense often serve to sacrifice individual freedom to the collective welfare. When H. Richard Niebuhr described the church in bondage to capitalism,[39] he was referring to an ideological, not strictly a political bondage. Conservative ideology fosters a spirit of nationalism by its appeal to the American Way of Life and its preoccupation with national security.

Reinhold Niebuhr was particularly sensitive to the hold of this ideology over American Protestantism, both liberal and conservative. An observation made many years ago has remarkable relevance to the religious and political situation today: "The effort to make voluntary charity solve the problems of a major social crisis, on the score that it represents a higher type of spirituality than coerced giving through taxation, results merely in monumental hypocrisies and tempts selfish people to regard themselves as unselfish."[40]

Whereas classical liberalism or conservatism celebrates free enterprise and private initiative, the emerging ideology of welfare liberalism accentuates the need for social planning and controls within a democratic context. This ideology stresses the safeguarding of human rights and human equality, but at the same time it places an almost inordinate trust in social planners, who are generally drawn from the disciplines of sociology and psychology, since it is assumed that these experts in human behavior will choose what is good for all.[41] While classical liberalism esteems the entrepreneur, welfare liberalism favors the functionary or "organization man" who will carry out the mandate of the corporation or government bureau. The team worker is prized over the rugged individualist. While the prime virtues in the older liberalism (what is now called conservatism) were thrift and industry, the prime virtues in this new ideology are utility, efficiency and loyalty. Welfare liberalism stresses the mastery of nature by technique; therefore, it may legitimately be regarded as the ideology of the technological society.[42]

Closely related is the ideology of socialism, which has made significant inroads throughout the world and which has cast a spell over various neo-orthodox, liberal and evangelical left theologians.[43] Socialism represents not only an economic philosophy but an ideology that seeks to convert the world into a utopia in which everyone will receive an equal portion of available goods. As the ideology of the revolutionary left, socialism purports to speak not for the aristocracy or the bourgeoisie but for the working masses. It champions a radical egalitarianism and interprets social conflict in terms of the class struggle. With Karl Marx and Friedrich Engels, its first two philosophers, it looks forward to a classless society when capitalism will be replaced by communism. In contrast to classical liberalism, it defends human rights over property rights; in contrast to welfare liberalism, it advocates state control of the means of production, not simply state regulation. Personal freedoms are subordinated to the cause of social justice. Socialism seeks to place technology in the service of the class struggle rather than in the service of business expansion (as in classical liberalism) or social stability (as in welfare liberalism).

Like conservatism and welfare liberalism, socialism is also a product of the Enlightenment. It emphasizes the last two of the Enlightenment values: liberty, *equality and fraternity*. David Beckmann has observed that the rich tend to support the liberty and efficiency of the market; the poor, on the other hand, favor a planned economy where equality and fraternity are fostered.[44] Ideological commitment is inseparable from the desire for economic gain and security, and this is why it will always be a part of the human condition.

Modern evangelicalism has been more successful in resisting the allurements of socialism than have neo-orthodoxy and liberalism. Yet this is in no small part because evangelicalism now represents the interests of the moneyed class. In Europe it has become largely removed from the concerns and expectations of the working masses, with the result that many of the working people are aligning themselves with the Socialist or Communist parties. The danger is not that evangelicalism will succumb to socialism but that it will become allied with the interest of the big property owners and corporations.

Another ideology that has infiltrated the church and become a significant factor in much of the inner turmoil within evangelicalism today is feminism. This is the ideology of women's liberation, which strives for a new social order characterized by unisex and the egalitarian family. Feminism generally tries to blur the distinctions between the sexes and consequently promotes the ideal of androgyny, in which men and women are urged to integrate within themselves the masculine and feminine attributes present in all human beings.[45] Divorced from marriage and reproduction, sex becomes a purely private experience contributing to the self-fulfillment of autonomous individuals. Rosemary Ruether, a moderate feminist, declares, "In androgynously developed persons it is not possible to rule out sex/love relations between women or between men."[46] Radical feminists generally support gay liberation, and some, such as Mary Daly, uphold the ideal of lesbianism for women. Ideological feminism also throws its weight behind abortion on demand, no-fault divorce and value-free sex education.

Among the conflicts precipitated by feminists in evangelical circles are women's ordination and desexing the language of worship. It is possible to argue on the grounds of faith itself that women as well as men may be called to the ministry of the Word and sacraments and that gender-inclusive language in worship may have a place, depending on the context. Feminists, however, make women's ordination (to the office of deacon, elder or pastor) a matter of human rights. They contend that it is the *right* of women to be ordained, whereas faith insists that the ministry of the Word is a special calling from God, a *privilege* extended only to some, and not to others, men or women.

On the matter of the language about God, feminists reject such symbols as Father, Lord and Son in reference to the deity on the grounds that these reflect an outmoded patriarchal culture. Most evangelicals retort that we cannot alter the language of revelation without ending in a new religion. To address God as Divine Providence, World Spirit or Source of Sustenance instead of Father (as some feminists recommend) is to depersonalize God. To refer to God as Father-Mother, another feminist substitute, is to make God androgynous.[47]

Many feminists sense an affinity to socialism, having come to the conclusion that women's rights are ultimately dependent on laws rigorously enforced by a federal agency with coercive power. They also generally support day-care centers and abortion clinics run by the state, as well as state-funded sex education programs.

Other feminists feel much closer to libertarianism and anarchism, which relegate decision making to local communities. Many of these people are attracted to neopaganism, where God and the world are practically equated. Communitarianism and nature mysticism form a part of this radical feminist vision, in which witchcraft is readily endorsed. The monotheistic religion of the creator God is replaced by the pantheistic religion of the Goddess.[48]

Another distinctly modern ideology which nevertheless draws upon the past is fascism.[49] Here the principal concern is with national rights over both human rights (as in socialism) and property rights (as in classical liberalism). Fascism champions the rights of the majority over the rights of minorities. It places national honor and security above all else and sees the state in the service of these ideals. It is also intent on preserving the racial or ethnic heritage of a nation. While profamily in its rhetoric, it ends by subordinating the family to the state. Fascism is often allied with a repressive patriarchalism in which marriage is seen as a vocation to fertility. It can also be regarded as a form of elitism, since it pins its hope on the privileged few whom destiny chooses to be leaders.

Fascism, like one part of feminism, is to be associated with neopaganism. It looks back before the Enlightenment, even before the rise of Christianity, to the ancient myths of the old pagan civilizations and barbarian tribes, where the instinctual drives and heroism were celebrated. Unlike socialism and classical liberalism, fascism glories in the irrational. Again, in contrast to socialism, it harbors a distrust of bureaucracy and rational controls and is attracted instead to a voluntarist activism and adventurism. In its economic philosophy, fascism sees the corporations and unions allied with the state for the purpose of creating a homogenous racial and national unit. While Marxist socialism is hostile to religion and seeks ultimately to destroy it, fascism is often outwardly friendly to religion but seeks to contain it or even to transform it.

Fascism is often considered counterrevolutionary rather than genuinely revolutionary, since it promotes a nostalgia for the ideals and values of the past. Yet this kind of distinction can be deceptive, because even though making use of traditionalist rhetoric, it aspires to fashion a wholly new social order.

Many scholars mistakenly label any authoritarian or military regime as fascist, but fascism is something narrower and deeper than state authoritarianism. It is distinguished by charismatic leadership and the call to heroic sacrifice for the tribe (or *Volk*). National Socialism and Italian Fascism were the two principal expressions of fascist ideology in the twentieth century. Falangism in Spain, Peronism in Argentina and Christian Nationalism in South Africa represent incipient fascism. The same can be said for the present regime in Iran, where the masses are mesmerized by a charismatic leader and where fidelity to a particular religioethnic heritage is made the badge of acceptance. This regime also has an adventurist or expansionist foreign policy in that it is intent on exporting its revolution.[50]

Fascist ideology was responsible for the cleavage in the German church in the 1930s when the so-called "German Christians" sought to accommodate their religious heritage to the rising tide of National Socialism. An attempt was made to purge Christianity of its Jewish roots. The Old Testament was denigrated, and Jesus was hailed as cosmopolitan or Aryan rather than Jewish. Other revelations beyond the Bible were posited, such as revelations in nature and history. It was against this perversion of the faith that the Confessing Church came into being, and the Barmen Declaration, drawn up by Karl Barth, became the battle cry of this protest movement.[51] A segment of evangelical Christianity was beguiled by the ideology of National Socialism, but another segment, by standing firm, helped to preserve a genuine Christian witness in those dark days.

I have not given here an exhaustive list of ideologies. A number of others could indeed be mentioned: anarchism, populism,[52] pacifism, environmentalism and libertarianism. The ones I have discussed were chosen because in my opinion they pose peculiar temptations to the church in our day, especially the evangelical church.

Ideological polarization has immense significance for the tensions in evangelicalism today. I believe that it can be shown that the traditionalist evangelicals are tied to or at least sympathetic with classical liberalism or conservatism. The new evangelicals (in common with many academic religious liberals) are attracted to welfare liberalism and socialism. The radical evangelicals are more at home with anarchism and communitarianism, with what Charles Reich calls "Consciousness III."[53]

In the contemporary American context, one can perceive a certain convergence of ideologies. The ideology of the new left and that of the American Way of Life (conservatism) have this in common: an unwarranted trust in technology and an abiding faith in the democratic consensus. The late Huey Long commented that if fascism ever came to America, it would come in the guise of democracy. When the will of the people is equated with the voice of God, we are already under the shadow of a new totalitarianism. Furthermore, when it is said that the will of the people must be interpreted by a socially enlightened elite, whether they be welfare planners, aristocrats or patriots, then individual liberties are in jeopardy.

The overarching ideology of our time might be called secular humanism, the enthronement of cultural values and the mastery of nature by human reason.[54] Salvation is understood in terms of the quest for personal and social well-being. Sin is seen as ignorance, which can be overcome through education, or sickness, which can be dispelled by therapy. This foundational ideology might also be aptly referred to as technological materialism, since the goal in life is the accumulation of material goods and comforts.[55] It sometimes poses as the ideology of the center, which seeks to unite all groups under the umbrella of the general will.[56] It may use the rhetoric of conservatism, but its program is actually closer to that of welfare liberalism and socialism—expanding technology in the service of the corporate state. Because it makes class interest and party loyalty subservient to the good of the larger whole—the people or nation-state (*Volk*)—it has the enigmatic and paradoxical appearance of a democratic fascism.[57]

One cannot predict the future of ideological movements and alignments, but what can be safely said is that the taint of ideology colors our religious commitment and accounts in no small part for the way Christians treat one another and why they are so often at loggerheads with one another.

THE NEED TO RESIST IDEOLOGY

Ideology is spiritually beguiling because it offers those whose faith is eroding a substitute faith. Wherever there is a religious or metaphysical vacuum, bogus religion or ideology enters to fill the vacuum. Indeed:

> Ideological systems provide what Max Scheler called *redemptive knowledge* (*Heilswissen*)—that is, knowledge that not only provides intellectual understanding but also provides existential hope and moral guidance. This is particularly seductive in an age of secularization and relativity, where the traditional religious bodies of "redemptive knowledge" have become implausible to many (especially to intellectuals) and where morality is a very uncertain business.[58]

What we need to realize is that there is a qualitative difference between simple or genuine faith and ideological commitment. The marks of an ideology are intolerance and fanaticism; the marks of faith are humility and openness to the unconditional. Unlike ideology, faith does not claim a premature possession of the truth, but it does profess to know the One who is the truth. While ideology seeks to impose its distorted perception of truth on others, faith simply points others to the truth in the hope that they will come to know in their own way and time. While politics is the passion of ideology, prayer is the passion of faith. Faith cares even for those who spurn the truth of faith, whereas ideology regards with contempt those who resist its allurements. Faith views salvation as an unmerited gift from God; ideology, on the other hand, regards its own program as the way to salvation.

Evangelicals need to understand ideology so that they can better resist it. Marxists contend that all religious commitment is ideologically tainted, but Christians insist that ideology can be transcended at least in part. With Reinhold Niebuhr, I hold that it is possible to rise above ideology in moments of "prayerful transcendence," but nonetheless theological systems and church programs can never be ideologically free. Yet in the humble recognition that even our theologies are mixed with human error and therefore need to be justified by grace, we can begin the process of distinguishing the truth of faith from ideological untruth. Christians should try to detach themselves from ideologies in order to be free to work within ideological movements for greater social justice as genuinely free agents. Yet as Jacques Ellul has many times pointed out, Christians will always be thorns in the flesh in the social movements in which they work, since their ultimate loyalty is not to the movement but to the living God.

It is important for us to be aware of the sources of ideology in social upheavals and conflicts of the past. Both the ideology of the moderate right (classical liberalism) and that of the left (welfare liberalism and socialism) focus on the invincibility of the human spirit, a trademark of the Renaissance and the Enlightenment. Christian faith, on the other hand, upholds the sovereignty and irresistibility of divine grace. Whereas all ideology aggrandizes humanity or at least part of humanity, whether this be the masses, the racially pure minority, or the enlightened social engineers, Christianity seeks to give all the glory to God, though recognizing that through faith we can have a share in this glory as humble recipients and servants of the Most High.

Ideology sees the source of hope in human reason or the instinctual life of man. Christian faith, on the contrary, regards humanity as ensnared in the web of sin, and this means that hope must lie outside humanity in God. Emil Brunner has perceptively remarked, "Religion does not merely criticize one form of civilization or another but casts doubt upon civilization itself and upon humanity, because it casts doubt upon man."[59]

This is not to suggest that the church should withdraw from social conflict. Its role is to inject a salutary word of caution and hope into this conflict. It must seek to remain above ideology, even while it works with the left or right in trying to bring about a greater degree of justice and freedom for all.

The best contribution that evangelicals can make to our pluralistic society today is to emphasize the uniqueness and disparateness of the Christian faith, to point people to a transcendent hope when they see this world as their only hope. Evangelicals should acknowledge and respect the pluralism in American life today without succumbing to the secular dogma that there are many ways to salvation or that no truth is absolute.

Our role as evangelicals is to sound a discordant note that calls into question the universal assumptions of our age. Evolution, for example, when elevated into a dogma that embraces even the moral and spiritual areas of life needs to be unmasked as woefully inadequate and palpably unchristian. Evangelicals have an obligation to stand against the utopianism which is characteristic of the ideological left even while they make common cause with socialists and others in the struggle for justice in our time. The holy community, which has traditionally been part of the Calvinistic and Puritan vision, always needs to be seen as a sign and parable of the kingdom of God, but not as the realization of this kingdom on earth.

Conscious as they are that power in the hands of sinful humanity corrupts, evangelicals are obliged to resist the growing centralization of power in all areas of national and social life. Yet their protest against the unwarranted accumulation of power should be aimed not only at the nation-state but also at the multinational corporations, the labor unions and even the churches.

Another strategy that evangelicals might well consider is the promotion of genuinely Christian schools as an alternative to the public school system, which is deeply penetrated by the values of secular humanism.[60] But so many Christian schools today prove to be the refuge of people who are resisting racial and class integration, and these schools thus end in promoting another kind of humanism or ideology—that of the right. The answer to secular ideology is not a chauvinistic American or even a Christian ideology but a genuinely religious attitude toward life and the world that points beyond ideological polarization.

Living as we do in a technological society, where the emphasis is on productivity, utility and efficiency, evangelicals need to stress the values of faith—integrity, piety, humility and love. In a church that has succumbed to the activist mentality, evangelicals need to emphasize that being in Christ takes precedence over busyness in the name of Christ.

It is important, however, that we oppose the demands of the ideological and religious right for prayer in the public schools. The kind of prayer that would be sanctioned by the state would be innocuous at best and blasphemous at worst. Christian prayer cannot be imposed upon non-Christians nor even upon believers, and even though pending legislation calls for voluntary prayer, it would not remain voluntary once zealots gained control of the particular schools in question.[61] Prayers stemming from coercion or from the desire to give no offense to others are surely not pleasing sacrifices to God.

Karl Barth has wisely seen that the church must always stand against the stream of the culture if it is to make its witness known.[62] When the culture becomes dominated by the ideological or religious right, then the church must tilt toward the left. When the ideological left gains control, the church must lend its support to the valid concerns of the right. It must always champion the oppressed, but when the oppressed become the new oppressors, it must then be ready to pronounce God's judgment upon them. It should seek to comfort the afflicted, but when the afflicted gain the comforts and peace that were withheld from them, then its task is to afflict the newly comfortable.

Finally, evangelicals should come to realize that one of the salient marks of the true church is racial and class inclusiveness. Too many evangelicals enamored with church growth have sought to build culturally homogeneous congregations. Such homogeneity is conducive to stability and expansion but often at the cost of obedience to the prayer of Christ that his people be one (John 17:20–22).

H. Richard Niebuhr has documented in his careful study *The Social Sources of Denominationalism* that it is not so much doctrinal disagreement as class conflict that lies behind the proliferation of denominations and sects in our time.[63] We need to recognize that classism is as much a sin as nationalism, racism and sexism and that the gospel will break down the barriers that divide the classes, races and nations if we will only take the risk of letting the gospel do its work (cf. Eph. 2:14–16). A case could be made that the movement from fundamentalism to evangelicalism and neoevangelicalism is motivated partly by a change in class status. The reason why so many young evangelicals are feminists is surely in part because they are moving from the patriarchal culture of the lower and lower middle classes into the more egalitarian culture of the upper middle class, where autonomy and independence are prized.[64]

One of the lasting contributions that evangelicals could make to the wider church and even to the secular culture is to demonstrate that racial, class and ethnic divisions can be surmounted in a fellowship of faith and love which the New Testament calls the koinonia. The best way to counter ideology is to prepare the way for a society where ideology is not a real temptation. The most powerful answer to Marxism would be for the church itself to become the classless society that socialists dream about but never seem to find.

THE GROWING CHURCH CONFLICT

As the values of our secularized society increasingly penetrate the church, the church is placed in the position of being obliged to strive to maintain its identity and the integrity of its message. On the left, Christian faith is threatened by an ever bolder secular humanism, and on the right by an emerging nationalism.

The evangelical community itself has proved to be vulnerable to ideological and cultural infiltration despite its claim that it has remained separate from the world and has thereby preserved the gospel in its pure form. The evangelical right is tempted to align itself with the political and ideological right, whereas the evangelical left is increasingly enchanted with the ideological left.

Liberal Protestantism, having severed itself from the historical and theological heritage of the church, is even more open to ideological seduction. Some segments of liberalism have been caught up in the ideology of the right. I am thinking here of Moral Re-Armament, Up With People, and Spiritual Mobilization (now defunct). Others have embraced the ideological left, with its uncritical support of radical feminism, abortion on demand and the revolutionary struggles of the third world. The magazine *Christianity and Crisis,* which at one time maintained a genuinely prophetic stance, seems in danger of succumbing to the ideological temptation on the left. The *National Catholic Reporter,* by so closely identifying with left-wing causes, including gay liberation, furnishes still another example of how ideology undermines a genuinely prophetic critique of society.[65] Susceptibility to Marxist ideology is becoming ever more apparent in the boards and agencies of the World Council of Churches and National Council of Churches.[66]

The growing church conflict (*Kirchenkampf*) crosses all denominational and ideological lines.[67] The life of the church is not at stake (Christ will always maintain his church), but the ability of the church to speak a sure word from God to the present cultural situation is seriously impaired. In the industrial nations of the West, the church is not threatened by persecution (as is the case behind the Iron Curtain and in many parts of the third world), but it is threatened by seduction by the principalities and powers of the world that sometimes appear in the guise of angels of light.

Where does the pivotal issue lie? Some argue that the church will become relevant again only when it identifies with the poor and the homeless of the world, only when it throws its weight behind the struggle of the dispossessed peoples of the world for liberation. They contend that the church, to maintain itself as the church, must take a firm stand in support of socialism, feminism and pacifism.

Others see the overriding issue as the safeguarding of the transcendent vision of the church. They fear that the church is succumbing to an idealistic or naturalistic monism in its encounter with current philosophies and other world religions. This is the concern of those who drew up the Hartford Appeal in 1975.[68]

Still others hold that the church will not free itself from heterodoxy until it reaffirms the infallibility and inerrancy of the Bible, its ruling standard for life and conduct. The issue is fidelity to the

Bible, and only when this fidelity is restored will we see a growing sensitivity to the world's needs and the rediscovery of transcendence. This view is represented by the International Council on Biblical Inerrancy and the recent books in defense of biblical inerrancy by Harold Lindsell, Norman Geisler, John Warwick Montgomery, R. C. Sproul and others.

My position is that the crucial issue today is the battle for the gospel. It is not simply the authority of the Bible but the integrity of the gospel that is at stake. This includes the ethical imperatives of the gospel as well as the doctrinal distinctives integral to the gospel.

We need to reaffirm what Paul Tillich calls "the Protestant principle," the protest against absolutizing the relative.[69] Both church and culture today are guilty of creating idols, of absolutizing ideas and values that supposedly serve the cause of human advancement. When either the state or the church, the Bible or the creeds, are invested with divinity, they become obstacles to worship that is done in spirit and in truth; indeed, they become substitutes for the true faith. As evangelicals, we believe that the Bible, the church and the creeds can become the channels or vessels of the Word of God, which alone is absolute; they can render an authentic and binding witness to the Word of God, but in and of themselves they are not to be confused with the very voice of God.[70] We cannot have the Word of God in our pockets, as is the case with the Bible or a church decree, but the Word can have us in his possession. We cannot possess or control the Word of God, but the Word of God can possess and control us. The Word can make us his fitting servants and instruments.

Today, our task is to emphasize the freedom of the gospel in the face of growing centralization of power and authority in the hands of the nation-state or the giant corporations. In America, it seems, the main enemy is the corporate state, the multinational corporations allied with a strong national government. A highly centralized state is not itself the main problem, though it is a contributing factor to the present malady. The real problem is the state in the service of secular humanism (the ideology of democratic socialism) or nationalism (the ideology of the right). It is not the state but state idolatry, it is not secular culture, but culture idolatry, that prove to be adversaries of the church and its gospel. I agree with Dorothy Sayers that people who say that this is a war of economics or of power-politics, are only dabbling about on the surface of things. . . . At bottom it is a violent and irreconcilable quarrel about the nature of God and the nature of man and the ultimate nature of the universe; it is a war of dogma.[71]

The time is approaching when the church in America, like the church in Germany in the 1930s, may be compelled to become a confessing church, one that confesses its faith out of fidelity to the divine commandment in the face of certain hostility and even persecution. A confessing church will invariably have a confessional statement of faith, though it is not the statement of faith but the gospel that is the real object of its confession. Abraham Kuyper gives this sound advice:

> When principles that run against your deepest convictions begin to win the day, then battle is your calling, and peace has become sin; you must, at the price of dearest peace, lay your convictions bare before friend and enemy, with all the fire of your faith.[72]

It may well be that the present divisions within evangelicalism will be overshadowed by future divisions. The authentic heirs of the evangelical heritage—those whose ultimate trust is in Jesus Christ alone and whose only message is the gospel that he gives us—may find themselves allied with fellow believers who happen to be in liberal churches and even in the Catholic and Eastern Orthodox churches. They may also find themselves opposed by their kinsmen in the faith, those who pride themselves on being evangelical or orthodox.

Before it brings about unity at a deeper level, the gospel creates division among people. The disunity that has its source in personal or denominational pride or in ideological or sociological alignments is an abomination to God. But the disunity that is brought about by the sword of the gospel may indeed be a blessing, since the true church then becomes distinguished from the false church, and people know where the real battle lines are (cf. II Cor. 2:15, 16; Heb. 4:12, 13).

The church today is called to speak a sure word from God concerning the critical social issues of our time: abortion, the population explosion, nuclear war, the poisoning of the environment, the breakdown of the family and the growing disparity between rich and poor. It is also imperative that it address itself to the crucial theological issues of today: the authority of the Bible, the uniqueness of Jesus Christ, the meaning of the cross of Christ, the decisive role of the sacraments and the mission of the church.

A church that claims to be evangelical, catholic and reformed will have to speak to these and other pressing issues. But what it speaks must be the Word of God and not the word of the "new demons," the harbingers of ideology, for then the church would in fact be the false, not the true church. The test of true prophecy is whether the church will recognize and successfully meet the challenges that the Spirit of God has placed upon it for our day.

V

Pathways to Evangelical Oblivion

Let us remember here that on the whole subject of religion one rule is to be observed, and it is this—in obscure matters not to speak or think, or even long to know, more than the Word of God has delivered.

JOHN CALVIN

To mingle in politics, before all else, is today to kill hope and to turn back God's gift.

JACQUES ELLUL

The intention should be not to justify Christianity in this present age, but to justify the present age before the Christian message.

DIETRICH BONHOEFFER

Are we to be primarily and almost exclusively concerned with evangelistic campaigns and with the attempt to make them more efficient by new methods and techniques? Or, should we not concentrate more . . . upon praying for, and laying the basis of Christian instruction for, revival as it is described in the Bible?

D. MARTYN LLOYD-JONES

OF ALL THE STRATEGIES that could insure the eclipse of evangelicalism as a movement of renewal in the church today, none is more dangerous than the way of repristination. This is the temptation to romanticize past periods in the history of the church or creeds and confessions associated with particular traditions in the church. It signifies a flight from responsibilities in facing the challenges of the present and future and a retreat into a supposedly safe enclave of the past. Every vital theological movement will seek to learn from the past; but it is another thing to enthrone the past. The latter is antiquarianism; the former is true conservatism. Evangelicals should not be reactionary in the sense of clinging to the past, but they should be conservative in the sense of drawing upon the past.

Repristination in the area of biblical studies is remarkably evident in evangelical circles. There is often a return to a precritical approach even while lip service is given to the proper place for historical and literary criticism. The reticence of evangelicals to question publicly the Pauline authorship of the pastoral epistles is deplorable so long as it is motivated by political instead of scholarly considerations. Many of those in the scientific creationist movement bring evangelicalism into disrepute by treating the first chapters of Genesis as literal rather than sacred history and then trying to reconcile the details of what is written with the latest findings of science.[1] John R. W. Stott wisely espouses the ideal of being a fundamentalist and a higher critic at the same time.[2] It is possible to hold to the fundamentals of the faith and yet be thoroughly critical in the examination of the materials in which the fundamental truth of the faith is given to us.

Restorationism is also apparent in the area of ecclesiology. A growing number of evangelicals are seeking to return to the undivided church of the first five centuries and make subscription to the so-called ecumenical creeds mandatory for all clergy and even for laity.[3] Some wish to revive the office of bishop (this in itself is not objectionable), and a few are even giving serious consideration to apostolic succession as the guarantee for a valid ministry.[4]

In a similar spirit, there is a movement to invest the priest or pastor with sacerdotal authority; as a result, the ministry acquires a supernatural aura. One evangelical minister serving in the United Church of Christ has described the body of Christ in his church paper in the following way: Christ is the head, the pastor is the neck and the laypeople comprise the lower members of the body. The conclusion is that one can reach Christ only through the mediation of the pastor.[5] Many Catholics in the post-Vatican II tradition would argue that this represents not authentic Catholic teaching but an exaggeration of certain valid emphases in Catholic thought in the High Middle Ages when the juridical model of the priesthood reigned supreme.[6] Most catholic restorationists in the evangelical churches do not go to this extreme, but it shows the dangers inherent in this kind of orientation.

Significantly, many of those in the new Oxford movement display uncritical admiration for Pope John Paul II, often depicting him as the model of Christian piety.[7] He is without doubt a man of courage and vision, but is his vision sufficiently biblical and fully ecumenical? His statements on moral issues today frequently reveal a biblical and pastoral orientation that is sorely lacking in both Protestant ecumenical and evangelical circles. At the same time, he closes his eyes to the implacable reality of the population explosion, refusing even to reconsider the traditional Catholic ban on all forms of artificial birth control. His stubborn resistance to the growing demand for clergy marriages in the face of declining vocations to the priesthood indicates a person who is fixated on the past rather than alive to the myriad possibilities that God brings to the church in the here and now.

Through their nostalgia for the early church, restorationists of the catholic type often end in making antiquity rather than divine revelation the norm for truth. By regarding church tradition or the consensus of the whole church as the criterion for judging and interpreting Holy Scripture, they succumb to one of the endemic errors of historical Roman Catholicism. Of course, the Catholic churches (Roman Catholicism, Eastern Orthodoxy, Anglo-Catholicism) are not alone in misunderstanding the respective roles of Scripture and tradition. Many of the cults (Mormonism, the Jehovah's Witnesses, the sectarian Church of Christ in the Philippines) are no less guilty in this respect. Authentic evangelical theology, by contrast, contends that the church is servant rather than master of the Word of God, that its task is to witness to and proclaim rather than contribute or add to the truth of Christian faith.

Those who call themselves catholic evangelicals, in the sense in which I use this phrase, wish to maintain continuity with the tradition of the whole church, but they nevertheless see the Word of God revealed in the Bible as having priority over the decrees and councils of the church. The church recognized but did not create the canon. It acknowledged the divine authority of the canonical books which they already possessed by virtue of their inspiration by the Holy Spirit. A church that is truly catholic is a church based on the apostolic doctrine contained in the New Testament, not a church supervised by bishops who supposedly stand in an unbroken succession to the original apostles. It is the doctrine that validates the ministry and not vice versa. I heartily concur with the Puritan father Richard Sibbes: "Beloved, that *that makes a church to be a catholic church . . . is the catholic faith.*"[8]

Antiquarianism is by no means confined to those who are attracted to the undivided church of the first five centuries. Others exalt the Protestant Reformation and its confessions to an excessive degree. The sixteenth century is no more sacrosanct than any other; to be sure, it heralded the rediscovery of the biblical message concerning salvation by the unmerited grace of God, but at the same time it precipitated a nearly fatal rupture in the ranks of believers that continues to this day.

The Reformation recovered the forensic or juridical meaning of the doctrine of justification, hitherto sorely neglected or virtually ignored in the Catholic theological tradition. Yet because of the polemics of the time, it failed to do justice to the mystical and eschatological dimensions of justification.

In Lutheranism, justification was emphasized to such an extent that sanctification was underplayed. Whereas justification was practically absorbed into sanctification in Catholic mystical theology, sanctification faded into insignificance in some strands of Reformation biblical theology. In his battle against the antinomians, Luther sought to correct this one-sided emphasis on justification: "They may be fine Easter preachers, but they are very poor Pentecost preachers, for they do not preach . . . 'about the sanctification by the Holy Spirit,' but solely about the redemption of Jesus Christ."[9]

We need to draw upon the abiding insights of the great Reformers without idolizing the Reformation. We must build upon the enduring truths of the Reformation without simply returning to that age. Similar advice can be given to those in conservative Methodism and the Holiness movement whose goal is to restore the pristine truths of Wesleyanism.

There is a place for a distinctly Lutheran, Calvinist, Wesleyan or Roman Catholic witness, but whatever the form, it should always point beyond itself to Jesus Christ, the one Lord of the church to whom all of us are subject. Calvinists should always ask where they can learn from their Arminian opponents. Instead of condemning the Reformation outright, Catholics should investigate the deficiencies in their own church that gave rise to the Reformation.[10] Those who champion the Reformed tradition should inquire why so many of its children are disavowing their heritage and embracing Pentecostalism. Until the church attains visible unity, we need to keep alive the distinctive hallmarks of our respective traditions, but this must be done in a spirit of self-criticism and humility. We should always remember that our foremost loyalty is to Jesus Christ and that when anything in our tradition becomes more of an obstacle than an aid to the proclamation of the gospel of Christ, we must then be willing to give up what had been previously cherished.

The lure of repristination is a problem, too, in the Roman Catholic Church, where many in reaction against the excesses resulting from Vatican Council II yearn for the triumphalist church of Vatican I. Charismatic Catholics (who sometimes identify themselves as evangelical Catholics) seem drawn to a restorationist posture, though it would be a mistake to characterize the mainstream of the Catholic charismatic movement in this way. Doctrines and practices dear to restorationist Catholics include papal infallibility, the Latin mass, novenas, the veneration and invocation of the saints (especially Mary), the veneration of the relics of saints, pilgrimages to shrines and the meritoriousness of monastic vocations. The great Marian doctrines, such as the Immaculate Conception and the Assumption of Mary, are also highly prized by these Catholics. One of their mottoes is "To Jesus through Mary."

Regrettable though these tendencies are, the growing reaction against creeping liberalism in the Catholic Church is understandable. For it is not only traditional formulas and practices but the gospel itself that is being called into question by some of those in the avant-garde. Karl Barth had serious reservations about various thrusts of Vatican II and warned against any rapprochement with the Enlightenment.[11] At the same time, evangelicals can appreciate Vatican II for its willingness to rethink traditional doctrine and practice in the light of the gospel and for its readiness to enter into dialogue with the "separated brethren" for the purpose of furthering the cause of Christian unity.

Those who are attracted to the spirit of repristination need to remember that some of the great saints of the church have called bishops and even popes to repentance, that the giants of Catholic tradition were nearly always involved in movements of radical church reform and were more often than not suspected of heresy. Catholics, particularly those who consider themselves evangelical, should bear in mind that a flight into the past is not the only alternative to a capitulation to the *Zeitgeist* of the present. The great saints of Catholic tradition displayed a readiness to follow Christ into the darkness of their age, fortified in the knowledge that he is already the victor against the prince of darkness. Both Protestant and Catholic evangelicals would do well to emulate these enduring models of holiness in the world.

Finally, we need to give attention to a restorationism in theological method. Right-wing evangelicals in particular are fascinated by the empirical rationalism of the later Enlightenment, especially as it came to America in the form of Scottish realism.[12] When John Warwick Montgomery maintains that "the sole ground" for judging the truth-claims of faith is "empirical probability,"[13] he is manifesting a philosophical bias endemic to the evangelical world. In these circles, the inductive method is prized over the deductive, and the Bible is treated as "a storehouse of facts" (Charles Hodge). Some in this camp, e.g., Norman Geisler, are also attracted to the philosophical method of Thomas Aquinas, since Thomas was more empirically oriented than many of his contemporaries, who stood in the tradition of Platonism and Neoplatonism. Among these same evangelicals, there is a concerted attempt to revive the cosmological proofs for the existence of God, which had supposedly been demolished by Hume and Kant in the eighteenth century.

Another strand in modern evangelicalism tends to maintain continuity with the idealistic rationalism of the early Enlightenment and the seventeenth-century Age of Reason. Rational clarity and logical consistency are valued more highly than empirical verification, the norm for truth in the later Enlightenment. Deduction is defended over induction, though the latter is not wholly discounted. Some who gravitate toward rationalism, e.g., Gordon Clark and Ronald Nash seek to rehabilitate the theory of innate ideas,[14] which ultimately goes back to Plato but which reappears in Augustine, Descartes and Leibniz, among others. Needless to say, deduction from metaphysical first principles is the method that has the approbation of these evangelicals. Gordon Payne's contention that biblical inerrancy "is established by logical reasoning from premises stated in the Bible" reflects this same kind of orientation.[15]

When theological method is so closely tied to philosophical method, theology is transmuted into philosophy of religion. A concomitant danger is that philosophical presuppositions are imposed upon Scripture, with the result that the real meaning and impact of the scriptural revelation are lost. The mystery and paradox in revelation are reduced to logical axioms capable of being understood by unbelievers as well as believers. The Word of God becomes a rational formula wholly in the control of the theologian, and theology becomes the systematic harmonizing of rational truths rather than an incomplete and open-ended explication of revelational meaning that always stands in need of revision and further elucidation.

Too often in the past history of the church, theologians have confused the living God of the Bible with the God of philosophical theism. It is possible to speak of a biblical theism (cf. Heb. 11:6), which is rooted, however, not in abstract speculation but in the event of the incarnation of the Word of God. The God of biblical faith is not a construct of the mind but a supramundane reality beyond the reach of human conception and perception. "Philosophical theism," Paul Holmer reminds us, "despite its long and hallowed history, is not the essence of Christian and Jewish religion; neither is the denial of that theism invariably and necessarily the denial of God Almighty."[16]

We can learn from the partial understandings and misunderstandings of the theology of the past, but our final criterion must always be the self-revelation of Jesus Christ attested in Holy Scripture. We can even learn from the methodologies of the philosophical theologians, but these must constantly be measured by the revealed wisdom in the Scriptures.

I agree with Paul Tillich that theology is neither an empirical-inductive nor a metaphysical-deductive science.[17] Nor is it a combination of induction and deduction, as some contemporary evangelicals would have it.[18] Yet I am reluctant to endorse the Tillichian understanding of theology as an elucidation of the symbols of church tradition correlated with the creative questions of the culture. For Tillich, the object of faith is the mystery of the New Being which transcends the subject-object cleavage and therefore can only be grasped in moments of ecstatic self-transcendence; this mystery, moreover, can be communicated only by ciphers or symbols which give a true awareness but not conceptual knowledge.

I see theology as a faith-responsive investigation which rests fundamentally neither on induction nor deduction nor even on intuition but on a receptivity to revelation, a receptivity created by the Holy Spirit and itself forming a part of revelation. God can be an object of knowledge but only because he makes himself so in the event of his self-revelation in Jesus Christ. Induction and deduction are employed in the service of faith, but faith gains its fundamental understanding from neither of these, indeed from no cognitive capacity within man but only from the Word itself.

We shall be immeasurably richer if we draw upon the wisdom of the fathers, the Reformers, the Pietists and Puritans, and even from the luminaries of Protestant orthodoxy, but let us take care that we do not simply repeat their errors. We need to take into consideration the modern philosophical critiques of the philosophies of the Enlightenment (given by Hume, Kant, Kierkegaard, Wittgenstein) as well as the theological critiques of the whole philosophical enterprise (Barth, Brunner, Reinhold Niebuhr). Instead of trying to restore the biblical-classical synthesis in which biblical meanings are united with the secular philosophical wisdom of Hellenism (a temptation of Renaissance and Enlightenment thinkers), we need to forge a new theological method that will be true to the Scriptures but also cognizant of the theological and philosophical revolutions in the past two centuries.

SEPARATISM

If many evangelicals have sought refuge in the allurements of restorationism, even more are tantalized by the appeal of separatism, a perennial temptation for earnest believers throughout the history of the church. Evangelicals especially are attracted to the ideal of a pure church in which the wheat has been separated from the tares, despite the fact that our Lord regarded this ideal as not realizable in earthly history (Matt. 13:24–30). Separatism leads to sectarianism (the delusion that we are the only true church) and ghettoism, in which the church becomes isolated from the theological and moral debates of the age. Carl Henry has rightly warned against the perils of "social isolationism" and "spiritual individualism" which so often afflict evangelicalism.[19]

It is disturbing but true that most current evangelical thought is not on the cutting edge of theology. It is characterized by a preoccupation with issues that no longer trouble the church at large. Some of these issues should be left buried in the past.

Many evangelicals appeal to II Corinthians 6:17, 18, where Paul gives salutary advice designed to keep believers from going astray: "Come out from them, and be separate from them, says the Lord" (v. 17 a RSV). Yet the apostle is not encouraging either corporate or individual withdrawal from society; instead, he is trying to steer believers away from marriage and intimate companionship with unbelievers. His admonition is similar to the warning in I John against love of the world, "the lust of the flesh and the lust of the eyes and the pride of life" (2:15, 16 RSV). Paul's concern is that believers maintain the values and goals of their faith which will invariably set them in opposition to the world; yet it is precisely in this opposition that believers can penetrate the bastions of the world and bring them into subjection to Jesus Christ.

Nothing is said in II Corinthians 6 about separation from other believers. While we are called to break fellowship with those in the community of faith who become immoral or apostate (I Cor. 5:9–13),[20] we are obliged to retain our ties with believers who hold to a slightly different understanding of the mission and goal of the church. Paul entered into dialogue with Peter and the other apostles at Jerusalem, but by no means was he contemplating the possibility of a new church (Acts 15).

The counterfeit religion of separatism has a long and checkered history in the life of the church. We see it in Tertullian, who finally broke with the Catholic Church and joined the Montanist sect, which elevated virginity over marriage and enjoined on its members all kinds of ascetic disciplines. Augustine was caught up in the struggle against the Donatists, who refused to readmit as members of the church those who had fallen away under persecution. "If you love the Head," declared Augustine, "you love the members." The Donatists manifestly failed this test, thereby proving that they were themselves a false church.

A sectarian mentality is evident in modern fundamentalism which is adamantly opposed to fellowship with persons and churches whose theologies are suspect. Dispensational fundamentalists speak of the "twilight of the Church" and urge regenerate Christians to withdraw from the established churches into enclaves of holiness in a hostile world. The Exclusive Plymouth Brethren have no compunction in terminating fellowship even with those in their own church who fraternize with other Christians. The disowning of apostates, which is supported by Scripture, is quite different from breaking dialogue and fellowship with Christians whose life-style reflects spiritual immaturity or who verge toward heterodoxy. The community of faith includes a vast array of people who still hold to the core of the faith but whose theological understanding is deficient or unbalanced. We should remember that Jesus himself continued to attend the temple and the synagogue even after he announced the message of his kingdom.

Many sincere but misguided Christians seek an ideal church and therefore give up on the local church because they regard themselves as superior morally and religiously to their brothers and sisters in the faith. But our commitment is not to a romantic idealism but to the evangelical faith, which sees the ideal as always ahead of us, something for which we should strive but never claim to possess. Evangelical Christianity holds that the true church is a church of sinners, that the church without spot or wrinkle (Eph. 5:27) is an eschatological goal, never a present achievement. Augustine on one occasion compared the church of Jesus Christ to Noah's ark: If it were not for the storm outside no one could stand the stench inside. Luther often likened the church to a hospital for sick souls. Instead of being already well, we as Christians are convalescents on the road to recovery. We still require the medicine of the Word and sacraments as well as the support of the koinonia. Once we suppose, however, that we can stand on our own apart from the life-support system of the church, then we shall suffer a relapse and our condition will be worse than it was previously.

Jesus' battle with the Pharisees was directed against the idea that the community of faith is a holy club in which only those who qualify morally and religiously are admitted. Our Lord expressly said that he had come to call not the righteous but sinners to repentance (Mark 2:17). The Pharisees, obsessed as they were with the moral and religious taboos of rabbinic Judaism, felt threatened by both the words and life-style of Jesus, whose goal was to break down the walls that divide people from one another (cf. Eph. 2:14–16). Jesus condemned the Pharisees for trusting in themselves and despising others (Luke 18:9).

Against John Nelson Darby and Ellen White, who in the nineteenth century called people out of the institutional churches, I side with Richard Sibbes, sixteenth- and seventeenth-century Puritan, who remained within the Anglican church; Philip Spener and Count Nikolaus von Zinzendorf, German Pietists who sought to reform the church from within; and Gerhard Tersteegen, the eighteenth-century German Reformed mystic, who continued to be loyal to a church that opposed him and even persecuted him.

Tersteegen, a layman and ribbon weaver by trade, was careful to hold his meetings for renewal at times that did not conflict with church services. Yet pastors in the area of Mülheim, Germany, were still alarmed enough to pressure the authorities to forbid Tersteegen from holding public meetings. For ten years Tersteegen was prohibited from preaching the gospel in Protestant Germany, but he sought to combat his accusers by prayer and goodwill, instead of setting up a new church. Eventually he was able to begin his meetings again after winning at least a modicum of respect from church and state authorities. Tersteegen declared, "A true mystic does not easily become a separatist, he has more important things to do."[21]

Despite their wide theological differences on matters of grace and free will, John Wesley and George Whitefield frequently exchanged pulpits and preserved an affectionate respect for one another. Even though they eventually had to maintain separate congregations and separate meeting places, they did not see these as separate churches. When Whitefield preached for Wesley, he tactfully avoided commending predestination or disparaging perfection. Whitefield's tabernacles were always open to Wesley, as were the chapels of the Countess of Huntingdon, a convinced Calvinist. When a censorious Calvinist asked Whitefield whether they would ever see Wesley in heaven, he received this retort: "I fear not, he will be so near the throne, and we shall be at such a distance, that we shall hardly get a sight of him."[22] Wesley and Whitefield were enabled to make an enduring and socially revolutionary witness in eighteenth-century English Protestantism, because their faith had, to a considerable degree, been perfected in love.

J. Gresham Machen felt constrained to break with Princeton Theological Seminary, because what he regarded as the true biblical witness was scarcely tolerated. At the same time, he strove to remain within the Presbyterian Church in the U.S.A., though he could not maintain that position. He was finally defrocked for trying to start a mission order within the denomination closely adhering to the tenets of the Westminster Confession. John Gerstner, retired professor of church history at Pittsburgh Theological Seminary, more than once threatened to withdraw from the United Presbyterian Church, U.S.A. because of the inroads of secularism in that denomination. Yet he decided to maintain his affiliation in order to work for reforms as best he could.[23]

The great Reformers, Luther and Calvin, also had to decide whether to continue to work for reform within the Catholic Church or to carry on their work outside. Actually the decision was forced upon them when the church in its defensiveness expelled both of them, even though they remained adamantly opposed to all forms of separatism and sectarianism. Luther was compelled to leave both his Augustinian order and the Catholic Church, because his doctrine was not tolerated. Far from being a radical or liberal, he was basically a conservative anxious to maintain continuity with the church's tradition but also eager to revivify this tradition in the light of the gospel of Jesus Christ. Luther was one of the last of the monks who embraced the Reformation doctrine to give up his monastic cowl, and he did so with sadness.[24]

The debate today on the charismatic renewal in the church re-

volves around whether the new wine of the Spirit can be poured
into the old wineskins of churches that have fallen under the spell
of a stultifying formalism. Some charismatics have elected to stay in
their respective churches and have proved to be a salutary leavening
influence. Others have chosen separation, contending that the
churches are controlled by spiritless rather than Spirit-filled
Christians.[25]

Karl Barth has called for a thorough reformation in the life and
thought of the church today. Yet he saw reformation not as the
overthrow of existing practices and attitudes (though sometimes it
would entail this) but rather as the renewal of what has become
moribund or inert but which is not destitute of saving grace. He contrasted reformation with restoration as well as with revolution, both
of which are often associated with separatism:

> Reformation is not the restoration and conservation of the old and
> sacrosanct. Nor is it revolution. Fundamental crises are the last thing
> that the church needs or that is good for it. Reformation is provi-
> sional renewal, a modest transforming of the church in the light of
> its origin.[26]

At the same time, Barth recognized that when the church becomes
the false church, as in the case of a significant segment of the German church under the Nazis, then the only pathway is restitution,
not reformation. Restitution means cutting away the cultural and
philosophical baggage that has subverted the church's message and
mission and returning to the beginnings. Such radical surgery, Barth
held, is necessary only in extreme situations. As a general rule, one
should not lightly discard those things that have for so many years
been employed in the service of the church's message, even the
philosophical concepts of Hellenism. Barth lent his support to the
ecumenical movement but always with reservations. Likewise, he
was favorably disposed toward the Second Vatican Council, but
again maintained a critical stance.

Like Barth and the Reformers, we must recoil from separatism not
only because it fosters unnecessary discord and divisiveness in the
church but also because it subverts the understanding of the truth of
faith. Right doctrine and the right attitude toward our neighbor are
inextricably intertwined, and when we break off relations with our
neighbor, this means that our perception of the mysteries of revela-

tion is seriously impaired (cf. I John 2:5, 6; 3:6; 4:8). Without love, Augustine maintained, one cannot properly understand the truths of Scripture. According to the eminent church historian and theologian of the Mercersburg movement, Philip Schaff, "Heresy is always latent schism, and schism is always latent heresy." When we separate from those we consider heretical, he suggests, we shall probably fall into heresy ourselves. Indeed, the implication is that the very desire to separate may be born out of a heretical distrust of the dogmas of the faith.

Robert Brinsmead, an ex-Seventh-Day Adventist, who has learned from bitter experience the virulent fruits of sectarianism,[27] makes an important distinction between the sectarian and catholic spirits: "Whereas the sectarian spirit is anxious to draw a line which identifies the spiritual elite, the gospel is accompanied by the catholic spirit, which is anxious to draw a circle that makes the Christian fellowship as wide as Christ intended."[28] The sectarian spirit not only subordinates the gospel to its distinctive doctrine but may actually present this doctrine as the gospel. Yet Brinsmead is keenly aware that sectarianism is not the greatest evil: "We would gain nothing if, after fleeing from the bear of sectarianism, we were bitten by the viper of compromise. The agony of divisions is better than the complacency of indifference."[29]

We may sometimes have to separate from the parent body (as Brinsmead did),[30] but we must never be separatists. If we separate we should do so for the purpose of a new church alignment that will be even more inclusive than the old. We should not so much will to separate from the church that has nurtured us, but we should be driven out and then only for the sole reason of standing firm for the truth of the gospel. Troublemakers are expelled or forced to leave a church because they persistently place their own interests above the common good. Saints are forced to leave because they willingly sacrifice their own interests for the sake of the gospel.

ACCOMMODATIONISM

Among all the factors that are causing evangelicals to leave mainline denominations today, none is more frequently cited than the capitulation to worldly mores and goals. What those who opt to leave do not always realize is that this problem afflicts the whole theological spectrum, from the far left to the far right. The peril of accommodationism often takes the form of revising or updating the thought and practice of the faith in order to bring them into harmony or at least correlation with the highest values of the culture. Richard Quebedeaux has aptly coined the phrase "worldly evangelicals" to denote those evangelicals who have succumbed to worldly standards in order to establish the credibility and relevance of their faith.[31]

Accommodationism is apparent in modernist attempts to rethink theology in order to make it meaningful to contemporary man.[32] On the left, we see feminist, political, third-world, relational, liberation and socialist theologies, all trying to show that their particular emphases are in tune with modern times. On the right, Christianity is depicted as a superior philosophy or the highest of the world religions, to which every earnest seeker after truth must surely give a serious hearing. Or the Christian faith is presented as the crown and fulfillment of the cultural values of peace, success and happiness.

Another form of accommodationism is aestheticism. Here the idea is to update worship and the communication of the gospel by means of the arts—music, drama, sculpture, etc. Some of the avant-garde, who concentrate on making worship contemporary, try to reach the world, especially modern youth, through gospel rock or liturgical jazz. The emphasis is on putting people into the proper frame of mind or creating the right kind of impression. It is said, for example, that people are more prone to worship God if they are in a worshipful mood.

The profound danger in such an approach was perceived by the eminent Congregational theologian P. T. Forsyth (d. 1921). His admonition against the culture-religion of his time has perhaps even more relevance today:

> This is the bane of much popular religion, and the source of its wide collapse. People are hypnotised rather than converted. They are acted on by suggestion rather than authority, which lowers their personality rather than rallies it, and moves them by man's will rather than God's.[33]

Aestheticism lies behind the current fascination with creative spirituality. It is instructive to observe that as the interest in spirituality rises, the concern about justification and the remission of sins correspondingly diminishes. Forsyth, who wrote at length on true spirituality, issued this prophetic warning:

> To put spirituality in the place of justification is to vaporise the Church. It is to detach the soul from the one decisive, final, and eternal act whereby it is placed within the eternal will of a God whose holy love founded our destiny and our peace before all worlds.[34]

Evangelicals as well as liberals have joined the cultural quest for spiritual fulfillment. As a result, their focus is on the journey *inward* to the ground and depth of all being rather than *outward* to God's redemptive act in Jesus Christ in history. Forsyth's cogent critique of this narcissistic kind of religion needs to be pondered anew:

> We can really develop our spiritual personality at last only by thinking about it less, and by being preoccupied with the realisation and confession of God's holy personality. The object of ethics is the development of personality, but the object of religion is the kingdom and communion of a holy God, which is the only means of securing, through a new creation, a personality worth developing at last.[35]

If we eschew the journey inward, however, it must not be to succumb to the opposite danger of spurning contemplation for productivity and efficiency, values prized by the technological society. Here evangelicals are perhaps even more derelict than their liberal and Catholic kinsmen in the faith. Activism is indeed one of the banes of evangelical religion today, and it is integrally tied up with anti-intellectualism. Evangelicals, it seems, want people who are energetic, not thoughtful. Busyness in the name of Christ appears to take precedence over being in Christ.

The custom of counting conversions is a distinctly modern phenomenon and is associated with the liberal ideology of achievement. The evangelist George Whitefield wisely refused to speak of the number of conversions at his revival meetings. Referring to some who claimed to "know when persons are justified," he remarked: "It is a lesson I have not yet learnt. There are so many stony-ground hearers which receive the word with joy, that I have determined to suspend my judgment, till I know the tree by its fruits."[36]

With a buoyant optimism fortified by rapid increases in membership and expanding building programs, evangelicals like to believe that God is blessing their institutions. Bus ministries which augment the Sunday School rolls are often pointed to as evidence of a spiritual church. The nagging question arises: Is our reliance on church growth techniques or on the surprising work of the Holy Spirit?

Karl Barth has these instructive words for evangelicals who are mesmerized by worldly standards of success:

> It is comforting to think that the good God likes to be on the side of the big battalions, so that we have only to look to these to find traces of the true Church. Certainly great membership rolls and good attendance and full churches and halls . . . are facts which naturally impress us . . . but what do they really have to do with the truth?[37]

Before liberal critics of evangelicalism congratulate themselves, let me hasten to free them from the delusion that falling membership and attendance show that their churches are closer to the truth. The declining fortunes of the liberal establishment are sometimes attributed to its prophetic stance or to the sociological fact that middle- and upper-class women bear fewer children. There may be some truth in these claims, but this is not the core of the problem of the demise of liberal Christianity. What is not sufficiently perceived is that God withdraws his blessing from churches that substitute public lectures for gospel preaching and a concern for the development of personality for a passion for souls. A vital church will repel because of its prophetic witness, but it will also attract because of its evangelistic zeal, and I am afraid that most liberal churches today have neither.

Yet evangelicals dare not view the weaknesses and misfortunes of fellow-Christians with sanctimonious detachment. Their own religion has by no means escaped the corroding influences of a blatantly secular culture. The fascination of a considerable segment of the evangelical community with worldly success and celebrities is nothing less than scandalous. A. W. Tozer laments that while Christ calls people to holiness, too many contemporary representatives of the old-time religion "call them to a cheap and tawdry happiness that would have been rejected with scorn by the least of the Stoic philosophers."[38] This prophet from the Christian and Missionary Alliance presents a rather bleak picture of modern evangelicalism:

> Evangelical Christianity is fast becoming the religion of the bourgeoisie. The well-to-do, the upper middle classes, the politically

prominent, the celebrities, are accepting our religion by the thousands . . . to the uncontrollable glee of our religious leaders who seem completely blind to the fact that the vast majority of these new patrons of the Lord of glory have not altered their moral habits in the slightest nor given any evidence of true conversion that would have been accepted by the saintly fathers who built the churches.[39]

The proper attitude for both evangelicals and liberals today is one of penitence and humility, born out of the knowledge that our supposed virtue and wisdom prove again and again to be a cloak for disobedience. When we begin boasting of our achievements, especially those of a moral and religious kind, this may well be a sign that we have forsaken our high and holy vocation. According to Barth, "The Church which does not ask itself whether it is not threatened by apostasy, and therefore in need of renewal, should beware lest it become a sleeping and a sick Church, even sick unto death."[40]

The same fascination with tangible success is present in unionism, the attempt to forge denominational mergers for the sake of greater efficiency in organization or a higher degree of cultural homogeneity rather than obedience to the will of God. Unionism places unity over truth, practice over doctrine. Its goal is denominational consolidation at the expense of dogmatic consensus. Unionism is a false ecumenism, since it controverts the ideal of the unity of truth and love.

Unionism has been one of the principal forces undermining the vitality of the liberal churches. Kierkegaard had this to say about this latest form of culture-Christianity:

> We are always hearing "Let us unite, in order to work for Christianity." And this is meant to be true Christian zeal. Christianity is of another view, it knows very well that this is trickery, for with union Christianity is not advanced, but weakened; and the more union there is, the weaker Christianity becomes.[41]

As might be expected, unionism is pervasive in the conciliar movement, since one of the aims of the great ecumenical bodies is to promote church union, even at the cost of blurring doctrinal distinctives. Christian unity is a biblical ideal, and much was said in the previous chapter on the need for making progress toward it. The question remains: Is the modern drive toward unity inspired by biblical fidelity or modern idealism? Forsyth uttered these prophetic words before the ecumenical dream became an organized movement: "A Christian optimism has grown up which had begun (like the social passion for brotherhood without righteousness, or with righteousness which was only fraternity) to dream of a speedy unity of the Churches without a prime regard to their belief."[42]

Unionism is endemic to liberalism, but the spirit of unionism is also beginning to penetrate the enclaves of evangelicalism. We hear much of the need to create a panevangelicalism that will present a united front against the liberal and modernist churches. But is this obedience to the prayer of Christ that his people be one in love and in truth? We also sometimes hear the call for a pan-Protestantism that will stand against a resurgent Roman Catholicism. Is this a true ecumenism motivated by the desire to convert the nations or a false ecumenism born out of a defensive mentality desirous of maintaining a particular tradition in the church?

Interchurch cooperation in the area of social services is indubitably a step toward the goal of Christian unity, but it can also be a device to avoid hastening toward this goal. I remember that when the ecumenical movement began to falter, the term "secular ecumenism" was increasingly used to denote the ecumenism of the future. Indeed, it seemed that the focus on overturning oppressive social structures and alleviating human suffering was more worthy than reaching agreement on the sacred mysteries of revelation, which for some appeared to be an impossible task and therefore no longer worth pursuing. Underlying this attitude was a disdain for doctrine and a distrust of biblical and ecclesiastical authority. Liberation theology today, which seeks to substitute praxis for logos, is a current manifestation of this same spirit which allows for latitude in doctrine but not in conduct.

A somewhat more subtle but no less pernicious form of accommodationism is psychologism, where the gospel is reduced to personal attitudes or interior experiences. We see this at least in part in the Faith at Work movement, which favors relational over doctrinal theology. It can also be discerned in the Clinical Pastoral Education movement, with its stress on psychic integration rather than eternal salvation. It is manifest, too, in the electronic church movement, where God is depicted as "an unlimited pool of power" that we need only to tap into in order to gain peace, health and prosperity.

The devotees of Clinical Pastoral Education promote what they call holistic salvation, where the accent is placed on the achievement or recovery of psychological wholeness. What is suspect in this emphasis is that the correlation between justification and regeneration on the one hand and normalcy as this is understood in the cultural sciences on the other is left unclear. It is an incontrovertible fact that not a few of the great saints in Christian history were considered mad or at least eccentric by cultural or psychological standards.

Bernard Ramm detects a distinct openness to psychologism among so-called young evangelicals. In reaction to the polemics of an earlier generation, they have come to believe that psychological wholeness is a more salutary goal than doctrinal correctness. The question is: Can we have an integrated personality apart from an integral vision of life? Are deep personal relations with others possible apart from a common faith and commitment?

It is disconcerting to realize that at so many evangelical conferences and retreats, group dynamics and small group discussion figure more prominently than scholarly lectures. Even prayer groups and Bible study groups are conducted in such a way that group process techniques tend to impede the free movement of the Holy Spirit. It is not an exaggeration to claim that John Dewey wields greater influence at many such meetings than either Karl Barth or John Calvin.

The fathers of the faith correctly perceived that the torments of the soul cannot be alleviated by therapeutic and medicinal techniques. "There is death," said Calvin, "even a spiritual death, which cannot be corrected by all the means and nostrums of the world. God has to put forth his hand, and that mightily."[43] Even Paul Tillich, who has pioneered in the dialogue between theology and psychotherapy, acknowledges that the latter, though helpful for mastering neurotic anxieties, is woefully incapable of overcoming the ontological anxiety of meaninglessness.[44]

Drawing on the insights of neo-orthodoxy and Tillichian theology, the modern pastoral care movement often stresses the unmerited forgiveness of God, indeed an integral part of the gospel, but at the expense of the demands of the gospel for personal holiness (cf. I Cor.

6:18–20; II Cor. 7:1; Heb. 12:14). The result is that people are soothed or tranquilized rather than challenged to live a godly and disciplined life. Kierkegaard foresaw that such an attitude could only lead to cheap grace and a hedonistic life-style:

> In *Christendom* Christianity has been employed as a stimulant oriented toward enjoying life. . . . Therefore Christendom is: refined life-enjoyment, dreadfully refined, for in paganism's enjoyment there was always a bad conscience. But in Christendom an attempt has been made to eliminate conscience by introducing atonement in the following manner: You have a God who has atoned—now you may really enjoy life. This is the greatest possible relapse.[45]

Accommodationism is also expressed in the politicizing of religion, in which the gospel is transmuted into a political-social program. This can be called the heresy of ideologism, and much has already been said about this in the last chapter. What is necessary to understand is that ideologism is as conspicuous in evangelical as in liberal circles. The Puritan vision of America as the new Israel destined to be a light to the nations is indeed pervasive in the evangelical right.[46] On the left, there is a fascination with messianic socialism, which has left its mark on the various liberation and third-world theologies. Both right- and left-oriented evangelicals are under the spell of utopianism, whose source is the millenarian tradition in Christian faith. We cannot afford to dismiss the millennial hope, but we must not confuse it with the blessed hope of the second advent of Christ, which will bring in the new heaven and the new earth (Isa. 65:17; Rev. 21:1). Evangelicals as well as liberals need to reflect on Forsyth's effort to disassociate himself from the social gospel of his day: "The largest and deepest reference to the Gospel is not to the world or its social problems, but to Eternity and its social obligations."[47]

Much of the accommodationism of today, as of yesterday, is rooted in the concern to make the faith palatable or desirable to its cultured despisers. Whenever apologetics preempts dogmatics as the central focus of the church, the slide toward an accommodation to the values and standards of the culture is almost inevitable. The apologetic thrust is highly visible not only among modernists but also among restorationists and separatists. Though claiming that Jerusalem has nothing in common with Athens, Tertullian was nonetheless a formidable apologist bent on demolishing the wisdom of Athens in order to insure the triumph of Jerusalem. Fundamentalists who call for a restoration of the old-time religion are as immersed in the apologetic enterprise as are the modernists. In seeking to combat rationalistic unbelief on its own ground, both parties betray the pitfalls of this kind of apologetic venture, which in the long run debilitates rather than strengthens the church.

An apologetic concern dominates the evangelical left almost as much as it does the right. Whereas the first tries to make the faith credible by the demonstration of a life-style of simplicity and caring, the second is intent on proving the superiority of the Christian world-view. The first often reduces Christianity to ethics; the second is in danger of confusing it with logic.

Kierkegaard, who did not abandon the apologetic task, claimed that so many apologists go wrong because they do not sufficiently perceive that the resistance to the Christian message is rooted in the sin in the human heart rather than in intellectual doubt:

> The arguments against Christianity arise out of insubordination, reluctance to obey, mutiny against all authority. Therefore, until now the battle against objections has been shadow-boxing, because it has been intellectual combat with doubt instead of being ethical combat against mutiny.[48]

Kierkegaard believed in witnessing indirectly by Christian presence but only as a preparation for the opportunity to witness directly by presenting the evangelical proclamation.

Karl Barth, who has been accused by evangelicals of giving up on apologetics, was acute enough to see that people need to be delivered before they can be persuaded. In his view, dogmatics must itself include the apologetic dimension, but the latter must not be construed as a foundation or stepping-stone to the former. He came to the conclusion that "even philosophers will not listen to a theologian who makes concessions, who is half-philosopher himself. But when you ring the bell of the Gospel, philosophers will listen!"[49] According to Barth, unbelief must not be taken too seriously, lest we imply that Jesus' victory over doubt, death and sin is incomplete. Such an attitude rests on the dubious assumption that the gospel is no match for the wisdom of the age, that the outpouring of God's grace is unable to break through the hardness of the human heart.

Barth can be criticized for ignoring the fact that an apologetic defense of the faith can awaken within the unbeliever a thirst for the Christian message, that apologetics can be a form of pre-evangelism. Yet we must not claim that apologetics can do anything more than silence criticisms and stir the conscience. In and of itself it is powerless to move the hardened sinner toward the grace of God unless grace is already present in the situation, working through the preaching of the Word of God. Harold J. Ockenga has rightly observed: "Christianity is intellectually defensible, but such intellectual apologetics do not make Christians. Christians are made by the Holy Spirit."[50]

The error of accommodationism is that it seeks to make the truth of faith contemporary whereas this truth is eternal and therefore always contemporary. The error of restorationism is that by seeing the truth encased in past formulations and practices handed down by the church, it invariably loses sight of the fact that this truth is living and therefore speaks anew to every age. Accommodationists can be accused of futurism, a desire to insure the revelance of the faith for future generations. Restorationists are guilty of archaism, the temptation to protect the faith against the allurements of the present and the future. An archaism that simply returns to the creeds and liturgies of the past can be as detrimental to the health and advancement of the churches as a futurism that in its passion to modernize the church fails to maintain continuity with its abiding tradition.

REVISIONIST VERSUS CONFESSIONAL THEOLOGY

The emerging conflict in theology today is between a revisionist and a confessional theology. The first is bent on revising or updating the life and thought of the church in the light of the new world consciousness. As David Tracy puts it, "a revisionist theology" seeks a "possible basic reconciliation between the principal values, cognitive claims, and existential faiths of both a reinterpreted post-modern consciousness and a reinterpreted Christianity."[51] For Langdon Gilkey, another revisionist theologian, the task of the church is to effect "a reinterpretation of our common Christian symbols of God, revelation, authority, salvation, law, and hope for the future—and their relation to historical change and becoming—in *non*supernaturalistic terms so that they can be means of grace to our time."[52] Confessional theology, on the other hand, has for its aim the overthrowing of the new world consciousness and its supplanting by fear and trust in the living, holy God revealed in the Scriptures. In this perspective, it is not the faith of the church but the ideologies of the world that need to be demythologized or reconceptualized.

Revisionist theology takes various forms. Feminist theologians are occupied in revising the language and content of faith on the basis of feminist experience. Liberation theology endeavors to reinterpret the faith in the light of the class struggle, the mythical vision of Marxism. In process theology, the aim is to rethink the classical doctrines of the faith, particularly the doctrine of God, in order to bring them into accord with the creative insights of Whiteheadian or Teilhardian philosophy.

Against the above approaches, evangelical theology is unashamedly confessional. It seeks to confess the great doctrines of Scripture and the church in a fresh language but with a continuity in meaning. This new language, moreover, is not a substitute for the language of Zion, the imagery of Holy Scripture, but instead a supplement to it. Evangelicals may also speak of revision, but what they have in mind is a revision not of Scripture or church dogma but of our present theological formulations in the light of Scripture and church tradition. A confessional theology does not simply seek to return to past times, nor does it try to accommodate to present times; instead, it heralds the fulfillment of all times in Jesus Christ.

A revisionist theology will necessarily be modernist in the sense that it represents an accommodation to the *Zeitgeist* (the spirit of the times). Though not accepting uncritically all the claims of modernity, revisionism does try to bring the faith into accord with the spirit of modernity. It often assumes the guises of latitudinarianism and universalism, both of which deny the absolute necessity of a personal commitment of faith in Jesus Christ for salvation.

Kierkegaard powerfully enunciated the evangelical reaction to the latitudinarian and universalist theology of his day:

> It is supposed that we shall all be saved, that we are Christians from birth—and instead of the fearful effort of having to make use of this

life for an eternal decision it is supposed that everything is already settled, and at most it is a question of whether out of gratitude we live a reasonably decent life, which in any case from the purely earthly and worldly point of view is the most prudent thing to do.[53]

Confessional theology strives to be liberal in the sense of self-critical, but it is adamantly opposed to the ideology of liberalism with its naive belief in moral progress and its almost unreserved trust in human reason. Whereas revisionist theology seeks the radical revision of the values and concepts of Christian tradition, confessional theology is radical in the sense of returning to the roots of the faith. At the same time, confessional theology is conservative, for it strives always to maintain the truth of Scripture and tradition.

Confessional theology is not, however, restorationist. It does not simply wish to return to past theological formulations or cultural attitudes that belong to a bygone era. It is confessional without being confessionalist in the sense of the old orthodoxy. It seeks to confess the abiding doctrines of the faith in the language of our day. It is also intent on applying the scriptural message to the critical social and spiritual issues of our time.

An evangelical theology of this kind does not deny or underplay the role of experience in faith (as is sometimes the case in neo-orthodoxy). It sees experience, however, not as the source but as the medium of a transcendent revelation. It believes that the revelation of God must be received in experience, though it does not derive its criterion for truth from experience. The gospel does not nullify experience but instead redeems it. Forsyth ably expresses the equivocal and yet crucial role of experience in evangelical theology: "Christian experience is the experience of the authority of the Gospel; it is not an experience which becomes the authority for the Gospel; whose authority can be most mighty when every reason drawn from human experience is against it."[54]

Our confession is not simply an intellectual commitment but is born out of the agony and joy of a transforming experience, thus becoming an existential witness. We cannot inwardly know the truth of the gospel apart from the evangelical experience, but this experience always points beyond itself to the reconciling and redeeming work of God in Jesus Christ in the history attested to in Holy Scripture.

Finally, confessional theology confesses not only the faith once for all delivered to the saints (Jude 3) but also the insufficiency and weakness of its response to this faith, even its sin. The evangelical theologian recognizes that he will be judged more severely than the others because his vocation is to enunciate not his own opinions but the very Word of God (cf. James 3:1). While the revisionist theologian is concerned about the judgment that the world gives, the confessional theologian believes that opposition by the world may be an invincible sign of the truth of his witness (cf. Matt. 5:10–12; 10:22; John 15:18–20).

A confessional theology is anchored in the assurance that faith itself provides and not in the certainty of its own grasp of the faith. It will be a theology of the cross rather than a theology of glory, though it makes a place for the proleptic experience of coming glory as an illumination and partial confirmation of faith.

Karl Barth here manifests the humility and searching attitude that should characterize all bona fide evangelical theology:

> Are we quite sure that what we, with hasty decision, call the gospel of Jesus Christ is the gospel? Are we quite sure that a victory of a so-called Christian view of the world would be a victory of God? Are we quite sure that a prosperous church is evidence of the progress and coming of the kingdom of God?[55]

The differences between confessional and revisionist theology become clear when seen in the context of H. Richard Niebuhr's typology set forth in his provocative book *Christ and Culture*.[56] A revisionist theology corresponds to the Niebuhrian category of "Christ of culture," since it focuses upon an underlying identity between the highest values of the culture and the message of faith. A confessional theology, on the other hand, is closer to the position of "Christ transforming culture," for its aim is the conversion of the values and thought forms of the culture into the service of the kingdom of Christ. At the same time, a confessional theology will also incorporate motifs associated with "Christ against culture," since it acknowledges that only by standing against the world can it overcome the world.

Christian action in the world most nearly resembles neither an ambulance service nor a peace corps devoted to rebuilding a society in disarray. Instead, it is more like a sortie from a fortress, which by its very presence poses an unmistakable challenge to worldly authority. The Christian should neither seek a new fortress (the way of sectarianism), nor be content to remain within the walls of the fortress (the way of restorationism). Nor should he abandon the fortress for the sake of greater relevance and acceptance by the world (the way of modernism). Instead, he should venture out with boldness doing battle with the principalities and powers of the world, thereby extending the influence and authority of the fortress (the church). The fortress is indeed a signpost of a kingdom that is not of this world, but it should be something more: It should serve as a launching vehicle for an invasion of the world, for bringing the world into submission to the Lord of the fortress. This was the transformationist vision of John Calvin and the Puritans, and it is this vision that we sorely need to recover today.[57]

VI

Toward the Recovery of Evangelical Faith

Protestantism stands or falls with the Bible, Romanism stands or falls with the papacy. We cannot go back to Romanism; still less can we surrender ourselves to the icy embrace of Rationalism.

PHILIP SCHAFF

We refuse to bow to the spirit of the age, but we ought at least to speak the language of that age, and address it from the Cross in the tone of its too familiar sorrow.

P. T. FORSYTH

The whole church must become a mobile missionary force, ready for a wilderness life. It is a time for us to be thinking of campaign tents rather than of cathedrals.

JOHN MACKAY

The Church will win the world for Christ when—and only when —she works through living spirits steeped in prayer.

EVELYN UNDERHILL

EVANGELICAL CHRISTIANITY can only survive by discovering anew the meaning of the biblical gospel for our day. It must also be willing to subordinate itself to the gospel, to alter its own strategies and programs in the light of the gospel. Unfortunately, latter-day evangelicalism is marked by the tendency to seek mastery over the gospel in order to advance itself. The gospel is either converted into a creedal formula possessed by the church or reduced to a therapeutic product dispensed by the clerics of the church. Unless this tendency is reversed, evangelicalism will most certainly lose its spiritual dynamic and momentum. The evangelical church may then see the new wine of the gospel being placed in new wineskins.[1]

As an evangelical passionately concerned with the future of this renewal movement, I venture to offer some correctives which, it seems to me, are needed if evangelicalism is to become all it was meant to be.

RECLAIMING HISTORICAL ROOTS

The Chicago Call conference (1977) reminded us that the rediscovery of historical roots is vital to a renewed evangelical faith. Among our spiritual forbears are the great theologians of Protestant orthodoxy—Chemnitz, Hollaz, Flacius, Polanus, Heidegger, Cocceius, Wollebius and Voetius. Certainly not all of these men can be considered rationalists. For the most part, they eschewed the later fundamentalist error of making an absolute equation between the words of the Bible and the revealed Word of God.[2]

Evangelicals should also recognize what they owe to the spiritual movements of purification subsequent to the Reformation—Pietism and Puritanism.[3] The Pietists and Puritans were reacting against both a deadening formalism and a stultifying creedalism in the church. Many evangelicals today seem to be fearful of the free movement of the Spirit, wishing to confine him to the formulas and credos of their own particular traditions. What we can learn from Pietism and Puritanism as well as from eighteenth- and nineteenth-century Evangelicalism is that the Spirit constantly breaks through our creedal and liturgical forms, overturning our traditional modes of understanding and behavior. Out of these renewal movements new forms of ministry emerged—house gatherings for prayer and Bible study (*collegia pietatis*), deaconess sisterhoods, institutes for lay evangelism, epileptic homes, homes for unwed mothers, orphanages, rescue missions and, much later, lay witness missions. It should also be borne in mind that the great missionary outreach to foreign lands (in which women played a significant role) had its fundamental source in these movements of inward purification.[4]

Surely, a reappropriation of the abiding insights of the Protestant Reformation of the sixteenth century is indispensable for a revivified evangelicalism today. The Reformation can indeed be considered evangelical in the most fundamental sense of that word: its focus was on doctrines that are integral to the gospel itself—*sola gratia* (salvation by grace alone), *sola fide* (justification by faith alone), *sola scriptura* (the primacy of Scripture over the church), and *Soli Deo gloria* (glory to God alone). Certainly these were not original with the Reformers, but they had fallen into obscurity, especially in the later Middle Ages when semi-Pelagianism was dominant.[5] No Christian can claim to be evangelical who does not stand with the Reformers in insisting on the priority and sovereignty of the grace of God and the infallibility and absolute normativeness of Holy Scripture.

It is a matter of debate among scholars whether the Reformation signified a recovering of New Testament Christianity or simply a modification and corrective to Latin Christianity. Brian Gerrish reminds us that the Reformers, unlike the revolutionary Spiritualists, were intent not on overthrowing the values and institutions of their times but instead on renewing them in the light of the gospel.[6] Ernst Troeltsch once remarked that the Middle Ages are the maternal womb of us all, including Protestants. According to Philip Schaff, the Reformation was "the legitimate offspring" and "greatest act" of the Catholic Church—the unfolding of the "true catholic nature itself."[7]

Yet although it is true that the Reformation cannot be adequately understood apart from the cultural and historical context of medieval Catholicism, it should also be stressed that the Reformation introduced something radically new for that time—the idea of the church as a community of faith instead of a hierarchical institution.[8] All Christians, said Luther, are members of the royal priesthood rather than being under the direction of a special priesthood. This means that all believers have the privilege of being intercessors, all may hear confessions, all may share in the ministry of mutual consolation.

In its stress on the universal call to discipleship, the Reformation broke irrevocably with the double standard of Catholic spirituality, in which a demarcation was made between the religious, who were expected to live according to the counsels of perfection (celibacy, poverty, obedience) and the ordinary believers, whose mandate was to maintain life in society. For the Reformers, all believers are summoned to the high and holy vocation of being witnesses and ambassadors of Jesus Christ.[9] Most Christians realize this vocation precisely in their secular occupations, which are no less sacred in their motivation and goal than the pastoral ministry.[10]

It can also be argued that the Reformation distinction between justification, fundamentally a forensic act by which God declares us just through the merits of Christ, and sanctification, the interior renewal by the Holy Spirit, represented a reappropriation of Pauline theology, which was only anticipated but never developed in Catholic and Eastern Orthodox theology. For the most part, justification was considered by Catholic scholars as something intrinsic rather than extrinsic. The Reformation view that we remain sinners even while covered by the perfection of the holiness of Christ stood in precarious tension if not diametrical opposition to the Catholic and Eastern Orthodox emphasis on deification, the idea that the sinner is transformed into godlikeness through grace.

While the Reformers continued to maintain the Catholic emphasis on the divine authority of Scripture, they insisted on its primacy over church tradition as well as religious experience. Here they could appeal to some of the church fathers for support, but when they went on to contend for the self-authenticating character of Scripture, the break with the Catholic Church was irremediable. Holy Scripture does not need to be interpreted by the teaching authority of the church to the laity; instead, Scripture interprets itself by the action of the Spirit to the whole church. The church magisterium can amplify and clarify the Word of God in Scripture, but this Word is fundamentally perspicacious to all who come to the Scriptures in faith.

Certainly we who stand in the tradition of the Reformation must not proudly exult in our particular heritage. We must not be blind to the tragic fact that the Reformation fractured Christian unity, that it discarded not only cultural and philosophical accretions that obscured the gospel of free grace but also some of the treasures in Catholic tradition which have yet to be taken seriously by Protestants (including the intercessory and exemplary role of Mary and the saints in Christian devotion). In addition, we should be willing to consider that the Counter-Reformation also laid hold of some important aspects of biblical truth, that it, too, produced models of piety worthy of emulation.

By no means should we be ashamed of the Reformation or downplay its enduring contributions (as do liberals who verge toward humanism and evangelicals captivated by positive thinking).[11] At the same time, when we celebrate this great reforming movement in Christian history, we must be poignantly aware of its failings as well as its successes, of its disobedience as well as its faithfulness to the mandate of the holy God.

In recovering our indebtedness to the Reformation, we must, of course, include the Anabaptists, with their pronounced stress on the Christian life. The Reformation message of justification by the free grace of God becomes rationalization for sin and cheap grace unless it is united with the New Testament call to radical discipleship, the salient emphasis of the Anabaptists. Whereas the mainline Reformers held up the Word and the sacraments as the two practical signs of the true church, the Anabaptists contended that the true church must also be distinguished by the marks of suffering for the faith, the effects of persecution by the world. A truly evangelical and catholic church will seek to incorporate the Anabaptist vision but within the context of the great Pauline and Reformation doctrines of salvation by grace through faith (cf. Rom. 1:16, 17; Eph. 2:8).

Yet evangelicals should not be content to draw upon both the mainline and left-wing Reformations; they can be immensely enriched by rediscovering the genuinely evangelical motifs in many of the church fathers and medieval theologians. Protestants often point to John Huss, John Wycliffe and Savonarola[12] as precursors of the Reformation, with their emphasis on scriptural authority and their attack on corruption in the church. To our detriment, most of us forget those who stand in the mainstream of Catholic tradition and yet who enunciated doctrines that exalt rather than detract from the gospel. The fathers of the church who successfully defended the faith against the ancient heresies—Gnosticism, Arianism and Neoplatonic mysticism—should be included among the pioneers and perfecters of the faith (cf. Heb. 11). Long before the Reformation contended for grace alone and faith alone, these biblical principles were stoutly affirmed by Ambrose, Augustine and Ambrosiaster. It was the last who declared, "It is ordained of God that whoever believes in Christ shall be saved, and he shall have forgiveness of sins, not through works but through faith alone, without merit."[13]

The doctors of the medieval church should also be regarded as sources for evangelical renewal in our day, even though we must read these men and women with biblical discrimination (but this applies also to the church fathers and Reformers). In Protestant evangelical circles, Thomas Aquinas is often accused of trying to construct a natural road to faith in God that would in effect supplant the road marked out by the biblical revelation. Yet Thomas insisted that though rational argument can demonstrate the reasonableness of belief in a supreme being and in a moral law, only faith can lay hold of the revelation of God in Jesus Christ that alone saves from sin and death. Moreover, he steadfastly affirmed that free will is inadequate for the act of faith, since the truth of faith is beyond reason. In accord with the Augustinian tradition, he was emphatic that faith is given to us by God apart from the merit of our preceding actions. "The reason," he said, "why God saves man by faith without any preceding merits" is "that no man may glory in himself but refer all the glory to God."[14]

Evangelical motifs can even be discerned in the tradition of Christian mysticism, though here we need to be particularly cautious because of the indebtedness of this tradition to Platonism and Neoplatonism. Yet we should remember that Luther was influenced positively in his spiritual development by John Tauler and the *Theologia Germanica*.[15] Both Calvin and Luther often referred to Augustine and Bernard of Clairvaux in support of their positions. Catholics of a somewhat mystical bent after the Reformation whose piety has been decidedly more biblical than Platonic include Cornelius Jansen, Pascal, Thérèse of Lisieux and Hans Urs von Balthasar.

The catholic heritage of the past is being increasingly rediscovered by Protestant evangelical scholars. Robert Webber's *Common Roots*, Thomas Oden's *Agenda for Theology*, and the Chicago Call conference in 1977, out of which came the book *The Orthodox Evangelicals*,[16] are all evidence of this trend. I also point the reader to my own books *The Reform of the Church* and *Essentials of Evangelical Theology*, particularly the second volume.[17]

A word of warning is appropriate at this juncture. In our endeavor to recover continuity with the whole tradition of the faith, we must resist the temptation to interpret the Bible in the light of classical Christianity rather than vice versa. A nostalgia for the past may blind us to errors in the past that have crippled the Christian witness in various periods of church history. Catholics as well as Protestants would do well to keep in mind that the church must continually be reformed in the light of the revelation given once for all in the past through the inspired witness of Holy Scripture.

The more prevalent failing in modern evangelicalism is to ignore the past altogether, to emphasize communication skills over the commentary on Scripture in the history of the church, to downplay nurture in the faith of the church in favor of strategies for expanding the church. Some of the new evangelical schools advertise programs in church growth and electronic media studies but are strangely silent regarding their offerings in systematic theology or the history of Christian thought. Evangelicalism will be caught up and submerged in the mainstream of popular culture-religion unless it rediscovers its identity as a bona fide branch of the holy catholic church. It needs to reclaim its glorious heritage, which extends from the first century of the church onward but which was given special visibility in the Protestant Reformation of the sixteenth century and the evangelical revival movements of the seventeenth and eighteenth centuries.

NEW STATEMENTS ON BIBLICAL AUTHORITY

If the neglect of historical roots is not widely recognized in the evangelical world, the question of biblical authority is readily acknowledged as a crucial issue. That the battle for the gospel today will also be a battle for the Bible is becoming abundantly clear. The erosion of biblical authority has seriously undermined the preaching ministry in both Protestant and Catholic communions. It has also had deleterious consequences in the areas of personal and social ethics. The facile acceptance by clerical as well as secular leaders of abortion on demand and deviate forms of sexuality signifies that in many circles biblical norms are now passé; indeed, the social sciences increasingly occupy the position formerly held by Scripture in determining what is normative in the areas of sexuality and family life.

It is commonplace today to try to draw a wedge between the historical expression of the faith given in Scripture and the object of faith, which is Jesus Christ. Yet we must recognize that we cannot have the divine content apart from the cultural and historical form in which this content comes to us. We must be frank enough to acknowledge a certain degree of historical and cultural contingency in the biblical witness to God in Christ; at the same time, we must insist that there is also an unchanging truth.

As I see it, there are three basic approaches to scriptural authority: the sacramental, the scholastic and the liberal-modernist.[18] In the first, the Bible is a divinely appointed channel, a mirror, or a visible sign of divine revelation. This was the general position of the church fathers, the doctors of the medieval church, and the Reformers. In the second, the Bible is the written or verbal revelation of God, a transcript of the very thoughts of God. This has been the viewpoint of Protestant fundamentalism, though it was anticipated in both Catholic and Protestant scholastic orthodoxy. In the third, the Bible is a record of the religious experience of a particular people in history; this reflects the general stance of liberalism, both Catholic and Protestant. Only the first position does justice to the dual origin of Scripture—that it is both a product of divine inspiration and a human witness to divine truth. We need to recognize the full humanity of Scripture as well as its true divinity. Indeed, it should be impressed upon us that we can come to know its divinity only in and through its humanity. As Luther put it, the Scriptures are the swaddling clothes that contain the treasure of Jesus Christ.

A careful examination of early Protestant orthodoxy as well as of Puritanism and Pietism reveals that the distinction between the word of God and the words of the Bible was quite common. Our spiritual forebears referred to the form and the content of Scripture, the shell and the kernel, the meaning and the words. David Hollaz distinguished between what God has revealed (the absolute principle) and the scriptural witness to this (the relative principle). He spoke of a divine revelation which is "contained in the writings of the prophets and apostles."[19] The Puritan Richard Sibbes could assert: "The word of God is ancienter than the Scripture. . . . The Scripture is but that *modus,* that manner of conveying the word of God."[20] For Sibbes, the truth of faith is not a propositional formula that remains lifeless until it is perceived by the hearer; instead, "divine truth is holy, full of majesty and power in itself."[21]

Philip Schaff, in whom Protestant orthodoxy and Pietism coalesce, is helpful in this regard. Schaff drew a distinction between the "matter" of Scripture and its "peculiar form." He pointed to the need to do justice to both the divine side of Scripture and its "human and historical character."[22] Portraying the Bible as "a mirror which reflects Christ," he held that "we must not look *at* the mirror, but *through* the mirror to the glorious object which it reveals."[23] Schaff stood close to Calvin in viewing the Bible as the unerring rule for faith rather than contending for an errorless book in the modern sense of technical accuracy. He referred to "the sufficiency and unerring certainty of the holy Scriptures" and the "unerring" truth which the Scriptures contain.[24] At the same time, he rejected a mechanical theory of inspiration in favor of an organic one, in which the Holy Spirit enters into the thought forms and life history of the authors.

The difference between liberalism and orthodoxy is the way in which each applies the form-content distinction to Scripture. The liberals (à la Harnack) seek to extract the content from the form and treat it apart from the form. Evangelical Christianity wisely recognizes that the divine content is available to us only in the language of Zion, that is to say, in the inspired symbolism and imagery of Holy Scripture. I affirm a union but not a fusion between the divine content and its worldly form.

Today, we should insist that Scripture be interpreted by Scripture, not by the new world consciousness of living in a male-female world (as some feminists advocate) or the emerging class consciousness of being poor in a world of affluence (as in the case of the liberationists). We must steadfastly refrain from accommodating the message of Scripture to any cultural ideology, whether on the right or left. The Scriptures stand in judgment over every cultural ideology. To be sure, God is also speaking to us in the times; but unless we first hear the Word of God in Scripture, we shall never recognize the hand of God in the times.

Neo-orthodoxy has helped us to recover the dynamic character of divine revelation, but it lost sight of an inspired text as the earthen vessel of this revelation. It is important to understand that there are three components in God's Word: words, meaning and power. All three must be present if we are to hear and know the veritable Word of God. Fundamentalism has placed the accent on the words, whereas liberal and neo-orthodox theology emphasize the spirit. We need today a new statement on biblical authority that will stress the organic connection between words and meaning, external symbols, and spiritual truth and power. Revelation is not simply a witness frozen in past formulations but an event in which the truth of this witness is unveiled to the perceiver in the here and now. Certainly this is the understanding conveyed by the psalmist: "Open my eyes, so that I may see the wonderful truths in your law" (119:18 GNB cf. Eph. 1:17, 18 NIV).

On the intractable problem of whether Scripture contains errors, we need to recognize that this conflict is rooted in disparate notions of truth. Truth in the Bible means conformity to the will and purpose of God. Truth in today's empirical, scientific milieu means an exact correspondence between one's ideas or perceptions and the phenomena of nature and history. Error in the Bible means a deviation from the will and purpose of God, unfaithfulness to the dictates of his law. Error in the empirical mind-set of a technological culture means inaccuracy or inconsistency in what is reported as objectively occurring in nature or history. Technical precision is the measure of truth in empiricism. Fidelity to God's Word is the biblical criterion for truth. Empiricism narrows the field of investigation to objective sense data,[25] and therefore to speak of revelation as superhistorical or hidden in history is to remove it from what can legitimately be considered as knowledge. The difference between the rational-empirical and the biblical understanding of truth is the difference between transparency to Eternity and literal facticity.[26]

We also seek a statement on scriptural authority that will do justice to the integral relation between Scripture and the tradition of the church. Just as the trunk and branches of a tree are as necessary for the life of the tree as its roots (though the roots have priority), so the whole of the tree is dependent for its life on water (the living Word of God), which is conveyed through the roots (the Bible) to the other parts of the tree. It is fallacious to assume, as do some evangelicals, that we can neglect the branches that have sprung from the roots and begin over again with the roots alone (a false conception of *sola scriptura*). At the same time, we should recognize that some branches become crooked and others die. Those that die need to be pruned, but they do not negate the strength and validity of the life of all. Though some traditions may become worthless or even dangerous, tradition itself is necessary to convey the truth of the Bible to the world.

One tradition that has served to impede the theological enterprise —the alliance with philosophy—can well be discarded. If there is to be authentic spiritual renewal in our churches today, evangelicals will have to divest themselves of dependence on current and past philosophical methodologies. We will be obliged to bring our philosophical and sociological presuppositions under the searchlight of Scripture. By no means dare we impose them on Scripture. Karl Barth has rightly observed that we should come to the Bible laying aside all overt philosophical presuppositions. He asserted this against both Bultmann and Tillich, for whom the insights of existentialist analysis were an invaluable aid in the study of the Bible.[27]

Within the church today (both Catholic and Protestant), there is a pressing need to transcend the cleavage between fideism and rationalism. We must realize that reason is involved in faith from the very beginning, because faith is a rational commitment as well as a decision of the will. At the same time, we should beware of seeking a rational or philosophical basis for faith. Reason is a useful instrument in explicating the truth of revelation, but it cannot prepare the way for the reception of this truth.

While affirming that the whole of creation reflects the light and glory of God (cf. Ps. 19:1–4; Rom. 1:19, 20), we must steer clear of any natural theology that supposes valid knowledge of God on the basis of this general light in creation. Indeed, the universal awareness of God made possible by the light in nature and conscience is the basis for the *misunderstanding*, not the *understanding* of God. Such knowledge of God as we can glean from nature gives us not a capacity but an incapacity for revelation. The light in nature can be a positive guide to the believer, since his eyes have been opened to the source of this light—Jesus Christ. Because of sin, our inward eyes are blinded to the objective glory of God reflected in nature, and yet we have enough intimation of this glory to render us inexcusable (Rom. 1:20; 2:1).[28] The natural knowledge of God is sufficient neither for a valid understanding nor for salvation but only for condemnation. Augustine confessed that before his conversion he did not really know God, that his ideas of God were only constructs of his mind.[29] The mixture of truth and untruth in pagan philosophy caused him to seek and resist God at the same time. In our era, Karl Barth has helped us to recover the truth that natural theology leads only to a dead end, which was fully recognized by Luther and Calvin and to a lesser extent by Augustine.

There is need today for a methodology that has its source of inspiration in Scripture, not in some philosophy extraneous to Scripture. In my opinion, Augustine and Anselm were true to the central thrust of the Bible when they propounded "faith seeking understanding" as the method of scientific theology. This must not be interpreted in a purely fideistic way as beginning with a leap of faith. Our point of departure is neither faith nor reason but divine revelation, which can be apprehended to be sure only with the eyes of faith. Yet the light of faith is a light that also illumines our reason, so that a reborn reason is capable of understanding the truth of revelation, not exhaustively but adequately. Christianity does not contradict rationality, for the Word of God is also the Logos or wisdom of God, but it does oppose rationalism, which seeks to bring revelation into accord with the canons of human logic.

The task of theology is not a systematic overview of God and the world but instead a true understanding of the will and purpose of God disclosed in Jesus Christ, an understanding that eventuates in obedience. The object is not to acquire observational knowledge about God (as in naturalistic empiricism) nor conceptual mastery of him (as in idealistic rationalism). Biblical theology is a more modest enterprise, for it seeks to know not the mystery of God in himself but the plan or purpose that God has for our lives, one that is revealed and exemplified in Jesus Christ. The goal of faith is not comprehension of the divine essence but conformity to the divine will. It is not so much transcendent wisdom (as in Gnosticism) as sacrificial discipleship under the cross. Our motto should be: "I believe and seek to understand in order to obey" (cf. Rom. 1:5; 16:26; II Cor. 10:5, 6; I Pet. 1:2).

It is also imperative that we begin to see the limitations of apologetics. Too often in the past, apologetics occupied the central role in Roman Catholic and Reformed theology. The evidence for the faith took precedence over the substance of the faith, and theology invariably became a philosophical justification for belief in God rather than a systematic explication of the revealed truth of God. Arguments and proofs for the gospel are hardly convincing to the man come of age, the liberated man of the world. Yet they can be useful as testimonies to the faith, which can make the outsider willing to listen to our gospel. Apologetics can also enable the insider to understand his faith better—in the light of attacks upon it.

Regrettably, in much current apologetics Christianity is recommended as a means to a higher end, such as personal integration or social harmony. Harry Blamires has some harsh words on this kind of defense of the faith:

> We must not *exploit* our Faith by advertising it as a technique for achieving earthly satisfactions. The Faith is not a recipe and not a program. It is a Way. Recipes and programs are made to help you to carry out earthly jobs successfully. But a Way is something you walk in.[30]

It is incumbent on us to recover dogmatics as the central task in theology, though not to the exclusion of apologetics. Apologetics will still have an important place in the theological enterprise, but it will now be seen as a branch of dogmatics, the branch that seeks to combat the attacks upon the faith from its cultured despisers. It is not to be construed, however, as a propaedeutic device that leads to faith; instead, it is a tool of discernment that enables believers to clarify their faith and answer objections to it. Apologetics can silence the criticisms of unbelievers, but it cannot move them to accept the truth claims of the faith. Those in the grip of unbelief are dead in sin and need not so much to be persuaded as to be resurrected. Only the Spirit of God can raise people from the dead, and he does this through the preaching and hearing of the gospel (Rom. 10:14–17; I Cor. 1:21).

It is significant that those who see apologetics as a stepping-stone to dogmatics or who contend that reason can gain some valid knowledge of God apart from revelation also allow a role for good works prior to faith. In his *Christian Commitment*, Edward John Carnell argues that the law of justice, available to everyone, leads to the law of consideration, which in turn leads to the law of love (salvation).[31] According to Norman Geisler, "If one follows the light he has, then God will give him the added (supernatural) light he needs to be saved."[32] Surely this represents the semi-Pelagianism against which the Reformers rallied. Many evangelicals today need to ask whether they really stand in the great heritage of the Reformation, Augustine and Paul.[33]

Paradoxically, with the ebbing of confessionalism there is occurring a resurgence of denominationalism, where the focus is on parochial rather than universal concerns. The confessions, it should be remembered, despite their polemical thrust, have provided a platform for dialogue with other Christians. Moreover, they are generally addressed to the whole church, not just to a particular constituency. Not surprisingly, we are also witnessing today the rise of an uncritical experientialism. When the church moves away from its confessional standards, it is prone to demand absolute loyalty to its leadership, its program or even to its polity. The other alternative is to enthrone personal experience or the light of conscience, and the church thereby becomes another club, a society of like-minded individuals.

The Chicago Call statement put it very succinctly: "We deplore two opposite excesses: a creedal church that merely recites a faith inherited from the past, and a creedless church that languishes in a doctrinal vacuum."[34] The indisputable fact is that this is precisely what we have today—churches that are merely creedal or churches without any creed whatsoever.

A genuine confession of faith will be aimed at the heresies of the time in which the confession is written. It will arise out of a poignant realization that the church is being threatened by false teaching, that the very identity of the church is at stake. Karl Barth has said that a confession will come "when a man realizes that . . . the faith of the Christian community is confronted and questioned either from within or without by the phenomena of unbelief, superstition and heresy."[35] In Germany at the time of the Barmen Declaration, the threat to the church was the cultural ideology of racism. In Western democratic culture, the threat seems to be a radical egalitarianism allied with a technocratic liberalism. Because the exact nature of this threat is not yet clearly seen, it is premature to plan a new confession of faith at this time. The signs are nonetheless unmistakable that we are fast approaching a confessional situation in this country. In all likelihood, the needed confession of faith will arise not from the councils of the church but from prophets specially chosen by God. It is to be hoped that it will cross all denominational lines and bring biblically oriented Catholics and Protestant evangelicals, both in the mainline denominations and in the smaller sects, to a doctrinal and moral consensus for our day.

The object of a genuine confession of faith is not to reiterate the views already held by a particular constituency. It is instead to challenge the partial conceptions and misconceptions of our people in the light of a vision given to the church by the Holy Spirit. A true confession will say something definite on ethics as well as dogmatics. It will address itself to life in society as well as to doctrinal issues. The task of the church is not to solve the problems of society but to relate to them and challenge them.

Many evangelical Protestant churches hold to the "Bible alone," disdaining all confessions. They rightly see that confessions may usurp biblical authority, and indeed, a true confession will always be under Scripture, not alongside Scripture. A confession is a broken symbol and should therefore always be open to revision and correction in the light of the new truth that the Spirit reveals through Holy Scripture. The answer to the temptations of a false confessionalism is not a creedless church, however, since this can lead to self-deception. Every church is creedal to some degree, if only implicitly. Yet we must guard against the danger of making the confession into a new law. Ideally, it should be a guide and norm for Christian belief and action in a particular period of history.

Pietism is inclined to downplay the role of confessions because of its emphasis on practical obedience. Such an attitude too easily prepares the way for latitudinarianism, which tolerates misunderstandings of the faith. The University of Halle, founded by Pietists, became in an amazingly short time a bastion of rationalism. Pietism, if it is to continue to be biblically vital, must be anchored in a solid confession of faith and nurtured by a concern for orthodoxy.

Yet latitudinarianism is not the only peril confronting those who seek to maintain the true faith. There can be a misplaced zeal, aimed at hounding the heretic rather than countering the heresy. In combating heresy, we should focus our attack on the false doctrine, not the person. We should seek to restore the heretic even while killing the heresy. Calvin sagaciously observed, "We delight in a certain poisoned sweetness experienced in ferreting out and in disclosing the evils of others."[36]

We should also not be too quick in judging the opinions of others, remembering that some of the most brilliant minds in the history of the church have been accused of heresy. It is the better part of wisdom to tolerate rather than root out the misguided speculations of others if these only remain on the periphery of church life and do not constitute a serious threat to the church's mission. Such opinions may not even be heresy, flagrant untruth, but only heterodoxy, an unbalanced emphasis on one segment of the truth to the detriment or exclusion of others.

At the same time, we should not remain indifferent to the threat of real heresy in the life and thought of the church. When a heretical doctrine begins to usurp the gospel in the church's proclamation, then the church must act or else become a false church. Philip Schaff, himself for a time under surveillance for theological deviation, has stated: "There are, indeed, differences which can never be reconciled; of two contradictory propositions one must be false and resisted to the end. Between truth and error, between God and Belial, between Christ and Anti-Christ there can be no compromise."[37]

The real division in the church today is not political or sociological but theological. Behind the class and ethnic barriers separating Christians in our time are deep-seated theological divisions that simply will not go away. It is the task of the church in this situation to explore these differences and to redefine the true faith against the various distortions of the faith that are so rampant.

The key to church renewal does not lie in simply returning to confessions of past ages. Such documents have been and continue to be guidelines for correct belief, but they do not carry the same authority and power for our day as they once did. The Holy Spirit always speaks a new word to his people, a word that does not negate the words he has spoken in the past but clarifies and fulfills the partial illuminations already given. Evangelicals in both Protestant and Catholic communions need to be prepared for a new confessional controversy that will divide Christians before it unites them on a deeper level.

Confessions of faith have not been given the attention they deserve because of the appalling neglect of ecclesiology in the circles of conservative evangelicalism. Perhaps one reason for this is the legacy of revivalism, with its emphasis on individual decision and commitment. The decision of faith was given priority over nurture in a Christian fellowship. The church, moreover, was generally regarded as a gathered fellowship of true believers where the accent was on community rather than on loyalty to a divine institution founded by Christ.

What we need today is to recover the classical marks of the church: catholicity, apostolicity, holiness and oneness. It is especially important for evangelicals, who are accustomed to elevate personal experience over church authority, to realize that the church, too, is a gift of God. It is well to remind ourselves, moreover, that the church is not many but one, that it is not parochial but universal, that it has apostolic foundation and therefore antedates the Reformation and the great revivals. The church is also holy, not because it is comprised of a people who have attained personal holiness, but because it is covered by the holiness of its Lord and head—Jesus Christ. The holiness of Christ must, of course, be reflected in all the members of his body, but we should recognize that our holiness is derivative and fragmentary. This is why the church is both sinful and righteous at the same time.

To these classical marks of the church, Luther and Calvin added the practical marks of the pure preaching of the Word and the right administration of the sacraments. Martin Bucer also argued for the inclusion of church discipline as a hallmark of the true church. In Pietism and Puritanism all of these were supplemented by two additional practical signs—fellowship and mission. It was rightly recognized that where the fellowship of love (koinonia) and the imperative to mission are absent, we do not have the church in its fullness. Today, Catholics and Protestants alike would do well to acknowledge that the church is indeed deficient apart from the fellowship of love, the urgency of evangelism and the practice of discipline.

A further salient mark of the holy catholic church, one that should perhaps be given special emphasis in our time, is racial and social inclusiveness. If a major source of division in the church is racial and class consciousness, then the church cannot be fully catholic or truly holy unless such barriers are overcome. Evangelicals who are attracted to church growth strategies often stress cultural and racial homogeneity as essential for a strong and vital church. This may be a valid sociological observation, but it is theological heresy, since the holy catholic church transcends and relativizes, without necessarily canceling out, those things that divide humankind (cf. Gal. 3:28). It is an incontestable fact that early Pentecostalism succeeded in overcoming racial and class antagonisms, but as Pentecostalism became steadily more institutionalized and ceased to be a free movement of the Spirit, it began to take on the restrictive patterns of the surrounding society, where racial, class and ethnic distinctions block significant human communication.

Mindful of the importance of each of these marks, we must strive for a renewed appreciation of the church in the plan of salvation. The church is not simply the herald or witness to Christ's salvation (as Barthianism envisages it) but is indeed a divinely chosen instrument and means of salvation. Calvin, who was not averse to referring to the church as "our holy mother," declared: "It is not enough to know that Jesus Christ has made amends for us, and even that all things necessary for our salvation were fully accomplished and performed by his death and passion, but we must also at the same time receive the benefit of it in such way as it is ministered to us."[88]

Neo-orthodoxy renewed theology, but it was not able to renew the life of the church. Yet the renewal of the church will entail theological renewal. Emil Brunner saw authentic community as nonstructural, and this accounts for his interest in the Oxford Group movement and the nonchurch movement in Japan.[39] Karl Barth conceived of the true church as a church in mission, which to him meant a church involved in the suffering of the world. Continuity with the tradition was not of great importance in their theologies, and this is perhaps one reason why they lost sight of the divinity of the church.

Evangelicals should also earnestly seek to recover the crucial place of the sacraments in the life of the church. For Zwingli, the sacrament augments faith but cannot give it. For Barth, Jesus Christ is the only sacrament, baptism and the Lord's Supper being ordinances concerned with the ethical mandate of the church. According to Calvin, by contrast, "The sacraments . . . are treasures which we can not esteem and prize too highly."[40] Calvin and Luther both insisted that the sacrament should be celebrated in the context of the Word and that it is effectual only where it is received in faith. Nonetheless, they recognized that God deigns to meet us in visible signs instituted by Christ and that intimate communion with Christ is nowhere more powerfully present than in holy baptism and the holy Eucharist.[41]

A viable doctrine of the church for our time will involve us in a passionate concern for church unity. If the church is one, holy and apostolic, we need to discover and demonstrate the unity that we already have as brothers and sisters in Christ. Too often in the evangelical world with which I am acquainted, the ideal is a pan-Protestantism or pan-Evangelicalism, but unity with our fellow believers in the Catholic and Eastern Orthodox churches is not in the picture. The charismatic movement has bridged some of these barriers, but its vision of a renewed church is on the basis of a common experience rather than doctrinal consensus. Doctrine, life and experience need to be held together in a catholic balance, and if any one of these is neglected we are on the slippery slope to heresy.

Because of the encroaching secularism of our time, it is incumbent on us to seek not only evangelical but catholic unity, not only spiritual but visible unity. Yet visible unity should not be conceived in terms of a monolithic, hierarchical institution; this would betray an accommodation to the values of the technological society with its penchant for centralization and consolidation for the purpose of greater efficiency and productivity. In my opinion, the Consultation on Church Union (COCU) has not escaped the spell of the technocratic culture in which we live, because the practical consequences of union seem to be given more prominence than biblical fidelity or doctrinal loyalty.

In Catholicism the conception of a monolithic and hierarchical church is based on a juridical understanding of authority, which did not become dominant in the church until the controversies in the Middle Ages and the Counter-Reformation. Avery Dulles gives a timely warning against the tendency in Catholicism to define the church primarily in terms of its visible structures, to see authority in the church as essentially hierarchical and juridical.[42] In this understanding, the clergy, especially the higher clergy, are viewed as the source of all power and initiative. The church becomes virtually identical with the kingdom of Christ, and the gospel becomes a new law.

The unity we should aim for is a pulpit and altar fellowship among all churches that is based on biblical, evangelical truth. We should allow for a certain diversity within this unity. There can be a pluralism of witness, though not a pluralism of dogma in the holy catholic church. Pluralism in theological matters should never be a goal in the life of the church; instead, it should be regarded as a means to the desired end of confessional unity or doctrinal harmony, which is not the same as theological uniformity. There can exist in a vital united church various liturgical rites and differing theological formulations but not doctrinal positions that are in open conflict with one another.

I can, for the most part, identify with this prophetic vision of Philip Schaff, who wrote before the ecumenical movement came into full bloom:

> Union is no monotonous uniformity, but implies variety and full development of all the various types of Christian doctrine and discipline as far as they are founded on constitutional differences, made and intended by God himself, and as far as they are supplementary rather than contradictory. True union is essentially inward and spiritual. It does not require an external amalgamation of existing organizations into one, but may exist with their perfect independence in their own spheres of labor.[43]

As Protestant evangelicals, we should endeavor to appreciate the catholic heritage of the church as well as the Reformation witness. My reservations concerning Roman Catholicism are that it is not sufficiently catholic, since it has not included the Reformation witness in its doctrinal and confessional stance. At the same time, there are promising signs that today the contribution of the Protestant Reformers is being re-evaluated and appreciated by Catholic scholars, and there may yet be an ecumenical breakthrough in this area. It should be borne in mind that the mainline Reformers never wished to found a new church, only to reform and purify the old one. Bullinger spoke for many when he declared, "We never departed from the catholic church of Christ."[44]

In our concern for church unity, we must avoid the pitfall of restorationism, which was examined at length in the preceding chapter. I take issue with the renowned Anglo-Catholic theologian Edward Pusey, who wrote, "We dare not go outside the first six centuries."[45] Nor do I empathize with John Nevin, who contended that Protestantism "must in the end fall back into the old Catholic stream in order to fulfil its own mission."[46] Instead, our vision should be fixed on the coming great church which stands in continuity with the church of the past but which represents a new work of the Holy Spirit in the latter days when the true church will be separated from the false church.

The quest for church unity must never supplant zeal for the truth. This is what divided Luther from Erasmus. Luther rightly recognized that the true church will be characterized by unswerving devotion to the truth of Holy Scripture, that compromise can be considered in the area of nonessentials but not of essentials. Erasmus, on the other hand, sought a church that would be informed by the latest scholarship, that would be open to the spirit of enlightenment and therefore closed to any firm dogmatic stance.

Church unity is especially urgent today on the mission field, as already noted in an earlier chapter. As the church confronts the great world religions and the new political religions, it needs to speak with an undivided voice. It is also obliged to demonstrate to the pagan world the love that Jesus taught and embodied. Christians at war with each other undermine the very gospel they proclaim.

A BIBLICAL, EVANGELICAL SPIRITUALITY

The Pietists rightly remind us that a reformation in doctrine is not enough. We also stand in need of a "reformation unto holiness." This is why Pietism, with its emphasis on practical holiness, claimed to be the fulfillment of the Reformation. At its best, this renewal movement kept alive the concern for spirituality within the churches of the Reformation.

Spirituality basically refers to the style or mode of life that emanates from faith in the living God. It concerns the practical appropriation of the truth of faith by the believer. In the Christian sense, its goal is conformity to the image of Christ.

True spirituality must always be on guard against misconceptions of the spiritual life. The legacy of Neoplatonism has given rise to many such misconceptions, which have reappeared with disturbing frequency in the history of Christian mysticism. A common understanding in these circles is that the goal in life is to transcend the material and to escape into the spiritual. The Eros philosophy of Hellenism has portrayed the spiritual quest as the reunion of the soul with the Eternal. But such a conception stands opposed to the biblical vision of Agape, the love that goes out to the despised and forsaken.[47] It is not the love that ascends to the highest but the love that descends to the lowest that is the biblical ideal. Self-sacrifice, not self-realization, is the hallmark of evangelical spirituality.

Catholic and Eastern Orthodox theologians have generally been aware of the danger of accommodating the faith to classical philosophy, though they have not always been able to avoid compromises that dilute or undercut the biblical motifs. In Catholic spirituality, it is common to hear warnings against "angelism," trying to be superhuman through heroic feats of asceticism. The biblical ideal indeed is not a superhumanity but a restored humanity. At the same time, as our Catholic brothers and sisters remind us, this will be a transfigured humanity, one that is transformed by the grace of God.

Besides Neoplatonic mystical spirituality, we must equally beware of modern, secular spirituality where the accent is on immersion in the world. Here we see a naturalistic mysticism, which celebrates the instinctual drives of man and the will to power and success.[48] The spiritual is seen as an aspect of the material, just as the supernatural is regarded as a dimension of the natural. The only transcendence is a transcendence within immanence. Prayer is regarded not as the elevation of the mind to God (as in classical mysticism) nor as supplication before a holy, all-powerful God (as in biblical prophetic religion); instead, it is viewed as the penetration through the world to God. Among scholars associated with this kind of outlook are J. A. T. Robinson, Thomas Altizer, Albert Schweitzer, Nikos Kazantzakis, Dorothee Sölle and Matthew Fox.[49]

The biblical view sharply contradicts both the classical and modern versions. In the biblical perspective, the spiritual embraces the material but at the same time transcends it. The spiritual enters into the material rather than calls us away from it (as in the classical view). At the same time, the goal of the material is to be taken up into the spiritual (in opposition to the modern view). The material is neither an obstacle to the spiritual (as in the classical view) nor the other side of the spiritual (as in the modern view). Instead, it is the vessel of the spiritual.

The atoning work of Christ is the basis of a biblical, evangelical spirituality. Here Christ is seen not simply as the representative of fallen humanity nor as the model of the new humanity but as Mediator, Expiator and Sin Bearer. Before he can be our example, he must be acknowledged as our Savior and Lord. True spirituality views the Christian life as primarily a sign and witness to the atoning work of Christ. The imitation of Christ is a token of our gratitude for his incomparable work of reconciliation and redemption on Calvary. It is not to be seen as a means to gain additional merits, insuring us a place in heaven.

Certainly true spirituality will also emphasize the outpouring of the Holy Spirit, for there can be no Christian life that is not inspired by the Spirit. In our theology of the Holy Spirit, we should strive for a balance between the gifts and the fruits of the Spirit. The gifts are necessary for the upbuilding of the church; the fruits are necessary as the evidence before the world of our incorporation into the body of Christ.

Spirituality will entail ethical action, but it must not be reduced to ethicism. Similarly, it will involve mystical communion with God, but it must not be dissolved into mysticism. We must seek in our time to recover the mystical dimension of the faith without succumbing to what Aldous Huxley calls "the perennial philosophy"—monistic mysticism.

Finally, as evangelicals who stand in the tradition of Reformation Protestantism, we should learn to appreciate Catholic spirituality without imitating Catholic forms of devotion. We likewise urge our brothers and sisters in the Catholic churches to draw upon the abiding values of evangelical devotion, including the spirituality of the Reformation, without jettisoning their own rich spiritual heritage. We need to be faithful to our own traditions but at the same time open to broadening our perspective and even having it corrected.

The Reformation, in its reaction to perversions and misunderstandings of biblical truth in the popular Catholic piety of the time, regrettably discarded much in the catholic heritage that is of enduring value. I have in mind such things as religious orders within the church,[50] celibacy, retreats and spiritual disciplines, including meditation and silence. In the evangelical perspective, the purpose of such disciplines is not to merit God's favor but to prepare ourselves to hear God's Word. It is not to insure a place for us in eternity but to make us more available for service in the world.

The doctrine of the saints was another casualty of a reforming zeal that understandably could not tolerate the idea, nurtured in Catholic popular devotion, of saints as mediators alongside of Christ. Some of the confessional documents of the Reformation sought to make a place for the role of the departed saints as intercessors, but for the most part even the idea of the communion of saints fell more and more into the background. The overriding concern of the Reformation was the holy gospel, not holy people. The role of Mary in the plan of salvation and in the life of the church was likewise neglected, though Luther at one time in his life was willing to make a place for a Christocentric form of Marian devotion.

An interest in spiritual formation presently engrosses a large part of both the liberal and evangelical communities. This can be a promising sign provided that the development of spiritual life is always based on the decisive act of God in Jesus Christ in biblical history. But when spirituality becomes divorced from its objective historical foundation, then we are engulfed in the peril of subjectivism. This is an omnipresent danger in the popular religion of our culture, whether it carries a conservative or liberal label.

Forsyth, a spiritual theologian of the first order, has this timely word of warning:

> To make the development of man the supreme interest of God, as popular Christianity sometimes tends to do, instead of making the glory of God the supreme interest of man, is a moral error which invites the only treatment that can cure a civilisation whose religion has become so false—public judgment.[51]

REDISCOVERING ETHICAL IMPERATIVES

What is missing in so much current spirituality is the ethical or prophetic note. Certainly the time is ripe to rediscover the ethical imperatives of the faith, for today there is an accelerated erosion of moral values. I am convinced that the current moral decay is associated with the rise of a moral relativism that denies a universal moral law or an absolute, binding moral norm.

We need to remember that faith not only has a kerygmatic but also a prophetic dimension. Our mandate as ambassadors of Christ is to bring the law of God to bear on the critical moral issues of the time. As concerned citizens of the state, we are then under the imperative to implement the divine commandment through legal measures that will insure a greater measure of justice in the land.

Among the burning social issues of our time is abortion on demand. Abortion has been condemned with a rare degree of consensus through Christian history from the first century onward. Both Karl Barth and Dietrich Bonhoeffer have described it as an undeniable evil. Although not explicitly condemning abortion, Scripture is quite clear that human personhood already begins at conception and that the unborn child is infinitely precious in the sight of God (Ps. 139:13–16; Isa. 49:1; Jer. 1:5; Luke 1:44; Gal. 1:15).[52] To countenance the wanton killing of innocent life on the grounds of freedom of choice is to abandon Christian norms in favor of a pagan, radical egalitarian ideology. In my opinion, the church should press for legislation that would put an end to the abortion traffic, which is creating a climate of opinion that regards human life as expendable if the common good demands it.

Yet while supporting laws that would severely restrict abortions, I do not share the absolutist position of some of my evangelical colleagues, who contend that the taking of a fetal life is always tantamount to murder.[53] The divine commandment cannot be frozen into a moral code that allows for absolutely no exceptions.[54] When the mother's life is at stake or when evidence indicates that genetic deformity or structural abnormality is so severe that the unborn child faces a life of agonizing pain or untold misery, we may hear God's permission for an abortion, but this is a possibility granted only by God; it is not ours to claim.[55] After birth, a distinction should be made between the deliberate taking of life and the withholding of medicinal aids or artificial supports necessary for the continuation of life.[56] The church needs to reach some consensus on this whole problem, but it should draw its main source of guidance from Holy Scripture, not from the biological and social sciences (though the latter should not be discounted).

Another intolerable social evil that casts a pall over the modern world is the nuclear armaments race. The church must certainly address itself to this spiritual issue if it is to maintain the relevance of the gospel for our age. The mainstream of Christian thought has never embraced an absolutist pacifism, but it has maintained that only some wars can be deemed just. Christian leaders, including the present pope, are fast coming to the conclusion that the concept of a just war is now passé in light of the emergence of weapons of mass extermination, which makes it impossible to discriminate between combatants and noncombatants and which eliminates any possibility of proportionality between the means used in warfare and the results effected. It is justifiable for a nation to defend itself against attack, but in responding to attack it is never justifiable for a nation to demolish civilian populations and to deform millions yet unborn, which would be the case in nuclear and biochemical warfare. The saturation bombing of Dresden was already a sign of a creeping callousness in warfare that can only be attributed to the triumph of nihilism over historic Christian values in the modern world.

Christians today are divided on what their response should be to the war strategies of the superpowers, which can only result in mass murder. Certainly the church should throw its weight behind an arms control program leading to a drastic reduction in biochemical and nuclear weapons and a verifiable ban on nuclear testing. It should also press for selective conscientious objection, so that nuclear pacifism is given legal recognition by the state. Withholding of income tax payments or refusal to register for the draft are actions that probably have to be left to the individual conscience. The call for a bilateral freeze on the manufacture of nuclear weapons would seem to be in accord with the divine commandment for our time. The policy of total obliteration and the building and deployment of first strike nuclear weapons should be unequivocally rejected.[57]

Whether the church should urge the unilateral dismantling of the nuclear arsenal of the West is quite another question, however, since such an action could well invite open aggression, even precipitating a nuclear attack, either against us or against weaker nations. Yet the church must not permit the state to rest content in the illusion that nuclear weapons can be an adequate deterrent to war, for even the possession of such weapons fosters a climate of fear and violence.

War takes on the character of a fateful tragedy when nations can no longer free themselves from their idolatrous dependence on weapons of terror and destruction (cf. Ps. 9:15, 16; Isa. 31:1–3). War could be avoidable if nations would turn to God in repentance and forsake their trust in military might (cf. Ps. 33:13–22). It becomes unavoidable when nations in their folly persist in their feverish war preparations, thereby reaping the retribution that follows from disobedience (cf. Matt. 26:52; Gal. 6:7, 8). A nation has the right and obligation to maintain the security of its people, but the line between a legitimate military defense and an acceleration in military expenditures that is no longer subject to rational controls is very thin indeed.

Christians, even pacifist Christians, cannot escape involvement in the tragedy of war, when discord between nations erupts into violence, but they can make their protest known in both words and deeds. If they embark on a program of civil disobedience, they must be ready to accept the penalty for their transgression—fines or imprisonment (as Martin Luther King was wise enough to discern). In this way, they will still give honor to the state as an authority set over us by God, even while taking issue with its policies. The Christian who seeks to make his witness within the power structures of government cannot necessarily be considered a greater sinner than the Christian who repudiates the social system that fosters the war mentality and withdraws into a communitarian enclave dedicated to nonviolence. It may be that the commandment of God will become ever more clear to the church as a whole in the dark days ahead, and Christians must be willing to follow the divine mandate wherever it might lead us.

The trouble with the "Ban the Bomb" movement today is that it is basically motivated by the desire for self-preservation rather than by obedience to the commandment of God. Whenever self-preservation is made into an absolute principle, we are no longer under grace but under law. We are also placing human survival over both fidelity to God's Word and a concern for the total welfare of our neighbor (including his or her eternal salvation). Especially disconcerting is the fact that many church groups today which align themselves with the peace movement in decrying the horrors of nuclear war are strangely silent on the mass murder of millions of unborn children through abortion. The credibility of their witness is thus seriously impaired, particularly among lower middle class and poorer people.

Where the Christian witness on peace differs most radically from the secular peace movement is in its focus on Jesus Christ as the key to real peace in the world. Only when people have been converted by the Spirit of Christ do they gain the motivation and power to be authentic peacemakers. This is why the Christian strategy for peace entails not only peacemaking, not only announcing the divine commandment against nuclear war but also, and above all, preaching the gospel of regeneration. This does not preclude Christians from working with secular people in the promotion of peace, but it does mean that we will try to stay clear of both utopianism and unrestrained pessimism (the secular temptations).

Even while disagreeing with the absolute pacifist and semianarchist position of the Sojourners fellowship, I fully concur with these words of Jim Wallis:

> His victory is the basis for our hope. I am convinced that the nuclear arms race will not be overcome by an appeal to fear. Its own basis is fear, and more fear will not finally prevail against it. Rather, nuclear violence will be overcome with hope. Christian hope sees the nuclear situation realistically, with no false optimism. But Christian hope knows that the victory of Christ is stronger than the nuclear powers. Prayer helps us to continue to believe that. Our actions must show the world that we believe.[58]

Among other critical social and moral issues which the church needs to come to grips with today are the growing use of torture as a means of human intimidation, euthanasia, the widening disparity between rich and poor, the virtually unchecked population explosion, the rape of the environment in the name of technological progress and the breakdown of the family, brought about partly by the sexual revolution.

This is not the place to delve into all of these critical moral issues, but a word should be said about moral decay in the area of sexual ethics and family life. The new permissive morality, which countenances any kind of sexual activity so long as it does not directly injure another person, is diametrically opposed to the Christian ethic, which calls men and women to live responsibly in a relationship either of holy virginity or holy marriage. In either case chastity, the channeling or sublimation of sexual desire, is the mode of life that has divine sanction. Christians today who justify fornication, extramarital relations, homosexuality or pornography on the grounds that these can all be stepping-stones to self-fulfillment reveal their distance from the thought world of the Bible.

This is not to argue for a return to Victorian morality, with its double standard and its suspicion of sex as something degrading. Pornography should be opposed not because it focuses upon nudity (which in itself is morally neutral) but because it portrays human beings not as persons but only as objects to be used for sexual gratification. Yet in opposition to the new religious and political right, I do not see any justification for opposing sex education in principle. Where the moral values of the Judeo-Christian tradition are shelved in favor of the value-free orientation of modern nihilism, then of course we must register a vigorous protest. But sexual ignorance is not a Christian solution to the growing problem of illegitimacy, venereal disease and abortions, and the sad fact is that most homes fail to provide the necessary information.

In contradistinction to new class liberalism today, I see no reason for not cooperating with Moral Majority and kindred groups in combating pornography, the abortion mills, no-fault divorce, incest, homosexuality, etc., because a society cannot long endure without a foundational moral code. I agree with Jacques Ellul that the common morality of a society is in most cases more salutary than destructive and therefore deserves the relative support of all people of goodwill.[59] On the other hand, this common morality or civil righteousness must not be confused with the higher righteousness of the kingdom, which calls us to works of mercy and sanctity beyond our obligations to society. While we should be generally supportive of the mores of a society, we must always look beyond these codes to the divine commandment, which stands in judgment over our morality as well as our immorality.

It is commonplace to hold that Christians live under grace, not a moral code, and yet the implications of this can be devastating for a society if it is supposed that grace annuls morality. To affirm *sola gratia* does not mean that we may therefore live in flagrant disregard of the moral codes that society sets up to protect itself. These codes comprise the dike that secures society from moral and social chaos.

Yet the moral codes and taboos of a society must not be accepted as absolute or unalterable. They should always be weighed in the light of the one norm that is absolute—God's self-revelation in Jesus Christ, which is both promise and command. Reinhold Niebuhr has urged that society's quest for order and justice be constantly judged and measured by the higher standard of sacrificial love; otherwise, this very quest may itself become an obstacle to the kingdom of God.[60]

I do not agree with Flo Conway and Jim Siegelman in their wholesale condemnation of modern fundamentalism, since I believe that it is prompted in part by a commitment to secular humanism.[61] When they can see only a right-wing conspiracy in the fundamentalist opposition to abortion on demand, pornography, the portrayal of homosexuality as a valid alternative life-style and the teaching of evolution as a metaphysical dogma, then they have failed to appreciate the genuine and often valid concerns of lower and lower-middle-class America regarding the intrusion of a humanistic and nihilistic mentality that threatens the values and freedoms of all religious people. The authors argue that the United States cannot long survive "as two nations—one fundamentalist, one secular."[62] But the alternative they propose to fundamentalist totalism is a secular pluralism, which in reality is a humanistic totalism that tolerates religion only insofar as it remains confined to charitable service or spiritual worship. Moral Majority, Religious Roundtable and other fundamentalist groups need to be critiqued and in some areas even opposed, but the only critique that will be convincing to evangelicals as well as many other Christians is one that arises out of a deep-seated commitment to biblical faith.[63]

In its ethical witness, the church should be conscious that if it is truly being faithful to the divine commandment, its word will always go against the values and ideals embraced by society, both right and left. Indeed, one of the tests of authentic prophecy is whether it calls into radical question the mythologies and idolatries dominating the culture of its time. True prophecy means speaking a word from God that judges speaker and hearer alike. The object of a genuine prophecy is liberation from ideological and religious bondage.

Finally, we as Christians need to keep in mind that our efforts to carry out our ethical responsibility are not a means to our salvation but a concrete sign and testimony of a salvation already won for us. We are summoned not to meritorious works but to an obedient life with the sole motivation of glorifying Christ and serving our neighbor for whom Christ died. The ethical goal is neither self-realization (eudaemonia) nor eternal security but the extension of the kingdom of God by upholding Jesus Christ before the world.

OVERCOMING POLARIZATION ON THE WOMEN'S ISSUE

The ethical seriousness of the faith is also put to the test in the drive for equal rights and working opportunities for women. When this drive tends to blur or disregard the very real differences between the sexes, then we have a theological issue of momentous import.

Women's liberation has precipitated at least two crises in the church: the first pertains to the issue of women in positions of spiritual leadership (elder, pastor) and the second to desexing the language about God. Of all the issues that threaten schism in the American church today, this is perhaps the most volatile. Indeed, some schisms have already resulted (especially in the Anglican and Presbyterian churches). The blame cannot be placed only on those who seek to cling to a waning patriarchalism. The strident demands of some feminists have contributed in no small measure to the widening splits in many local churches as well as denominational bodies.

Behind the current dissension in the churches and in society at large over the role of women lies the all-pervasive sin of sexism. Many evangelicals, to their shame, have difficulty even in recognizing sexism as a sin. Yet treating women as inferiors, which is basically what sexism is, reveals the arrogance of power, the urge to dominate and control—one of the more ugly manifestations of sin. We also need to realize that sexism contravenes the faith affirmations that *all* people are created in the image of God, *all* are called to be witnesses and ambassadors of Jesus Christ.

Sexism is rampant in nearly every area of society. It is most blatant in the traffic in prostitution and pornography, where women are reduced to nothing more than sex objects serving male gratification. It is also apparent in the still appreciable disparity in the salaries of men and women who perform the same services and in a host of other ways.

Sexism is indissolubly linked to the often harsh patriarchalism inherited from both Hebraic and Hellenic cultural traditions. In the patriarchal ethos, woman is not so much the helpmate of man as his servant, always there to do his bidding. Marriage is seen in the service of biological fertility, and a childless marriage or even a marriage without male heirs is considered a signal misfortune. In most patriarchal societies of the past and many in the present, women are even denied the right to vote.

Modern feminism signifies a vehement, almost violent, reaction against the sexism and patriarchalism that have been part of the heritage of virtually all of Western civilization (as well as most other cultures). Whereas in patriarchalism woman is the property of man, in feminism woman is the equal, even the rival of man. The independence of woman from man is one of its cardinal principles. Mutual responsibility is seen to be in the service of the Enlightenment ideal of autonomy. Career development is championed over the often humdrum service in home and family, which is for the most part considered demeaning.

Feminist ideology generally favors the mythical vision of androgyny over complementarity, which supposes that male and female are incomplete apart from the other. In androgyny man and woman seek to discover the masculine and feminine elements present within all human beings and to integrate these within themselves.[64]

Just as patriarchalism, where the male is seen as dominant over the female, is associated with an ideology of restoration, so feminism represents an ideology of accommodation. Its motto is not a return to the past but an openness to the future. In Christian circles feminism takes the form of a revisionist theology in which the Spirit of God is identified with the new consciousness of a world free from exploitation and oppression.

The biblical alternative to both patriarchalism and feminism is the covenant of grace in which marriage is patterned after the covenant that God made with Israel. Marriage is now seen as a partnership in kingdom service in which man and woman realize a common vocation under the cross. Even in the single state, it is contended, man and woman cannot live unto themselves alone but must live in interdependence, not independence. Against both heteronomy (subjection to external authority—the patriarchal model) and autonomy (freedom from all outward authority—the feminist ideal), biblical faith upholds theonomy, in which man and woman are joined together in service to the living God. Faithfulness to God means not servile subjection to the will of a tyrant but following the lead of a loving Father. No longer servants, men and women are now sons and daughters, brothers and sisters, members of a community characterized by loving fellowship rather than an authoritarian chain of command.

The concept of subordination is not abrogated in biblical faith but instead drastically transformed. Just as Christ demonstrated his lordship by laying down his life for his church, so the husband is called to exercise his headship in the role of a servant.[65] It is still his task to provide protection and guidance for his family, but as much as possible he should do this indirectly. He should seldom if ever arbitrarily impose his will on his family but instead endeavor with them to discover the will of Jesus Christ, the one Lord of both church and family. Similarly, a wife must still subordinate herself to her husband and the children to their parents, but this subordination now takes the form not of servile submission but of loving assistance.[66] The church as the bride of Christ responds to her bridegroom in love and gratitude; the wife responds in a like manner to the love of her husband (cf. Song of Solomon 7:10–13).

In the biblical scheme, man and woman are essentially equals by virtue of their creation in the image of God and a common calling to the service of the kingdom (cf. Gen. 1:27; 5:1, 2; Gal. 3:28, 29). They are equal heirs to a salvation already secured through faith in Christ (I Pet. 3:7). Yet biblical equality does not eradicate biological differentiation, but instead seeks to harness the unique capabilities and talents of each sex for the purpose of creating community. Biblical faith affirms both biological and psychic differences between the sexes,[67] but this does not necessarily relegate woman to a background role. The Bible allows for the fact that women, too, may be called to leadership positions, both civil and spiritual, but that in assuming such responsibilities, they must do so as women and not try to imitate men.[68]

The move to obliterate the ineradicable differences between the sexes today is detrimental to both sexes and renders genuine community between them impossible. The search for a unisex utopia can only end in the masculinization of women and the feminization of men. Dietrich Bonhoeffer has some timely words on this subject:

> There is something wrong with a world in which the woman's ambition is to be like a man, and in which the man regards the woman as the toy of his lust for power and freedom. It is a sign of social disintegration when the woman's service is thought to be degrading, and when the man who is faithful to his wife is looked upon as a weakling or a fool.[69]

Regarding the debate on the language about God, evangelicals must hold firm to the biblical principle that form and content are inextricably bound together, that the personal and mainly masculine metaphors pertaining to God given in Holy Scripture cannot be jettisoned without turning Christianity into an immanentalistic or naturalistic religion. The biblical terms "Father, Son and Holy Spirit" are not merely symbols that point to an undifferentiated ground of being (as in monistic mysticism) but instead analogies revealed by God himself concerning his own person and activity. When Jesus himself taught his disciples to pray addressing God as Father, we are bound to do likewise if we wish to identify ourselves with the same community of faith.

To substitute an inclusive language in reference to God for the personal metaphors of Scripture signifies a move away from Trinitarianism. To think of God as Father-Mother rather than heavenly Father is binitarian. To envision God primarily or exclusively as Spirit or heavenly Parent or Divine Providence is to end in unitarianism.

Feminists seek to do away with not only masculine but also hierarchical metaphors, thus contradicting the biblical principle of the infinite qualitative difference between God and man. God is not the creative depth of being but the Sovereign Creator who brought us into the world out of nothing. He is not simply Friend or Companion but Lord and Master, and he is the latter before he is the former.

When feminists attack the biblical symbol "Lord" in reference to both God and Christ, they are robbing the church of a politically revolutionary symbol, for to confess Jesus as Lord calls into question all worldly claims to absolute power. The confession of Jesus as Lord is a challenge not only to fascist and communist dictatorships but also to the totalitarianism of the democratic consensus, the idea that the will of the people is sovereign. The ancient Roman Empire was not alarmed by the various mystical cults of its time, because they did not pose a challenge to civil authority; yet it did feel immensely threatened by the confession of Jesus as Lord, which dethroned the gods of the pantheon and effectively undermined the idolatry of the emperor. Pagan Rome felt compelled to stamp out the Christian "heresy" in order to survive as a cultural entity.

Although sacred Scripture generally envisions God in masculine terms, this is not always the case. There are also metaphors pointing to the divine motherhood.[70] In the Wisdom literature, the Wisdom of God (practically equivalent to the Word of God) is always portrayed as feminine—as mother and sister (cf. Prov. 7:4; 8:32–36; Sirach 24:18; Wisd. of Sol. 7:12 RSV; Matt. 11:19). Moreover, the Spirit of God in the Hebrew Scriptures and the glory of God (*Shekinah*) in later rabbinical literature are likewise represented as feminine, not masculine.

W. A. Visser't Hooft rightly argues that to try to overcome personal metaphors for an inclusive language in which God is portrayed as neuter is ultimately to depersonalize God.[71] This was the way of the deists and many Neoplatonic mystics, and the end result was the impersonal Absolute of philosophical speculation, far removed from the living, personal God of biblical faith.

Yet Visser't Hooft is ready to acknowledge that the fatherhood of God is not a closed or exclusive symbolism: "It is open to correction, enrichment, and completion from other forms of symbol, such as 'mother,' 'brother,' 'sister' and 'friend.'"[72] He is willing to allow for describing or even addressing God in certain contexts by feminine symbols so long as these are subordinated to the masculine symbols of faith, which in the Bible are dominant.[73] In his view, we need to make room for a certain amount of spiritual imagination in describing God by metaphors other than masculine and hierarchical, but we do not transgress the limits of biblical faith provided that "Father, Son and Spirit" remain central.[74]

The threat to the church today lies in a neo-Gnosticism and naturalistic mysticism in which the boundaries between the infinite and the finite, the supernatural and the natural, are overcome, and the sovereignty and transcendence of God are then called into question. It is crucial in this age of immanentalistic mysticism to preserve the metaphors and symbols of transcendence if the church is to maintain its identity and integrity. It is also imperative that we oppose the feminist appeal to new revelations in nature and inward experience and affirm the uniqueness and decisiveness of the one final revelation of God in the biblical history culminating in Jesus Christ.[75]

RENEWAL THROUGH BIBLICAL PREACHING

There can be no biblical renewal in our churches today (Catholic or Protestant) without a renewal of biblical preaching. If the problems associated with naturalistic mysticism and radical feminism are fairly recent arrivals on the religious scene, the crisis in preaching has been looming for decades. The anecdotal nature of much preaching today has led Daniel Jenkins, a pastor and theologian in the United Reformed Church in England, to predict that within one or two generations people will begin turning away from the churches out of a depressing awareness that they have not been spiritually fed. Many factors have precipitated the present disarray in Roman Catholicism, evident in the loss of vocations and decreasing attendance at mass, but certainly we should not discount the slow but irrefragable erosion of biblical, kerygmatic preaching in that communion through the centuries.

The demise of biblical preaching has both sociological and theological roots. Part of the legacy of revivalism was the turning of the focus from an objective message to personal experience. Individual conversion rather than the conversion of the world in Jesus Christ became the paramount concern. Both, of course, are important, but the loss of an objective, historical content seems the greater peril today. Romanticism also played a significant role in undermining biblical, evangelical preaching. For Schleiermacher, who regarded himself as a Pietist of a higher order, the purpose of preaching is not to herald a definite message but to evoke a sense of the mystery of God.[76] The transcendentalist movement in America posed a similar threat, placing the emphasis on internal experience rather than external authority, on the perfecting of the self rather than the deliverance of the world through the redemptive work of God in biblical history.[77] Most sermons today are constructed with an eye on the impression they will make on the subject, not the glory they will give to the object of faith—the living God.

Growing ritualism in worship is also responsible for undermining evangelical preaching. Sermons are reduced to moral homilies, and the main action is what goes on in the Mass or Eucharist. The retreat into liturgy can be observed not only in Roman Catholic, Anglo-Catholic and Lutheran churches but also in mainstream evangelical Protestantism.

Biblical preaching consists in the diligent and faithful exposition of the biblical text, taking into consideration its literary and historical background as well as assessing its theological significance for the present age. An effort will always be made to examine the text in the light of the law and the gospel, which are either implicit or explicit in the whole of Scripture. Preaching that is true to the scriptural imperative entails more than fidelity to the text and to the central message of the Bible: it also presupposes a personal encounter between the preacher and the Holy. Biblical preaching includes not only *soundness* in exposition but also spiritual *fervor* and *power*. What is at stake is not only the viability of the message but also the credibility of the messenger.

In an age when the average sermon has degenerated into an after-dinner speech, random thoughts on the contemporary scene, or a soothing pep talk to carry us through the week, we need to rediscover the sacramental character of gospel preaching. James Hastings Nichols has trenchantly observed that the Reformation made preaching into a third sacrament, one that effectively took the place of absolution.[78] Indeed, it was through the renewed preaching of the gospel that people of that time received deliverance from guilt and inner torment. Puritan preachers were commonly referred to as "physicians of the soul." Such a designation can help to remind us all, preachers and congregations alike, of the seriousness and cruciality of the homiletic task.

Biblical preaching at its best will be expositional, evangelical and prophetic. It will seek not only to expound the text but to relate the text to the gospel, the central content of Scripture. It will also take care to apply the imperatives of the gospel to the society in which we live as well as to our personal lives. It will therefore include the note of divine judgment as well as divine grace.

Preaching will be in the context of worship. Indeed, preaching serves the worship of God and not vice versa. Calvin said that the purpose of worship is to glorify God and lead people to Christ. This is also the purpose of preaching.[79]

We are living in an age where the focus of ministry is upon counseling and group manipulation rather than upon preaching. Expertise in psychology and in church management are deemed more important than immersion in the Word of God. If there is to be a genuine revival of biblical preaching, the spiritual hunger of people for the Word of God will have to be rekindled.

A BIBLICAL AND RELEVANT ESCHATOLOGY

Paradoxically, in popular evangelical circles, while there is a ready acceptance of the modern virtues of psychological maturity and efficiency, indicating a preoccupation with the immanent at the expense of the transcendent, in the area of eschatology the thrust is otherworldly and escapist. Nonetheless, the selfist mentality persists, for in this kind of eschatology people are led away from concern for social justice to an egocentric obsession with personal security. We need an eschatology that will give hope and significance to this present age without denying that this-worldly hopes can only be provisional and that the blessed hope signifies the end of this age. We need to perceive Pentecost as the second stage of the advent of Christ and the latter-day Pentecost before his second advent as the dawn of the glory of the millennium.

In constructing an eschatology capable of bringing hope to a spiritually destitute humanity, we have to keep in mind that what God has done in the past is not to be subordinated to what God will do in the future. What he will do in the future is the outcome of what he has done in the past and what he is doing in the present. He has already set up his kingdom in our midst, Pentecost has already occurred, though, to be sure, his kingdom has yet to be consummated. Though mindful that the full realization of the kingdom lies in the eternal future, we must include in our message that the kingdom has already come, the new age is already here, even though the old has not yet passed away. This means that we can even now proclaim liberty to the captives (cf. Luke 4:18), for the devil was dethroned when Jesus rose from the dead.

In forging a new eschatological vision, we should not minimize the role of the church. Evangelicals of the dispensationalist variety often refer to the "twilight of the church" and issue a call to separation from the institutional church, which they regard as apostate. We should remember Christ's promise that the gates of hell will not prevail against his church (Matt. 16:18 KJV). We should consider that the church is not condemned to be an ever dwindling minority but is destined to include a vast multitude of people of all races and nations (Col. 1:6; Rev. 7:9). The New Testament vision of the church is that it will withstand and overcome the principalities and powers, that it will finally inherit the world (Matt. 5:5).

We should, of course, be alert to the opposite error of unduly exalting the church, of seeing the eschatological victory already finalized in the church. This imbalance is present in both Reformation and Catholic traditions, stemming partly from Augustine, who practically identified the church with the kingdom of Christ. The church is the vessel of the kingdom, the herald of the kingdom, but it will not become the kingdom until the wheat is separated from the tares on the last day. The kingdom, which might be regarded as the invisible church, is hidden in the church as a historical institution. It is both more narrow and more extensive than the visible church, since the latter contains some who are faithless and does not yet include on its membership rolls many who are faithful. Already partially realized in the fellowship of love, the kingdom is still coming as the messianic rule of Christ over the whole of creation. The church as well as the world looks forward to the coming of the kingdom (Rom. 8:19–22), though only the former is granted the right understanding of this.

Our eschatology will not be sufficiently realistic or fully biblical unless it does justice to the ineradicable and persistent dualistic motif in Scripture—the idea of two kingdoms arrayed against one another. The kingdom of Christ is not the only one in this world; there is also the kingdom of evil, the kingdom of the devil which continues to hold the world in subjection. Even though the principalities and powers have been overthrown by the cross and resurrection victory of Christ, they continue to exert real power by virtue of the spell that they cast over those who have not truly awakened to the full dimensions of Christ's victory. Jesus Christ is already Lord over all earthly powers (Rev. 17:14; 19:16), but the salvific fruits of his victory extend only to the community of faith, where his Lordship is acknowledged and his will obeyed.[80] His rule continues to be challenged even by a devil who is in his death throes, whose power is more psychological than ontological, whose time is already practically at an end. Yet just as a mortally wounded beast can be all the more dangerous in its desperation, so the devil presents a still greater peril as he struggles to rebound from defeat. Evangelical theology must indeed take this into consideration if it is to avoid the utopianism and spurious idealism of neoliberal and neo-Barthian theology.[81]

Finally, we should strive for a new statement on the millennium that will do justice to the total biblical vision. The millennium signifies the end-time age, but this age is already here in part, because Christ's reign has already begun. The millennial age overlaps the present age, for Christ's messianic kingdom has already been established, though it does not yet extend throughout the entire earth.

The universal revelation of its power and glory will not take place until Christ comes again, but partial revelations of the millennial triumph within worldly history are apparent wherever there is a marked breakthrough in Christian mission. We must do justice to the millennial hope without abandoning the present world to the devil.

We are challenged today to avoid both a crippling pessimism and an unrealistic optimism. The end times will be marked by growing persecution and tribulation for Christians, but they will also witness wholesale conversions to the gospel. The rapture of the church will be manifest in the way it emerges triumphant over the anti-God powers in the last days. The millennium means the victory of the church, not its defeat at the hands of worldly power.

PROMISE OF RENEWAL

The impending collapse of Western civilization does not mean the defeat of the holy catholic church. Nor does the decline of the mainline denominations signify the end of Christianity. Never before have so many missionaries gone out from the churches of Western nations to the third world and other mission areas. Christianity may be declining in Europe, but it is on the march in Africa and southeast Asia. The church is even advancing behind the Iron and Bamboo curtains, despite periodic and often severe persecution. We have reason to hope even amid the encroaching desert of secularism and nihilism, because Pentecost is a continuing reality in the life of the people of God, a reality that the world is powerless to extinguish. The transforming power of Pentecost is currently manifest in the burgeoning evangelical movement in this country and other countries throughout the world.

The growing cleavage in the church could be a signal opportunity for the church to redefine itself against the beguiling forces of secular humanism and modernism. Heresy has always been the catalyst which orthodoxy has needed to put its house in order and rediscover the abiding relevance of the gospel. When a false church emerges on the horizon, the true church will also become more visible.

We should recognize that the evangelical movement could itself fall into heresy if it continues its slide into sectarianism. It is imperative that the evangelical church reappropriate those elements that belong to the church in its fullness—catholicity, apostolicity, holiness and love.

The true church, the church of Jesus Christ, will be centered in the gospel, anchored in church tradition and imbued with the fire of Pentecost. It will be evangelical in the sense that it will be devoted to the proclamation of the gospel as attested in Holy Scripture. It will also be catholic, for it will strive both to maintain continuity with the tradition of the whole church and to include the whole world under the banner of the gospel. It will be Reformed in that it will commit itself to continual reformation in the light of the criterion of God's self-revelation in Jesus Christ. It will be inclined to view the Protestant Reformation as the model of a church striving for biblical reform.[82] It will also be Pentecostal (but not in the sectarian sense), since it will live on the basis of the outpouring of the Holy Spirit upon the community of faith, bearing in mind that it is the Spirit who "will convince the world of sin and of righteousness and of judgment" (John 16:8 RSV).

A church that is truly catholic, evangelical and Reformed will make room for the liberal spirit—the spirit of inquiry and openness. Indeed, such a church will eschew all obscurantism and maintain a self-critical stance concerning its own formulations of the truth of faith.[83] At the same time, it will vigorously oppose liberalism as a theological movement that seeks to bring the faith into accord with modernity, that strives for a biblical-cultural synthesis in which the claims of faith are justified at the bar of reason. It will concur in the judgment of P. T. Forsyth: "What is called liberal theology . . . works on the whole against the preaching of the Gospel, and becomes little more than an enlightened Judaism."[84]

Liberal theology in the sense of modernism identifies the Spirit of God with the interior spirit of the age and holds that the life of the time appoints the creed of the time. Evangelical theology, on the contrary, maintains that there is an infinite qualitative distinction between the Spirit of God and the spirit of the time and that the creed of the church must be based on the light of the Word of God, even though it is addressed to the age in which we live. We do not draw our agenda from the world, but we bring God's agenda, as delineated in the Scriptures, to the world.

An evangelical catholic church will also be committed to the ideal of church unity. Revivification by the Holy Spirit is nowhere more evident than in love for our brothers and sisters in the faith. Indeed, such love is a sign that spiritual renewal has already begun to take place. Philip Schaff declares, "If we love Christians of other creeds only as far as they agree with us, we do no more than the heathen do who love their own."[85] The key to renewal in the church lies not only in love, however, but also in humility. "We look hopefully for a reunion of Christendom and a feast of reconciliation of churches," Schaff continues, "but it will be preceded by an act of general humiliation. All must confess: We have sinned and erred; Christ alone is pure and perfect."[86]

In our striving for church unity, we must not lose sight of our mandate to counter doctrinal error, for nothing subverts the cause of unity more than a latitudinarianism which signifies giving up on real church unity in favor of mutual tolerance. Yet in our ongoing battle with heresy, we should be poignantly aware of the fact that there are heresies on the right as well as on the left. Luther reminds us that the Christian must always be fighting on two fronts. Today, the two enemies are an obscurantist biblicism on the right and modernism on the left. If we focus on only one of these threats, the overwhelming temptation will be to forge an alliance with the opposite heresy and thus begin to compromise the faith unwittingly.

I have discussed at length the centrifugal forces threatening the unity of the evangelical catholic church: restorationism, separatism and accommodationism. But there is also a centripetal power drawing evangelical Christians from all communions into a deeper unity —namely, the movement of the Holy Spirit in these last days, the awakening to evangelism and mission. We can face the future with confidence because of the irreversible victory of Jesus Christ and the continuing life-transforming reality of Pentecost, which confirms this victory in the hearts of all who believe. Just as the devil is making his final stand against a church emboldened and renewed by the Holy Spirit, so Jesus Christ is preparing to bring down the curtain on the history of the old aeon and complete his mission—the salvation of a lost and despairing humanity and the creation of a new heaven and a new earth.

Notes

NOTES TO THE PREFACE

1. Clark Pinnock, "God Made in the Image of Man," in *Christianity Today*, Vol. 26, No. 14 (September 3, 1982), p. 35.

2. Howard A. Snyder, *The Community of the King* (Downers Grove, Ill.: InterVarsity Press, 1978), p. 180.

NOTES TO CHAPTER I—Introduction

1. The subordination of Scripture to tradition is evident in James Barr. He rejects the traditional model "God → revelation → scripture → church" and substitutes "God → people → tradition → scripture." In his view, revelation is derived from all these sources. See James Barr, *The Scope and Authority of the Bible* (Philadelphia: Westminster Press, 1980), p. 60.

2. That Kierkegaard was a theologian of grace as well as of Christian discipleship is made abundantly clear by Vernard Eller in his brilliant work *Kierkegaard and Radical Discipleship: A New Perspective* (Princeton, N.J.: Princeton University Press, 1968). See especially pp. 172 ff.

3. Cf. Forsyth: "The great dividing issue for the soul is neither the Bethlehem cradle nor the empty grave, nor the Bible, nor the social question. For the Church at least . . . it is the question of a redeeming atonement. It is here that the evangelical issue lies." P. T. Forsyth, *The Cruciality of the Cross* (London: Independent Press, 1948), p. 39.

4. While revealing his distance from "theologians of the word" such as Calvin, Barth, Brunner and Nygren, David Tracy acknowledges the deep similarities between Catholic and liberal Protestant theologians both

in structure and in spirit. See David Tracy, *The Analogical Imagination* (New York: Crossroad Publishing Co., 1981), pp. 180, 213, 214, 217, 220, 379, 444. Tracy seeks to bring together motifs from Thomist and process thought, but he displays a distinct preference for the latter (see pp. 439, 440, 443, 444).

5. Our words are nevertheless accepted and justified by God if they are born out of a sincere faith in Jesus Christ and are in accordance with the New Testament witness to God's redemptive act in Christ. Despite the lack of perfect correlation, they may be accepted as the vehicle or instrument of God's Word. Yet a qualitative distinction will always remain between God's eternal Word and the earthen vessel of the human witness (II Cor. 4:7). What saves is not our broken testimony but the divine blessing upon our testimony.

NOTES TO CHAPTER II—The Problem of Evangelical Identity
1. This appears to be the stance of many of those associated with the International Council on Biblical Inerrancy. This doctrine, which even its supporters acknowledge is not specifically stated in Scripture, can never be the foundation for faith but only an inference from faith, and even then it needs to be qualified.

2. It would be a mistake to regard these preachers as charlatans. For the most part, they are sincere and God-fearing people. Moreover, I acknowledge that through their ministries there are genuine healings and conversions. But their overall impact is to reinforce traditional values and mores rather than to bring a prophetic word to bear on what the culture holds most dear. By shoring up the moral codes by which society lives, the media preachers perform a distinct service, but they dismally fail to move society toward a new social vision which calls for drastic changes in our mode of life.

An illuminating critique of the electronic church and modern popular religion is given in Richard Quebedeaux, *By What Authority* (San Francisco: Harper & Row, 1982). While much of what the author says rings true, he can be faulted for being at times too negative, for not giving adequate recognition to the evangelistic concern of the electronic church movement and the genuinely Christian motivations of many of its leaders. He is nonetheless accurate in perceiving the impact of New Thought on a significant part of this movement.

3. For a judicious assessment of the new religious right by an evangelically oriented scholar, see Gabriel Fackre, *The Religious Right and Christian Faith* (Grand Rapids, Mich.: Eerdmans, 1982).

4. One of the most devastating exposés of pornography was published in *The Humanist*, an antireligious journal. See Sarah J. McCarthy,

"Pornography, Rape, and the Cult of Macho," in *The Humanist*, Vol. 40, No. 5 (October 1980), pp. 11–20. Similarly, one of the most telling indictments of abortion is to be found in the leftist *Progressive*, which is humanist in its value orientation but not necessarily antireligious. See Mary Meehan, "Abortion: The Left Has Betrayed the Sanctity of Life," in *The Progressive*, Vol. 44, No. 9 (September 1980), pp. 32–34. This does not alter the fact that secular humanism on the whole is militantly supportive of the right to abortion.

5. For a penetrating critique of secular humanism in American society, see John X. Evans, "Definition as Dr. Jekyll and Mr. Hyde," in *Center Journal*, Vol. 1, No. 2 (Spring 1982), pp. 53–83. The author states the case for a Christian humanism against secularist inhumanism.

6. Hans Küng argues with some cogency that the principal threat today is nihilism, the dissolution of all values and norms. See his *Does God Exist?*, trans. Edward Quinn (Garden City, N.Y.: Doubleday, 1980), pp. 341–477.

7. Pascal was associated with the Jansenist movement within the Roman Catholic Church. Jansenism sought to recover the Augustinian emphases on the sovereignty of grace and unconditional election, but it was condemned by Pope Urban VIII in 1642 and again by Pope Clement XI in 1713.

8. G. W. Bromiley, professor emeritus of church history and historical theology at Fuller Theological Seminary, tries to establish that Thomas Aquinas is really a theologian of grace, not of works, and of revelation, not of revelation *and* reason. While some of his interpretations are debatable, it nonetheless shows how one evangelical theologian in our day is able to appreciate the contribution of one of the foremost thinkers in Roman Catholicism. See G. W. Bromiley, *Historical Theology: An Introduction* (Grand Rapids, Mich.: Eerdmans, 1978), pp. 208–209.

9. An evangelical note can be detected in the spirituality of the nineteenth century French Carmelite nun Thérèse of Lisieux, who upheld the "little way" over the heroic way and who spoke of a lift or elevator to heaven, the lift of free grace, rather than the mystical ladder to heaven. See Thérèse of Lisieux, *Story of a Soul: the Autobiography of St. Thérèse of Lisieux*, trans. John Clarke (Washington, D.C.: Institute of Carmelite Studies, 1975); and Ida Friederike Görres, *The Hidden Face*, trans. Richard and Clara Winston (New York: Pantheon Books, 1959).

10. Peter M. Schmiechen, "The Challenge of Conservative Theology," in *The Christian Century*, Vol. 97, No. 13 (April 9, 1980), pp. 402–406. For my reply to Schmiechen, see Donald G. Bloesch, "To Rec-

oncile the Biblically Oriented," in *The Christian Century*, Vol. 97, No. 24 (July 16–23, 1980), pp. 733–735.

11. I would argue that these motifs are integral to the evangel or gospel itself. Even if they are not explicitly affirmed, they are definitely implied. A theologian or church that questions these motifs is surely on the way to heterodoxy if not outright heresy. Yet it would be wrong to condemn any person or group as apostate so long as the confession was made that Jesus is Lord and Savior.

12. Pelagius' position is intellectually viable but not theologically legitimate, since a Christian can hold to it only by ignoring or misinterpreting certain biblical passages that bear on the matter of human bondage and freedom.

13. Albert Schweitzer is reported to have said to Karl Barth at a historic meeting between the two in Münster, Germany: "You and I started from the same problem, the disintegration of modern thought; but whereas you went back to the Reformation, I went back to the Enlightenment." George Seaver, *Christian Revolutionary* (New York: Harper & Bros., 1944), pp. 42–43.

14. Dietrich Bonhoeffer, *Sanctorum Communio*, trans. R. Gregor Smith (London: Collins, 1963), p. 187.

15. Dietrich Bonhoeffer, *No Rusty Swords*, trans. Edwin H. Robertson and John Bowden (New York: Harper & Row, 1965), p. 172.

16. See Kenneth S. Kantzer, "The Future of the Church and Evangelicalism," in Donald E. Hoke, ed., *Evangelicals Face the Future* (South Pasadena, Calif.: William Carey Library, 1978), [pp. 127–146], pp. 127–129. Kantzer points out that the word "Evangelical" was in use by the adherents of the Reformation before "Protestant," which did not enter the vocabulary of western European languages until after 1529.

17. The term *evangelisch* now applies in German-speaking Europe to the state-supported Lutheran, Reformed and United churches and has a sociological more than a theological meaning. The term *pietistisch* (pietist) generally is the German equivalent of the Anglo-American *evangelical*. But in recent years *evangelikal* has come into use in German-speaking lands to indicate the resurgence of a conservative orthodoxy that is united with Pietism.

18. For a graphic account of the Evangelical revival in England, Scotland and Wales in the eighteenth century, see A. Skevington Wood, *The Inextinguishable Blaze* (Grand Rapids, Mich.: Eerdmans, 1960).

19. The reference here is to evangelicalism in its ideal form, in what it seeks to be, in what it is at its best. Most of the evangelical leadership

today, particularly the academic leadership, would understand evangelicalism in the way it is here delineated.

20. The gulf between vital evangelical Christianity and formalistic
orthodoxy or ecclesiasticism is evident in this confession of George
Whitefield: "God showed me that I must be born again, or be damned! I
learned that a man may go to church, say his prayers, receive the sacrament, and yet not be a Christian. How did my heart rise and shud-
der. . . . With what joy . . . was my soul filled, when the weight of
sin went off, and an abiding sense of the pardoning love of God . . .
broke in upon my disconsolate soul!" Arnold Dallimore, *George
Whitefield*, Vol. I (London: Banner of Truth, 1970), pp. 73, 77.

21. In other words, it is not only *what* we believe but *how* we believe
that is important for evangelicals. It is not simply the *truth* of faith but
the *conviction* of faith that is decisive in this perspective.

22. Jerry Falwell and his associates candidly admit: "It is possible to
attend a fundamentalist church and hear a great deal of preaching about
and against all sorts of things and almost never hear the Gospel." *The
Fundamentalist Phenomenon*, ed. Jerry Falwell with Ed Dobson and Ed
Hindson (Garden City, N.Y.: Doubleday, 1981), p. 181.

23. This is not to deny the place for personal testimonies in the context of a biblical sermon, but the testimony of our experience must always point beyond itself to God's great act of deliverance in Jesus Christ.
Paul reminds us that we are to "preach not ourselves, but Christ Jesus
the Lord" (II Cor. 4:5 KJV; cf. I Thes. 2:4–6).

24. Neo-orthodox theologians have often been fond of saying that
liberalism and fundamentalism are two sides of the same coin—trust in
reason over revelation. While there is some truth in this allegation, it
must nonetheless be recognized that most people who follow fundamentalist teachings are still basically evangelical, whereas most liberals
have jettisoned apostolic doctrine altogether.

NOTES TO CHAPTER III—The New Conservatism

1. Evangelicalism has a greater range and depth than many of its adherents have been willing to acknowledge. An evangelical contingent is
even present in the Unitarian-Universalist Association, the Seventh-Day
Adventist Church and the United Pentecostal Church. My two-volume
work *Essentials of Evangelical Theology* (San Francisco: Harper & Row,
1982, 3rd printing) has been used as a text at the United Pentecostal
Seminary in Jackson, Mississippi, though the professor responsible, Dan
Lewis, has since left because of his growing reservations with the doctrinal stance of that denomination. An evangelical surge has also been

evident in the Coptic Church of Egypt. See Edward E. Plowman, "Egypt: A Crisis in the Coptic Church," in *Christianity Today*, Vol. 22, No. 19 (July 21, 1978), p. 50. Evangelical stirrings can even be detected among the Jehovah's Witnesses. See "Witness Under Prosecution," in *Time* (February 22, 1982), p. 66; and "The Watchtower Cracks Again," in *Christianity Today*, Vol. 26, No. 4 (February 19, 1982), pp. 27, 32.

2. See *The Fundamentals: A Testimony to the Truth*, ed. by R. A. Torrey and others (reprint ed., Grand Rapids, Mich.: Baker Book House, 1980).

3. This point is made by Ramsey Michaels in Roger Nicole and J. Ramsey Michaels, eds., *Inerrancy and Common Sense* (Grand Rapids, Mich.: Baker Book House, 1980), pp. 49–70; and James Barr, *The Scope and Authority of the Bible* (Philadelphia: Westminster Press, 1980), pp. 81, 82.

4. Whereas premillennialism teaches that Jesus' second coming inaugurates the thousand-year period of peace on earth referred to in Revelation 20, amillennialism sees this as symbolic of the age of the church (between the first and second coming), and postmillennialism regards it as a period within world history before the second advent. On the postmillennialism of the Puritans see Iain Murray, *The Puritan Hope* (London: Banner of Truth, 1971). That a premillennial strain was also apparent among the Puritans is documented by Richard Lovelace in his *The American Pietism of Cotton Mather* (Grand Rapids, Mich.: Eerdmans, 1979), pp. 64–72.

5. John Opie, Jr., "The Modernity of Fundamentalism," in *The Christian Century*, Vol. 82, No. 19 (May 12, 1965), pp. 608–611.

6. Harold Lindsell seeks to show the affinity between Christianity and capitalism in his *Free Enterprise: Judeo-Christian Defense* (Wheaton, Ill.: Tyndale House, 1982). Robert Webber, on the other hand, contends that true Christianity will always be in conflict with free-enterprise capitalism. See his *The Moral Majority: Right or Wrong?* (Westchester, Ill.: Cornerstone Books, 1981).

7. Ernest R. Sandeen, *The Origins of Fundamentalism* (Philadelphia: Fortress Press, 1968).

8. George Marsden, *Fundamentalism and American Culture* (New York: Oxford University Press, 1980).

9. Among these are James Boice, pastor of the Tenth Presbyterian Church, Philadelphia (which has withdrawn from the United Presbyterian Church in the U.S.A.) and R. C. Sproul of the Ligonier Valley Study Center near Pittsburgh.

10. In his *Neo-Evangelicalism* (Des Plaines, Ill.: Regular Baptist Press, 1965), Robert P. Lightner distinguishes neoevangelicalism from true evangelicalism or fundamentalism.

11. See Jerry Falwell, *Listen, America!* (Garden City, N.Y.: Doubleday, 1980); and *The Fundamentalist Phenomenon*, ed. Jerry Falwell with Ed Dobson and Ed Hindson (New York: Doubleday, 1981).

12. See their article "Inspiration," in *The Presbyterian Review*, Vol. 2, No. 6 (April 1881), pp. 225–260. For the reprint see Archibald A. Hodge and Benjamin B. Warfield, *Inspiration*, Introduction by Roger R. Nicole (Grand Rapids, Mich.: Baker Book House, 1979).

13. Geisler identifies himself as orthodox as opposed to both neoevangelical and fundamentalist in his *Decide for Yourself* (Grand Rapids, Mich.: Zondervan, 1982). Yet his acceptance of dispensationalism marks him as closer to historical fundamentalism.

14. On the resurgence of fundamentalism, see George W. Dollar, *A History of Fundamentalism in America* (Greenville, S.C.: Bob Jones University Press, 1973).

15. For a penetrating introduction to the debate on evolution today, see Huston Smith, "Evolution and Evolutionism," *The Christian Century*, Vol. 99, No. 23 (July 7, 1982), pp. 755–757. A perceptive critique of evolutionary dogma is given by Magnus Verbrugge in his "Animism in Science," *The Journal of Christian Reconstruction*, Vol. VIII, No. 2 (Winter 1982), pp. 79–107. Also see L. Duane Thurman, *How to Think About Evolution and Other Bible-Science Controversies* (Downers Grove, Ill.: InterVarsity Press, 1978). For a hard-hitting attack on the theory of evolution from a non-Christian source, see Fred Hoyle and C. Wickramasinghe, *Evolution from Space* (London: Dent, 1981).

16. Jack Rogers and Donald McKim try to show that inerrancy in its modern sense has little solid support in the history of theology. See their *The Authority and Interpretation of the Bible* (San Francisco: Harper & Row, 1981). John Woodbridge of Trinity Seminary seeks to refute their position in his *Biblical Authority: A Critique of the Rogers/McKim Proposal* (Grand Rapids, Mich.: Zondervan, 1982). In polemical debates of this kind, the temptation is to disregard evidence contrary to one's own position. Part of the problem lies in whether there is a common understanding of truth and error that has remained unchanged through the centuries.

17. Karl Heim, whose affinities are with German Pietism, is widely respected among Anglo-Saxon evangelicals for his work in defense of a supernatural world-view. See his *The Transformation of the Scientific*

World View, trans. W. A. Whitehouse (London: SCM Press, 1953); and *Christian Faith and Natural Science*, trans. N. Horton Smith (New York: Harper & Row, 1953).

18. Even Benjamin Warfield, much to the chagrin of many of his orthodox colleagues, was willing to affirm theistic evolution. Bernard Ramm states the case for a progressive creationism in his *The Christian View of Science and Scripture* (Grand Rapids, Mich.: Eerdmans, 1954).

19. Carl Henry, *The Uneasy Conscience of Modern Fundamentalism* (Grand Rapids, Mich.: Eerdmans, 1947).

20. Even some right-wing and confessionalist evangelicals have aligned themselves with postmillennialism. The Christian Reconstructionist movement headed by Rousas J. Rushdoony is emphatically postmillennial and looks forward to the building of a holy community before the second coming of Christ. Its magazine is *The Journal of Christian Reconstruction*, and its seminary is the Geneva Divinity School in Tyler, Texas.

21. George Eldon Ladd offers an evangelical alternative to the historical-critical method in his *The New Testament and Criticism* (Grand Rapids, Mich.: Eerdmans, 1967). Also see Gerhard Maier, *The End of the Historical-Critical Method* (St. Louis: Concordia Publishing House, 1977); and his "Concrete Alternatives to the Historical-Critical Method," in *Evangelical Review of Theology*, Vol. 6, No. 1 (April 1982), pp. 23–36.

22. Bernard Ramm, *Special Revelation and the Word of God* (Grand Rapids, Mich.: Eerdmans, 1961), pp. 154–160.

23. Carl Henry, *God, Revelation and Authority*, 6 vols. (Waco, Tex.: Word Books, 1976–83).

24. Paul K. Jewett, *The Ordination of Women* (Grand Rapids, Mich.: Eerdmans, 1980), pp. 44–47, 122, 127.

25. See J. D. Douglas, ed., *Let the Earth Hear His Voice* (Minneapolis: World Wide Publications, 1975), p. 3.

26. Horace Hummel, *The Word Becoming Flesh* (St. Louis: Concordia Publishing House, 1979).

27. Donald Gelpi contends that "it is dangerous and misleading to demand that the divine response be the gift of tongues, just as it is dangerous and misleading to call the gift of tongues, which is the least of the gifts, the 'fullness of the Spirit.'" In his *Pentecostalism: A Theological Viewpoint* (New York: Paulist Press, 1971), p. 185.

28. Don Basham explores conflicting views on demons in his *Deliver Us From Evil* (Washington Depot, Conn.: Chosen Books, 1972), pp.

219–220. Basham is open to the view of Derek Prince that demons are disembodied spirits of a pre-Adamic race of beings corrupted by Satan and his angels.

29. Michael Harper, *None Can Guess* (Plainfield, N.J.: Logos International, 1971), pp. 149, 153.

30. See James S. Tinney, "The Prosperity Doctrine: An Accretion to Black Pentecostalism," in *Evangelical Review of Theology*, Vol. 4, No. 1 (April 1980), pp. 84–92.

31. The Assemblies of God and the Church of God in Christ, which ministers to the black community, are the two largest Pentecostal denominations in this country. The former had a growth rate of 70 percent from 1970 to 1980. See Dean Merrill, "The Fastest-growing American Denomination," *Christianity Today*, Vol. 27, No. 1 (January 7, 1983), pp. 28–34.

32. Key books by J. Rodman Williams include *The Era of the Spirit* (Plainfield, N.J.: Logos International, 1971); *Pentecostal Reality* (Logos International, 1972); and *The Gift of the Holy Spirit Today* (Logos International, 1980).

33. In his *Reflected Glory* (Grand Rapids, Mich.: Eerdmans, 1976), Thomas Smail, active in the charismatic movement in the Church of Scotland, makes a good case that the church of Jesus Christ is charismatic as well as evangelical and catholic. See also his attempt to restore a Trinitarian balance to current Pentecostalism in his *The Forgotten Father* (Grand Rapids, Mich.: Eerdmans, 1981).

34. Books by Catholic charismatics in which evangelical themes are in evidence include Simon Tugwell, *Did You Receive the Spirit?* (New York: Paulist Press, 1972); and Ralph Martin, *A Crisis of Truth* (Ann Arbor, Mich.: Servant Books, 1982).

35. See *Theology Today*, Vol. XXX, No. 4 (January 1974), p. 333. Both Tillich and Bultmann belong in the category of neoliberalism. Reinhold Niebuhr and his brother H. Richard Niebuhr can be placed on the extreme left of neo-orthodoxy.

36. Other names by which it was known even in its early stages were neo-Reformation theology, neo-Calvinism and neo-orthodoxy.

37. Helmut Thielicke in Germany also belongs in the tradition of progressive or neo-Lutheranism. Thielicke, however, is more open to the contribution of Reformed theology than the Lundensian school and is even willing to give a prominent place to the third use of the law, the law as a guide for the Christian life. See Helmut Thielicke, *Theological Ethics*, Vol. I, ed. William H. Lazareth (Philadelphia: Fortress Press, 1966), pp. 123–139.

38. Paul Lehmann maintains that Niebuhr makes contemporary sense of the basic insights of classical orthodoxy. Paul Lehmann, "The Christology of Reinhold Niebuhr," in Charles W. Kegley and Robert W. Bretall, eds., *Reinhold Niebuhr: His Religious, Social, and Political Thought* (New York: Macmillan, 1956), pp. 252–280. Edward J. Carnell, on the other hand, sees Niebuhr at variance with historical orthodoxy at many points. See his *The Theology of Reinhold Niebuhr* (Grand Rapids, Mich.: Eerdmans, 1951).

39. C. C. Ryrie, *Neo-orthodoxy: An Evangelical Evaluation of Barthianism* (Chicago: Moody Press, 1956), pp. 14, 15.

40. Bernard Ramm, *The Evangelical Heritage* (Waco, Tex.: Word Books, 1973), pp. 103, 104, 111.

41. See Bruce Demarest, *General Revelation* (Grand Rapids, Mich.: Zondervan, 1982).

42. Neo-orthodox theologians have at times described the Bible as the medium of the Word. Or they say that the Bible contains the Word of God, or that it becomes the Word by the action of the Spirit. The most common designation, especially among Barthians, is that the Bible is a witness to the Word.

43. Joseph Haroutunian, *God With Us: A Theology of Transpersonal Life* (Philadelphia: Westminster Press, 1965).

44. Neo-orthodox theologians can be criticized for not doing justice to another dimension of sin—self-loathing. For significant works on the subject of sin by neo-orthodox scholars see Emil Brunner, *Man in Revolt*, trans. Olive Wyon (New York: Scribner, 1939); Reinhold Niebuhr, *Moral Man and Immoral Society* (New York: Scribner, 1932); Reinhold Niebuhr, *The Nature and Destiny of Man*, Vol. 1 (New York: Scribner, 1951); Joseph Haroutunian, *Lust for Power* (New York: Scribner, 1949); and E. La B. Cherbonnier, *Hardness of Heart* (Garden City, N.Y.: Doubleday, 1955). This last work sees pride and self-contempt as two sides of the same coin—hardness of heart.

45. Theologians who presently teach at Dubuque include Donald Bloesch, Donald McKim and Arthur Cochrane. All are active members of the Karl Barth Society of North America.

46. Whereas Barth's first attempt at systematizing theology was entitled *Christian Dogmatics* and his second *Church Dogmatics*, his final work was significantly called *Evangelical Theology*. See Karl Barth, *Evangelical Theology: An Introduction*, trans. Grover Foley (Garden City, N.Y.: Doubleday Anchor Books, 1964).

47. See Gregory G. Bolich, *Karl Barth & Evangelicalism* (Downers

Grove, Ill.: InterVarsity Press, 1980); and Donald G. Bloesch, *Jesus Is Victor!* (Nashville: Abingdon Press, 1976).

48. Barth's theology was the main force behind the Confessing Church movement in Germany, but this renewal was short-lived.

49. Only those restorationists who ignore history and simply wish to return to the ideal church of the past, i.e., the New Testament church, fall under my stricture. I believe in a restoration of New Testament doctrine but not of all practices in the New Testament church.

50. See Jerry Falwell, ed., *The Fundamentalist Phenomenon*, pp. 28 ff.

51. See Robert Webber and Donald Bloesch, eds., *The Orthodox Evangelicals* (Nashville: Nelson, 1978).

52. Jaroslav Pelikan, *The Riddle of Roman Catholicism* (Nashville: Abingdon Press, 1959), pp. 45–57.

53. The catholic evangelicalism that I espouse concurs with the Puritans and the Reformed tradition generally that every Communion must be preceded by rigorous self-examination and that therefore it is not appropriate for Communion to be offered every Lord's Day, though this is the ideal. In contrast to the Puritans, however, catholic evangelicalism sees the usefulness of the church year in guiding the pastor in the selection of the text, but does not regard this as a law that must be rigidly obeyed.

54. Both Richard Sibbes, the Puritan, and Philip Spener, the Pietist, remained in their own churches to bring renewal from within. Their approach is to be contrasted with that of the radical Pietists and Separatists, who urged withdrawal from the established churches. John Wesley also sought to work for reform within his own Church of England, but the Methodist movement could not be contained within the parent body.

55. Schaff, who was associated with the Mercersburg movement, still maintained his earlier connections with the Evangelical Alliance. Unlike his colleague John Nevin, he had only kind words for John Wesley, regarding him as a preacher in the apostolic tradition. See Philip Schaff, *History of the Christian Church*, Vol. VIII (Grand Rapids, Mich.: Eerdmans, 1958), p. 815.

56. Others in the past who approached this ideal of catholic evangelicalism include John Nevin and Wilhelm Loehe. Both Nevin and Schaff were identified with the Mercersburg movement within the German Reformed Church in this country, which sought a restoration of emphases and practices associated with the pre-Reformation Catholic tradition. The Mercersburg movement is best understood as a reaction against

the rampant individualism and subjectivism in American Protestantism. It has been criticized for its neglect of the area of preaching in favor of a more sacramental orientation. See Howard G. Hageman, *Pulpit and Table* (Richmond, Va.: John Knox Press, 1962), p. 97. The newly formed Mercersburg Society is seeking to keep this tradition alive in the United Church of Christ.

57. Max Thurian is the theologian of the Taizé Community, a Protestant monastery in Burgundy, France.

58. A. W. Tozer, famed preacher and spiritual writer in the Christian and Missionary Alliance, sought to draw from the wellsprings of the Catholic mystics, whom he credits with leading him to the gospel.

59. Klara (Mother Basilea) Schlink, sister of the noted Lutheran theologian Edmund Schlink, is cofounder of the Evangelical Sisterhood of Mary in Darmstadt, Germany, an evangelical convent, which brings together Reformation theology and the fervor and concerns of evangelical revivalism, including Pentecostalism. For a report on this as well as other current religious communities, see Donald G. Bloesch, *Wellsprings of Renewal* (Grand Rapids, Mich.: Eerdmans, 1974).

60. Max Lackmann, German Lutheran pastor, was the former head of the League of Evangelical-Catholic Reunion. For many years he maintained a close association with The Gathering (*Die Sammlung*). See Max Lackmann, *The Augsburg Confession and Catholic Unity*, ed. and trans. W. R. Bouman (New York: Herder & Herder, 1963).

61. See Richard Lovelace, *Dynamics of Spiritual Life: An Evangelical Theology of Renewal* (Downers Grove, Ill.: InterVarsity Press, 1979).

62. See Robert E. Webber, *Common Roots: A Call to Evangelical Maturity* (Grand Rapids, Mich.: Zondervan, 1978).

63. See Bela Vassady, *Christ's Church: Evangelical, Catholic and Reformed* (Grand Rapids, Mich.: Eerdmans, 1965).

64. Peter Gillquist is a bishop in the Evangelical Orthodox Church and an editor for Thomas Nelson. Several of the leaders in this movement came out of Campus Crusade for Christ.

65. See Ralph Martin, *A Crisis of Truth* (Ann Arbor, Mich.: Servant Books, 1982).

66. This is the magazine of the Assembly of Covenant Churches, which was originally a part of the New Covenant Apostolic Order, the parent body of the Evangelical Orthodox Church. Unlike the last, the Assembly of Covenant Churches seeks consciously to stand in the tradition of the mainstream Protestant Reformation. Among its spiritual leaders is Ray Nethery, an active participant in the Chicago Call conference in May, 1977.

67. For example, it can be shown that I stand partly in both neo-evangelicalism and neo-orthodoxy, even though I belong mostly to catholic evangelicalism.

68. In my opinion, Calvin and Luther are closest to what I have described as a catholic evangelicalism. They sought the reform of the Catholic Church, not the creation of a sect divorced from catholic tradition. Throughout their ministries, moreover, they were concerned for the unity of the whole church. This was more true of Calvin and Melanchthon than of Luther. On the efforts of the mainline Reformers on behalf of church unity see John T. McNeill, *Unitive Protestantism* (Richmond, Va.: John Knox Press, 1964).

69. In his *After Fundamentalism: The Future of Evangelical Theology* (San Francisco: Harper & Row, 1983), Bernard Ramm forcefully argues that Barth's theology can serve as a model for a renewed evangelicalism.

70. See p. 34.

71. See Ronald J. Sider and Richard K. Taylor, *Nuclear Holocaust and Christian Hope* (Downers Grove, Ill.: InterVarsity Press, 1982). Sider is presently working on a new book with the tentative title *What Does It Mean to Be Pro-Life?*

72. J. Gresham Machen, *Christianity and Liberalism* (Grand Rapids, Mich.: Eerdmans, 1923). In my opinion, there are two kinds of Christianity: orthodoxy and heterodoxy. The latter, which contains Christian elements, is moving in the direction of another religion, but it still may be regarded as a variation of Christianity, though a deviant one. When heterodoxy becomes heresy, however, when an unbalanced emphasis becomes a formal repudiation, then we have moved out of the circle of Christian faith. For a further discussion on this subject, see pp. 124–126.

Notes to Chapter IV—Evangelical Disunity

1. Carl Henry, *God, Revelation and Authority* IV (Waco, Tex.: Word Books, 1979), p. 590.

2. The traditional Reformed position on baptism is stated by G. W. Bromiley in his *Children of Promise: The Case for Baptizing Infants* (Grand Rapids, Mich.: Eerdmans, 1979). Paul Jewett, who also belongs to the Reformed family, makes a case for believer baptism in his *Infant Baptism and the Covenant of Grace* (Grand Rapids, Mich.: Eerdmans, 1978). For a book that tries to overcome the gulf between paedobaptists and baptists see Donald Bridge and David Phypers, *The Water That Divides* (Downers Grove, Ill.: InterVarsity Press, 1979, 2nd printing).

3. See Karl Barth, *Church Dogmatics* IV, 4, trans. G. W. Bromiley (Edinburgh: T. & T. Clark, 1969).

4. See note 20, p. 160. It should be noted that Jonathan Blanchard, the first president of Wheaton College, was, for the most part, a post-millennialist.

5. See Robert G. Clouse, *The Meaning of the Millennium: Four Views* (Downers Grove, Ill.: InterVarsity Press, 1977).

6. I am here using "pietism" in its distinctly contemporary meaning, since historical Pietism was noted for its social involvement.

7. This split between personal piety and social concern was not present in earlier evangelicalism. See Donald Dayton, *Discovering An Evangelical Heritage* (New York: Harper & Row, 1976); and David Moberg, *The Great Reversal*, rev. ed. (Philadelphia: J. B. Lippincott, 1977).

8. R. C. Sproul distinguishes between the confessional, presuppositional and classical methods; the last seeks to establish the infallibility of Scripture "on the inductive basis of historical-empirical evidence." In John Warwick Montgomery, ed., *God's Inerrant Word* (Minneapolis: Bethany Fellowship, 1974), [pp. 242–261], p. 250.

9. Augustine can be used to support both groups. Norman Geisler, Gordon Clark and Ronald Nash all appeal to Augustine, though a case can be made that Augustine was much more skeptical of the role of reason in coming to a right understanding of God. See Robert E. Cushman, "Faith and Reason," in Roy W. Battenhouse, ed., *A Companion to the Study of St. Augustine* (reprint ed. Grand Rapids, Mich.: Baker Book House, 1979), pp. 287–314.

10. For a delineation of the increasing divergence of Lutheran orthodoxy from Luther, see Jaroslav Pelikan, *From Luther to Kierkegaard* (St. Louis: Concordia Publishing House, 1950).

11. Kuyper declared that the conviction of faith "is *not* the outcome of observation or demonstration." Abraham Kuyper, *Principles of Sacred Theology* (Grand Rapids, Mich.: Eerdmans, 1954), p. 131. G. C. Berkouwer is representative of this tradition today.

12. Francis Schaeffer, *Escape From Reason* (London: Inter-Varsity Fellowship, 1968).

13. See Brian Gerrish, *Tradition and the Modern World* (Chicago: University of Chicago Press, 1978), pp. 61, 62.

14. It is possible to hold to *ex opere operato* without falling into magic, but only when the rite is united with faith and the Word.

15. See James E. Tull, *The Atoning Gospel* (Macon, Ga.: Mercer University Press, 1982), pp. 190–192.

16. It is a matter of debate whether Charles Hodge can be included among the total inerrancy advocates. He likened what appear to be factual inconsistencies in the text to a speck of sandstone in the Parthenon which was nonetheless built of marble. See Charles Hodge, *Systematic Theology*, Vol. I (New York: Scribner, 1898), p. 170. Hodge, moreover, distinguished between what the writers thought and believed as children of their times and what they genuinely taught under the inspiration of the Spirit. Yet the polemics of his day led him to assert that Scripture can be perfectly harmonized not only with itself but also with the external evidence of science. For a perspicacious critique of Charles Hodge as a "transitional theologian" who prepared the way for the rigid inerrantist position of A. A. Hodge and Benjamin Warfield, see Jack B. Rogers and Donald K. McKim, *The Authority and Interpretation of the Bible* (San Francisco: Harper & Row, 1979).

17. Formerly known as *Present Truth,* this magazine was begun by ex-Seventh-Day Adventists who on rediscovering the Reformation doctrines of *sola gratia* and *sola fide* felt obliged to withdraw from their communion. On its quarrel with the Holiness movement, see *Present Truth,* Vol. 2, No. 1 (February 1973).

18. Paxton has since left Verdict ministries and now works with Lee S. Ferro, Jr., a Florida Presbyterian pastor, in TAP (Theological Assistance Program), but his theological thrust remains the same.

19. See Donald G. Bloesch, *Is the Bible Sexist?: Beyond Feminism and Patriarchalism* (Westchester, Ill.: Crossway Books, 1982).

20. See Letha Scanzoni and Virginia Mollenkott, *Is the Homosexual My Neighbor?* (San Francisco: Harper & Row, 1980).

21. See the statement against weapons of mass extermination drawn up by Arthur C. Cochrane, "Mass Extermination," in *The Reformed Journal,* Vol. 30, Issue 6 (June 1980), pp. 4, 5.

22. For the divergence of attitudes toward war in the evangelical community, see Robert G. Clouse, ed., *War: Four Christian Views* (Downers Grove, Ill.: InterVarsity Press, 1981).

23. Vernon C. Grounds, "An Evangelical's Concern about Evangelical Unconcern," in *MPL Journal,* Vol. III, No. 3 (1982), p. 11. Compare this forthright statement of James R. Cook, spokesman for the Church of God (Anderson, Indiana): "It seems inconsistent for Christians to decry the Nazis' murder of six million Jews and to ignore the implications of our own military build-up. Currently, the United States has enough nuclear warheads deployed or stock-piled to incinerate the world's population eighteen times over. And some American military leaders have spoken publicly about reserving the option for a first strike!" Barry L.

Callen, ed., *The First Century Church of God Reformation Movement,*
Vol. 2 (Anderson, Ind.: Warner Press, 1979), p. 794.

We should also, of course, deplore the schizophrenic mind-set of the
left which raises an outcry against nuclear weapons development but
which is disturbingly silent on the grave evil of abortion, which involves
the yearly mass slaughter of millions of unborn children throughout the
world.

24. See Billy Graham, "Graham's Mission to Moscow," in *Christianity
Today,* Vol. 26, No. 11 (June 18, 1982), pp. 20–23.

25. This is not to dispute the right of church bodies to demand from
their adherents a high standard of life, but we must not confuse the
moral standards that form part of the revealed law of God with the
mores and folkways that have their basis in the dynamics of human culture rather than the mystery of divine revelation.

26. See *Christianity Today,* Vol. 23, No. 5 (December 1, 1978), p.
52.

27. Pierce Beaver also reports that he "has often heard from Asians
and Africans the assertion that the scandal of disunity, unbrotherliness,
and internecine strife robs the spoken word of power. People of new nations seeking unity and stability fear what they believe to be the inherent divisiveness of Christianity." R. Pierce Beaver, *The Missionary Between the Times* (Garden City, N.Y.: Doubleday, 1968), pp. 11, 12.

28. Paul Holmer, *The Grammar of Faith* (San Francisco: Harper &
Row, 1978), p. 2.

29. See Karl Mannheim, *Ideology and Utopia,* trans. Louis Wirth and
Edward Schils (New York: Harcourt, Brace & World, 1953). In contrast
to Mannheim, I see ideology as encompassing not only the conservative
defense of the established order but also its revolutionary opposition.

30. Langdon Gilkey, *Message and Existence* (New York: Seabury
Press, 1981), p. 30.

31. Hans Küng, *Does God Exist?,* trans. Edward Quinn (Garden
City, N.Y.: Doubleday, 1980), p. 124.

32. For a discerning critique of Reinhold Niebuhr's understanding of
ideology, see Dennis P. McCann, "Political Ideologies and Practical
Theology: Is There A Difference?" in *Union Seminary Quarterly Review,* Vol. XXXVI, No. 4 (Summer 1981), pp. 243–257. McCann contrasts Niebuhr with the liberation theologian Juan Luis Segundo.

33. Cited by Robert T. Coote, "Carl McIntire's Troubled Trail," in
Eternity, Vol. 20, No. 5 (May 1969), p. 36.

34. See *Christianity Today,* Vol. 15, No. 1 (October 9, 1970), p. 42.

35. *The Christian Century*, Vol. 86, No. 19 (May 7, 1969), p. 660.

36. See James Davison Hunter, "The New Class and the Young Evangelicals," in *Review of Religious Research*, Vol. 22, No. 2 (December 1980), pp. 155–169.

37. See Peter Berger, *The Sacred Canopy* (Garden City, N.Y.: Doubleday, 1967); "Ethics and the Present Class Struggle," *Worldview*, Vol. 21, No. 4 (April 1978), pp. 6–11; "The Worldview of the New Class: Secularity and its Discontents," in B. Bruce-Briggs, ed., *The New Class?* (New Brunswick, N.J.: Transaction Books, 1979), pp. 49–55; and "The Class Struggle in American Religion," *The Christian Century*, Vol. 98, No. 6 (February 25, 1981), pp. 194–199.

38. For a contemporary scholarly exposition of this ideology, see George Gilder, *Wealth and Poverty* (New York: Basic Books, 1981).

39. H. Richard Niebuhr, "Toward the Independence of the Church," in H. Richard Niebuhr, Wilhelm Pauck and Francis P. Miller, *The Church Against the World* (Chicago: Willett, Clark & Co., 1935), pp. 123–156.

40. Reinhold Niebuhr, *The Contribution of Religion to Social Work* (New York: Columbia University Press, 1932), p. 29.

41. What I call welfare liberalism parallels Peter Berger's "new class" (see note 37), though the latter includes aspects of socialism as well. Welfare liberalism also roughly corresponds to Charles Reich's Consciousness II, whereas classical liberalism would be analogous to his Consciousness I. Reich speaks, too, of Consciousness III, in which harmony with nature takes priority over the quest for mastery over nature. One part of feminist ideology would be in tune with Consciousness III. See Charles Reich, *The Greening of America* (New York: Random House, 1970).

42. Most modern ideologies, including classical liberalism, ably serve the goals of the technological society, though not all are so obviously in harmony with these goals as welfare liberalism.

43. I am including communism and Maoism within the wider ideology of socialism. For a forceful exposition of the socialist creed by an American devotee, see Michael Harrington, *The Twilight of Capitalism* (New York: Simon & Schuster, 1976).

44. David M. Beckmann, *Where Faith and Economics Meet* (Minneapolis: Augsburg Publishing House, 1981), pp. 61–80.

45. Even though holding to the ideal of androgyny, Helen Luke breaks with most feminists by contending that before union is realized the differences between the sexes must be frankly acknowledged:

"Those who assert that the only difference between men and women is biological, and that in every other way they are equal and have the same inborn potentialities, have disastrously missed the point." Helen M. Luke, *Woman Earth and Spirit: The Feminine in Symbol and Myth* (New York: Crossroad Publishing Co., 1981), p. 2. Luke is taken to task for her assertion that there are immutable psychic differences between the sexes by Rita M. Gross in her review of Luke's book in *The Christian Century*, Vol. 99, No. 8 (March 10, 1982), pp. 276–279. In my opinion, the logic of Luke's position leads to an overcoming of the male-female polarity.

Another feminist who tries to maintain the distinctions between male and female is Ann Belford Ulanov. See her *Receiving Woman: Studies in the Psychology and Theology of the Feminine* (Philadelphia: Westminster Press, 1981).

46. Rosemary Ruether, "From Machismo to Mutuality," in Edward Batchelor, Jr., ed., *Homosexuality and Ethics* (New York: Pilgrim Press, 1980), p. 31.

47. See Donald G. Bloesch, *Is the Bible Sexist?: Beyond Feminism and Patriarchalism* (Westchester, Ill.: Crossway Books, 1982).

48. See Naomi Goldenberg, *Changing of the Gods* (Boston: Beacon Press, 1979); Starhawk, *The Spiral Dance: A Rebirth of the Ancient Religion of the Great Goddess* (San Francisco: Harper & Row, 1979); Charlene Spretnak, ed., *The Politics of Women's Spirituality* (Garden City, N.Y.: Doubleday Anchor Books, 1982); Rosemary Ruether, "The Way of Wicca," *The Christian Century*, Vol. 97, No. 6 (February 20, 1980), pp. 208–209; and Virginia Mollenkott, "An Evangelical Feminist Confronts the Goddess," *The Christian Century*, Vol. 99, No. 32 (October 20, 1982), pp. 1043–1046.

49. See Stanley G. Payne, *Fascism: Comparison and Definition* (Madison: University of Wisconsin Press, 1980).

50. Where the present regime in Iran falls short of fascist ideology is in its tendency to subordinate the glory of the state to the cause of the Shiite Moslem faith. Yet it is an open question whether the Iranian state is in fact subordinate to the faith or vice versa. Probably the most accurate picture is that both fascist and theocratic religionist forces are at work in today's Iran and that it is still too early to ascertain which will come out on top.

51. See Arthur C. Cochrane, *The Church's Confession Under Hitler*, 2nd ed. (Pittsburgh: Pickwick Press, 1976).

52. Populism advocates government interference not only in the economic sphere of life (as does socialism) but also in the area of personal

behavior (as does conservatism). Populism, in contrast to fascism, is an-tielitist, but like fascism it seeks to unite a concern for the common good with the preservation of the national and cultural heritage.

53. See note 41.

54. This is an appropriate, not a mistaken designation. For a first-rate scholarly critique of secular humanism see James Hitchcock, *What Is Secular Humanism?* (Ann Arbor, Mich.: Servant Books, 1982). Hitch-cock fails to explore the impact of secular humanism on modern warfare. Another provocative study is Robert Webber, *Secular Humanism* (Grand Rapids, Mich.: Zondervan, 1982). Webber warns against both the secular humanism of the left and the secularism behind growing mil-itarism and nationalism.

55. See Howard A. Snyder, *The Liberating Church* (Downers Grove, Ill.: InterVarsity Press, 1982). See especially pp. 31, 113–114, 139–140, 210–211. Snyder trenchantly develops the dominant characteristics of this life- and world-view.

This underlying ideology or metaideology might also be called "tech-nocratic liberalism" (Robert Bellah), since it realizes the Enlightenment dream of the mastery of nature by practical reason.

56. This position is already anticipated in the social thought of the Enlightenment thinker Jean-Jacques Rousseau, who believed that the will of the people is indestructible and infallible. See Lester G. Crocker, *Rousseau's Social Contract* (Cleveland: Press of Case Western Reserve University, 1968).

57. An instructive book in this connection is Bertram Gross, *Friendly Fascism: The New Face of Power in America* (New York: M. Evans & Co., 1981).

58. Peter L. Berger and Hansfried Kellner, *Sociology Reinterpreted* (Garden City, N.Y.: Doubleday Anchor Books, 1981), p. 144.

59. Cited in *The British Weekly and Christian World*, Vol. XCV, No. 4290 (May 8, 1969), p. 9.

60. The latest secularist intrusion in the public schools is values clarification, "in which children are encouraged to regard all questions of belief as 'open' matters of opinion." The result is to cause children to question the religious and moral beliefs handed down to them by their parents and church. See James Hitchcock, *What Is Secular Humanism?*, p. 108.

61. For a perceptive evangelical critique of the Moral Majority agenda to introduce teacher- or student-directed voluntary religious exercises in the classroom context, see John Warwick Montgomery, "School Prayers: A Common Danger," in *Christianity Today*, Vol. 26, No. 9 (May 7,

1982), p. 59. I see a definite place for teaching the moral values of the Judeo-Christian heritage in the public schools, and our founding fathers would have no objection to this. There can be no such thing as a value-free education.

62. See Karl Barth, *Against the Stream,* trans. E. M. Delacour and Stanley Godman (London: SCM Press, 1954).

63. H. Richard Niebuhr, *The Social Sources of Denominationalism* (New York: Henry Holt & Co., 1929).

64. See note 36.

65. This journal has not, to my knowledge, lent its support to other forms of sexual aberration such as incest and sadomasochism, which are defended by certain segments of the secular liberal community. These criticisms of both *Christianity & Crisis* and *National Catholic Reporter* should not be taken to mean that an authentic prophetic voice can never be heard from their pages. Moreover, when this voice does break through the ideological verbiage, it is one which is seldom available in magazines of a different orientation.

66. For a timely indictment of the World Council of Churches, see Robert Webber, *The Moral Majority: Right or Wrong?* (Westchester, Ill.: Cornerstone Books, 1981), pp. 57–86.

The National Council of Churches is now giving serious consideration to including the Metropolitan Community Church in its membership despite the latter's upholding of a gay life-style. Eastern Orthodox members have rightly objected that because such a life-style conflicts with biblical norms, this must be regarded as "a theological issue."

67. Cf. Paul Vitz: "It is beginning to look as though there is a world-wide fundamental conflict between Christianity and the modern state—a conflict which has little to do with whether the state espouses a leftist or rightist political philosophy." *Psychology as Religion* (Grand Rapids, Mich.: Eerdmans, 1977), p. 114.

68. For an assessment of the Hartford Appeal by eight of its participants, see Peter L. Berger and Richard John Neuhaus, eds., *Against the World For the World* (New York: Seabury Press, 1976).

69. I do not share Tillich's belief that the object of faith is the unconditional beyond all human understanding; instead, it is the incarnate Word of God, Jesus Christ, who enters into our understanding and remolds it. The absolute that I affirm became incarnate in a particular place and time in history.

70. Reformation theology holds that by the action of the Spirit the Bible can indeed transmit the Word of God. There is no absolute equation of the Word of God and the Bible, but there is an inseparable rela-

tion. The Bible is the vessel, the channel, the medium of the Word of God. The infallible criterion in Reformation theology was not the original autographs (as in later fundamentalism) but the unity of the Bible and the Spirit.

71. Dorothy Sayers, *Creed or Chaos?* (New York: Harcourt, Brace & Co., 1949), p. 25. Even though these remarks were made several decades ago, they are surprisingly relevant to the present scene.

72. Cited in G. C. Berkouwer, *A Half Century of Theology*, trans. Lewis B. Smedes (Grand Rapids, Mich.: Eerdmans, 1977), p. 12.

NOTES TO CHAPTER V—Pathways to Evangelical Oblivion
1. Karl Barth is helpful in describing the early chapters of Genesis as saga rather than either myth or exact history. Saga is the poetic elaboration of what is essentially divine intervention into history. It is not unhistorical (as is myth) but superhistorical. What it purports to speak about is not accessible to historical investigation.

2. John R. W. Stott, "Are Evangelicals Fundamentalists?" in *Christianity Today*, Vol. 22, No. 21 (September 8, 1978), pp. 44–46. Stott reveals his break with evangelical rationalism by contending that instead of embracing the Aristotelian golden mean or either one of the extremes, we should "hold fast to both extremes, so long as they are equally biblical, even if our human mind cannot reconcile or systematize them. For biblical truth is often stated paradoxically and the attempt to resolve all the 'antinomies' of Scripture is misguided because impossible." Stott is here endorsing Charles Simeon's advice. John R. W. Stott, *Christ the Controversialist* (London: Tyndale House, 1970), p. 46.

3. Restorationist evangelicals should take note of Geddes MacGregor's *The Nicene Creed Illumined by Modern Thought* (Grand Rapids, Mich.: Eerdmans, 1981). MacGregor, who tends to endorse an emanationistic monism, is still a devout defender of the Nicene Creed. Because ancient creeds can be defended by modern liberals and others who stray into heterodox and heretical modes of thinking, such documents cannot serve as the confession of faith that is needed in our time.

4. Those who hold to apostolic succession believe that the authority in the Christian church is derived from the apostles through an unbroken succession of bishops, and unless one receives the rite of laying on of hands from a bishop who stands in this succession, one is not validly ordained.

5. In his later speculation, John Nevin, Mercersburg theologian, moved toward the position of a hierarchical order that proceeds down from Christ through the bishops to the people. He appealed to Cyprian

in support of this view. This theory of hierarchy was at variance with the views that both Nevin and Schaff had previously expressed. See James Hastings Nichols, *Romanticism in American Theology* (Chicago: University of Chicago Press, 1961), pp. 275–276.

6. Note that in the encyclical *Vehementer* of Pope Pius X (1906), the church was defined as "an unequal society," ruled by pastors and teachers, in which the "multitude of the faithful" had "no other right than that of allowing itself to be led, and, as a docile flock to follow its shepherds." Wilhelm Pauck, *The Heritage of the Reformation* (Glencoe, Ill.: Free Press, 1950), p. 193.

7. See Kenneth L. Woodward, "Today's Oxford Movement," *Newsweek*, Vol. 97, No. 2 (January 12, 1981), p. 80.

8. Richard Sibbes, *The Complete Works of Richard Sibbes*, Vol. II, ed. Alexander Balloch Grosart (Edinburgh: James Nichol, 1862), p. 241.

9. Martin Luther, *Luther's Works*, Vol. 41 (Philadelphia: Fortress Press, 1966), p. 114.

10. For examples of recent ecumenical Roman Catholic writing in which the Reformation is treated appreciatively, see Harry J. McSorley, *Luther: Right or Wrong?* (Minneapolis: Augsburg Publishing House, 1969); Hans Küng, *Justification*, trans. Thomas Collins, Edmund Tolk and David Granskou (New York: Thomas Nelson, 1964); Louis Bouyer, *The Spirit and Forms of Protestantism*, trans. A. V. Littledale (Westminster, Md.: Newman Press, 1961); Stephen Pfürtner, *Luther and Aquinas on Salvation*, trans. Edward Quinn (New York: Sheed & Ward, 1964); and John Murray Todd, *Luther, a Life* (New York: Crossroad Publishing Co., 1982).

11. See Karl Barth, *Ad Limina Apostolorum*, trans. Keith R. Crim (Richmond, Va.: John Knox Press, 1967), pp. 27–28; 35–37; 39–40.

12. See George M. Marsden, "Scotland and Philadelphia: Common Sense Philosophy from Jefferson to Westminster," in *The Reformed Journal*, Vol. 29, No. 3 (March 1979), pp. 8–12. Also see the discussion on the Common Sense philosophy in Jack B. Rogers and Donald K. McKim, *The Authority and Interpretation of the Bible* (San Francisco: Harper & Row, 1979), pp. 235–248.

13. John Warwick Montgomery, *The Shape of the Past: A Christian Response to Secular Philosophies of History* (Minneapolis: Bethany Fellowship, 1976), pp. 143, 293–295.

14. See Ronald H. Nash, *The Word of God and the Mind of Man* (Grand Rapids, Mich.: Zondervan, 1982). Nash, following the evangelical rationalism of Gordon Clark and Carl Henry, asserts that our knowl-

edge of God is univocal, not merely analogical, and that the propositions in Scripture are identical with divine revelation. He criticizes my position for undercutting cognitive revelation, though he acknowledges that I affirm it. Against the evangelical rationalists, I contend that although we find the truth of revelation in Scripture, this revelation is not to be identified with the very words of Scripture, for this is to confuse the infinite and the finite.

15. In a letter to *The Christian Century*, Vol. 96, No. 6 (February 21, 1979), p. 197.

16. Paul L. Holmer, *The Grammar of Faith* (San Francisco: Harper & Row, 1978), p. 162.

17. Paul Tillich, *Systematic Theology*, Vol. I (Chicago: University of Chicago Press, 1951), p. 8.

18. See Paul Feinberg, "The Meaning of Inerrancy" in Norman L. Geisler, ed., *Inerrancy* (Grand Rapids, Mich.: Zondervan, 1979), [pp. 265–304], pp. 272–276.

19. Carl Henry, "What Must We Do To Save the Day?" in *Eternity*, Vol. 21, No. 12 (December 1970), p. 24.

20. The Christian is enjoined to break fellowship with an erring brother or sister both to maintain the purity and integrity of the church and to bring the erring one back into the fold. See I Cor. 5:1–5, 11–13; II Thess. 3:14, 15.

21. In Walter Nigg, *Great Saints*, trans. William Stirling (Hinsdale, Ill.: Henry Regnery Co., 1948), p. 216.

22. Cited in A. Skevington Wood, *The Inextinguishable Blaze* (Grand Rapids, Mich.: Eerdmans, 1960), p. 188.

23. The Presbyterian Church (U.S.A.), perhaps more than any other denomination today, impresses me as being two churches under one umbrella. The shadow of schism lies over this as well as several other mainline denominations. As the evangelical movement becomes stronger, the tensions between liberals and conservatives will multiply.

24. H. G. Haile, *Luther* (Garden City, N.Y.: Doubleday, 1980), p. 248.

25. Charismatics who are separatists have an affinity to the ancient Gnostics and Montanists, who distinguished between grades of believers. In these sects, the psychics were those who lived by carnal standards, whereas the pneumatics were those who lived in the full dispensation of the Spirit.

26. Karl Barth, *The Christian Life*, trans. Geoffrey W. Bromiley (Grand Rapids, Mich.: Eerdmans, 1981), p. 194.

27. This is by no means to suggest that all Seventh-Day Adventists have been sectarian. Brinsmead has observed that while Seventh-Day Adventism began as a heresy, it is one of the few churches today that is steadily moving toward orthodoxy.

28. Robert Brinsmead, "The Gospel versus the Sectarian Spirit," *Verdict*, Vol. 4, No. 3 (March 1981), p. 16.

29. Ibid.

30. Other church leaders and scholars in recent times who have felt called to sever their ecclesiastical connections include Martin Marty, Jaroslav Pelikan, James Boice, R. C. Sproul, Charles Keysor, and Paul and Elizabeth Achtemeier.

31. See Richard Quebedeaux, *The Worldly Evangelicals* (San Francisco: Harper & Row, 1978).

32. See Shailer Mathews, *The Faith of Modernism* (New York: Macmillan, 1924); and William R. Hutchison, *The Modernist Impulse in American Protestantism* (New York: Oxford University Press, 1982).

33. P. T. Forsyth, *The Principle of Authority*, 2nd ed. (London: Independent Press, 1952), p. 51.

34. Ibid., p. 348.

35. Ibid., p. 382.

36. Arnold Dallimore, "Whitefield and the Testimony of the Eighteenth Century," *Banner of Truth*, No. 79 (April 1970), p. 21. Also see Arnold Dallimore, *George Whitefield*, Vol. I (London: Banner of Truth Trust, 1970), p. 137.

37. Karl Barth, *Church Dogmatics* IV, 1, ed. G. W. Bromiley and T. F. Torrance, trans. G. W. Bromiley (Edinburgh: T. & T. Clark, 1956), p. 709.

38. A. W. Tozer, *Born After Midnight* (Harrisburg, Pa.: Christian Publications, 1959), p. 141.

39. Cited in David J. Fant, Jr., *A. W. Tozer: A Twentieth Century Prophet* (Harrisburg, Pa.: Christian Publications, 1964), p. 150.

40. Karl Barth, *Against the Stream*, trans. E. M. Delacour and Stanley Godman (London: SCM Press, 1954), p. 228.

41. Søren Kierkegaard, *The Last Years: Journals 1853–1855*, ed. and trans. Ronald Gregor Smith (New York: Harper & Row, 1965), pp. 136–137.

42. P. T. Forsyth, *The Justification of God* (London: Independent Press, 1948), p. 38.

43. John Calvin, *Sermons on the Epistle to the Ephesians* (Edinburgh: Banner of Truth Trust, 1975), p. 140.

44. See Paul Tillich, *The Courage to Be* (New Haven: Yale University Press, 1952).

45. Søren Kierkegaard, *Søren Kierkegaard's Journals and Papers*, Vol. I, A–E, ed. and trans. Howard V. Hong and Edna H. Hong (Bloomington, Ind.: Indiana University Press, 1967), p. 217.

46. For a trenchant critique of the religious right, with its uneven blend of a bastardized Puritanism and nationalism, see Dale Vree, "Ideology versus Theology," in Peter Williamson and Kevin Perrotta, eds., *Christianity Confronts Modernity* (Ann Arbor, Mich.: Servant Books, 1981), pp. 57–78.

Ronald Wells sees a similar fusion of chauvinistic Americanism and latter-day Calvinism in Francis Schaeffer's *A Christian Manifesto* (Westchester, Ill.: Crossway Books, 1981). See Ronald A. Wells, "Francis Schaeffer's Jeremiad," in *The Reformed Journal*, Vol. 32, No. 5 (May 1982), pp. 16–20. Both Vree and Wells fail to do justice to the genuinely biblical foundations of the Calvinist and Puritan vision of a holy community, but they have good reason to be apprehensive of the association of this ideal with the American dream. For a thoughtful retort to Wells in defense of Francis Schaeffer, see Wayne G. Boulton, "A Different Schaeffer," *The Reformed Journal*, Vol. 32, No. 8 (August 1982), pp. 3, 4. Boulton contends that Wells gives away too much in his assertion that Protestantism is "the religious form of Renaissance humanism." Boulton prefers the way Schaeffer states the problem: *"Liberal* theology is only humanism in theological terms" (p. 4). Though I can empathize with Boulton and Schaeffer in their warnings against liberalism and humanism, I cannot go along with Schaeffer's blanket condemnation of liberal theology. To contend that all liberal theology is covert humanism is a gross oversimplification.

For an in-depth study of the concept of "manifest destiny," which has been used to justify American imperial ambitions, see Albert K. Weinberg, *Manifest Destiny: A Study of Nationalist Expansionism in American History* (Baltimore: Johns Hopkins University Press, 1935). Also see Robert Jewett, *The Captain America Complex: The Dilemma of Zealous Nationalism* (Philadelphia: Westminster Press, 1973). For Jewett, the source of modern American "zealous nationalism" lies in radical millenarian Puritanism and Social Darwinism.

47. Cf.: "The ministry is not meant to be a social and philanthropic institution, to organise and run all kinds of movements and campaigns for the external reform of mankind. It is intended to be the soul of the

world, not its arms and feet; an inspirer, a teacher, a healer, not an engineer." Forsyth is here endorsing a statement in the *Missionary Record of the United Free Church of Scotland*. In P. T. Forsyth, *The Church and the Sacraments* (London: Independent Press, 1947), p. 186.

48. Søren Kierkegaard, *Søren Kierkegaard's Journals and Papers* I: 359.

49. *Karl Barth's Table Talk*, ed. John D. Godsey (Edinburgh: Oliver & Boyd, 1963), p. 19.

50. Cited in *Decision*, Vol. 11, No. 1 (January 1970), p. 13.

51. David Tracy, *Blessed Rage for Order* (New York: Seabury Press, 1978), p. 32. Tracy also speaks of the "dramatic confrontation, the mutual illuminations and corrections" between the contemporary consciousness and a reinterpreted Christianity, but it seems that confrontation and mutual correction serve the goal of a possible rapprochement.

52. Langdon Gilkey, *Catholicism Confronts Modernity* (New York: Seabury Press, 1975), p. 60.

53. Søren Kierkegaard, *The Last Years*, p. 124.

54. P. T. Forsyth, *The Principle of Authority*, p. 334. Cf.: "The classic type of Christianity is the experience of moral redemption and not merely ethical reform. Or rather it is the experience of a redeemer. Because it is not the *sense* of the experience that is the main matter, but the *source* of the experience, and its content. It is not our experience we are conscious of—that would be self-conscious piety—but it is Christ. It is not our experience we preach, but the Christ who comes in our experience." P. T. Forsyth, *Positive Preaching and the Modern Mind* (London: Independent Press, 1953, 4th impression), p. 45.

55. Karl Barth and Eduard Thurneysen, *Come Holy Spirit*, trans. George W. Richards, Elmer G. Homrighausen and Karl J. Ernst (Grand Rapids, Mich.: Eerdmans, 1978), p. 63.

56. H. Richard Niebuhr, *Christ and Culture* (New York: Harper & Row, 1951).

57. Jerry Falwell, despite his tacit alliance with the political right, shares this vision more than many of his evangelical and liberal detractors, who often seem content to abandon the world to secularism. Falwell would come closer to the Puritan and Calvinist vision if he would expand his conception of holiness to include the social righteousness of the Old Testament prophets in which the plight of the poor takes priority over both business expansion and national security.

NOTES TO CHAPTER VI—Toward the Recovery of Evangelical Faith

1. Evangelical Christianity as an empirical phenomenon in history is the preeminent vessel of the holy catholic church, but it is not to be equated with the very body of Christ itself. As an earthen vessel, it is not absolutely indispensable to the being or the advancement of the holy catholic church.

2. According to Heppe, both the older Reformed and Lutheran theology clearly distinguished between the Word of God and Holy Scripture, though this was mainly a historical rather than a dogmatic judgment. Heinrich Heppe, *Reformed Dogmatics*, trans. G. T. Thomson (London: Allen & Unwin, 1950), pp. 14, 15.

3. See Donald G. Bloesch, "The Legacy of Pietism" in his *The Evangelical Renaissance* (Grand Rapids, Mich.: Eerdmans, 1973), pp. 101–157.

4. The Reformation applied all of its energies to the task of church reform and consequently was not able to do justice to the imperative of evangelism.

5. See Heiko Oberman, *The Harvest of Medieval Theology* (Grand Rapids, Mich.: Eerdmans, 1967).

6. Brian A. Gerrish, "Historical Theology and Some Theologians," in *Criterion*, Vol. 21, No. 2 (Spring 1982), pp. 8–14.

7. Schaff also argues that the Catholic Church in the Counter-Reformation gave up catholicity in favor of particularity. See Philip Schaff, *The Principle of Protestantism*, ed. Bard Thompson and George H. Bricker (Philadelphia: United Church Press, 1964), pp. 73, 74.

8. This is also Schaff's thesis. See Philip Schaff, *Christ and Christianity* (New York: Scribner, 1885), pp. 126, 132, 133.

9. The Second Vatican Council affirmed the universal call to discipleship in its "Decree on the Apostolate of the Laity." See *The Documents of Vatican II*, ed. Walter M. Abbott and Joseph Gallagher (New York: America Press, 1966), pp. 489–525.

10. Luther and Calvin nonetheless made a place for the special ministry of the Word and sacraments, but this special ministry differs from the general ministry only in function, not in spiritual status or priestly quality.

11. Robert Schuller, who combines aspects of New Thought with evangelical tradition, not surprisingly keeps himself at a distance from the Reformation of the sixteenth century. He accuses the Reformers of leading a reactionary movement, whereas what is needed today is a rec-

onciling movement. Robert Schuller, *Self Esteem: The New Reforma-tion* (Waco, Tex.: Word Books, 1982), pp. 39, 146, 162, 174, 175. In-terestingly, Clark Pinnock sees promise in this book, believing that Schuller helps us to find a point of contact between the gospel and mod-ern man—the cultural pursuit of self-esteem (on jacket cover). For a tren-chant critique of Schuller's book, see Carl F. H. Henry's review in *Eternity*, Vol. 33, No. 10 (October 1982), pp. 42, 43.

12. David Schaff comments: "Defective as Savonarola's exegesis was, the biblical element was everywhere in control of his thought and de-scriptions." Savonarola saw himself as a biblical preacher and teacher: "I preach the regeneration of the Church, taking the Scriptures as my sole guide." David S. Schaff, *History of the Christian Church*, Vol. VI (Grand Rapids, Mich.: Eerdmans, 1957), p. 689.

13. This statement is cited in the Augsburg Confession in support of the position of the Reformation. See Theodore G. Tappert, ed. and trans., *The Book of Concord* (Philadelphia: Fortress Press, 1959), p. 32.

14. Thomas Aquinas, *Commentary on Saint Paul's Epistle to the Ephesians*, trans. Matthew L. Lamb (Albany, N.Y.: Magi Books, 1966), p. 96. Thomas nonetheless made a place for merit after the first grace. With the aid of justifying and sanctifying grace, the Christian is able to merit glory.

15. See Bengt R. Hoffman, *Luther and the Mystics* (Minneapolis: Augsburg Publishing House, 1976).

16. See Robert Webber and Donald Bloesch, eds., *The Orthodox Evangelicals* (Nashville: Nelson, 1978).

17. Donald G. Bloesch, *Essentials of Evangelical Theology*, Vol. II (San Francisco: Harper & Row, 1982, 2nd printing).

18. I first enunciated this distinction in *Essentials of Evangelical The-ology*, Vol. II, pp. 270–275.

19. Cited in Gerhard Maier, *The End of the Historical-Critical Method*, trans. Edwin W. Leverenz and Rudolph F. Norden (St. Louis: Concordia Publishing House, 1977), p. 59. Hollaz could not break free from scholastic rationalism, but he did make a place for the dynamic ele-ment in revelation. It should be noted that Maier affirms the infallibility and verbal inspiration of Scripture but not "anthropological inerrancy" (p. 72).

20. Richard Sibbes, *The Complete Works of Richard Sibbes*, ed. Alexander Balloch Grosart (Edinburgh: James Nichol, 1862–64), VII: 197.

21. Sibbes, *The Complete Works of Richard Sibbes* IV: 383.

22. Philip Schaff, *Christ and Christianity*, p. 171.

23. Ibid., p. 135.

24. Philip Schaff, *The Principle of Protestantism*, pp. 106, 225.

25. Arthur Holmes rightly protests against "the limitation of knowledge to what fits a scientific model, whether in the narrow rationalism of a Cartesian deductive system or in the narrow empiricism of Locke and his positivistic descendants." Arthur F. Holmes, *Christian Philosophy in the Twentieth Century* (Nutley, N.J.: Craig Press, 1969), p. 71.

26. The Bible does not negate history but points beyond history to Eternity. Revelation enters into history, but it does not become bound to history. History is the vessel of Eternity but not an aspect of Eternity. To believe otherwise is to abandon supernaturalism in favor of either naturalism or idealism. History is the occasion but not the source of our knowledge of the messianic identity of Christ as attested in Matthew 16:17. The cross of Christ is not simply a noteworthy event in history but an event in which Eternity impinges upon time or in which time opens up to Eternity. It signifies the fulfillment of time (*kairos*), not simply another moment in time.

27. Barth's approach is also to be contrasted with Van Til, who asserts that we should come to the Bible with the presuppositions of classical Calvinism. For Barth we should come only with simple faith, keeping our own system open-ended and tentative. Here we see the difference between presuppositionalism and confessional theology. Arthur Holmes reveals his distance from Van Til in his *Christian Philosophy in the Twentieth Century*, p. 239.

28. This is the basic position of Calvin, and it seems to be reaffirmed by Karl Barth in his *The Christian Life*, trans. Geoffrey W. Bromiley (Grand Rapids, Mich.: Eerdmans, 1981), pp. 122 ff.

29. "When I thought of You," he said, "it was not as of something firm and solid. For my God was not yet You but the error and vain fantasy I held." *Confessions* IV, Chap. VII, No. 12. Quoted by Henri Bouillard in his "A Dialogue with Barth: The Problem of Natural Theology," in *Cross Currents*, Vol. 18 (Spring 1968), p. 215.

30. Harry Blamires, *The Secularist Heresy* (Ann Arbor, Mich.: Servant Books, 1980), p. 50.

31. In Carnell's view, "Men could know God if they would only will to know him, for the divine tribunal reveals itself in both conscience and the judicial sentiment." He refers to the judicial sentiment as "the narrow point of contact between God and man." Edward John Carnell, *Christian Commitment* (New York: Macmillan, 1957), pp. 209, 237. In his later writings, Carnell increasingly distanced himself from the per-

sonalistic idealism of the Boston school and showed a growing appreciation for existentialist and neo-orthodox theologies.

32. Norman L. Geisler, *Options in Contemporary Christian Ethics* (Grand Rapids, Mich.: Baker Book House, 1981), p. 32.

33. Donald K. McKim in his critique of Bruce A. Demarest, *General Revelation* (Grand Rapids, Mich.: Zondervan, 1982) perceptively asks: "But is this not actually incipient Semi-Pelagianism in which one prepares oneself, through reason, to receive the gift of faith?" *Reformed Review,* Vol. 36, No. 2 (Winter 1983), pp. 103–104.

34. Robert Webber and Donald Bloesch, eds., *The Orthodox Evangelicals,* p. 13.

35. Karl Barth, *Church Dogmatics* III, 4, ed. G. W. Bromiley and T. F. Torrance (Edinburgh: T. & T. Clark, 1961), pp. 78–79.

36. John Calvin, *Institutes of the Christian Religion,* Vol. I, ed. John T. McNeill, trans. Ford Lewis Battles (Philadelphia: Westminster Press, 1960), Book II, viii, 48, p. 412.

37. Philip Schaff, *Christ and Christianity,* p. 18.

38. John Calvin, *Sermons on the Epistle to the Ephesians* (Edinburgh: Banner of Truth Trust, 1973), p. 199.

39. See Emil Brunner, *The Misunderstanding of the Church,* trans. Harold Knight (Philadelphia: Westminster Press, 1953).

40. John Calvin, *Sermons on the Epistle to the Ephesians,* p. 175.

41. An admirable statement on the theological significance of the Eucharist is John Nevin's *The Mystical Presence* (Philadelphia: United Church Press, 1966).

42. Avery Dulles, *Models of the Church* (Garden City, N.Y.: Doubleday, 1974), pp. 31–42, 179 ff.

43. Philip Schaff, *Christ and Christianity,* p. 16. My one reservation is that it is not clear whether Schaff sees theological variety in the service of confessional unity.

44. Cited in Geoffrey Bromiley, *Historical Theology* (Grand Rapids, Mich.: Eerdmans, 1978), p. 263.

45. Cited in David S. Schaff, *The Life of Philip Schaff* (New York: Scribner, 1897), p. 89. Even while regarding Anglo-Catholicism as "an entirely legitimate and necessary reaction against rationalistic and sectaristic pseudo-Protestantism," Philip Schaff faults it for "its utter misapprehension of the divine significance of the Reformation, with its consequent development, that is, of the entire Protestant period of the church." *The Principle of Protestantism,* pp. 158, 160.

46. Cited in James Hastings Nichols, *Romanticism in American Theology* (Chicago: University of Chicago Press, 1961), p. 206. It should be noted that Philip Schaff opposed the idea that the unity and catholicity of the church could be achieved by a return to a past period of church history.

47. See Anders Nygren, *Agape and Eros,* trans. Philip Watson (Philadelphia: Westminster Press, 1953).

48. This kind of mysticism is present in certain strands of liberation theology where the accent is on the struggle of the proletariat to wrest power from the bourgeoisie. It is also evident in neotranscendentalism (Unity, New Thought, Christian Science, Psychiana), which emphasizes the need for developing self-esteem with its dividends of health and prosperity.

49. See Kenneth C. Russell, "Matthew Fox's Spiritual Trilogy," in *New Catholic World,* Vol. 225, No. 1348 (July-August 1982), pp. 189–192. Leading figures in the intellectual world who prepared the way for the new mood include Friedrich Nietzsche, Walt Whitman, William Blake and Carl Jung.

50. In evangelical perspective, a monastery will function as a training center for mission rather than a testing ground to prepare oneself for heaven. Its goal will be not the ascent to divinity but the apostolate to the nations.

51. P. T. Forsyth, *The Justification of God* (London: Independent Press, 1948), p. 117.

52. My position is diametrically opposed to that of Joseph Fletcher: "A fetus is a parasite, tolerable ethically only when welcome to its hostess. If a woman doesn't want a fetus to remain growing in her body, she should be free to rid herself of the unwelcome intruder." In a letter to Charles Fager in Charles Fager, "So Who's the Radical?" in *National Catholic Reporter,* Vol. 9, No. 18 (March 2, 1973), p. 12.

Much more Christian is the position of Lewis Smedes, who sees the fetus or conceptus in the early stages of pregnancy as on the way to becoming a person, though not yet a full-fledged person. Yet because human personhood is latent in all fetal life, this life must be treated with the utmost respect. Biological life and a human person are not identical, but the first is the life-support system for the second. Smedes therefore takes a strongly antiabortion stance, but he stays clear of the absolutist position that sees all abortion after conception as equivalent to infanticide (which is implied by Francis Schaeffer and C. Everett Koop). Lewis Smedes, *Mere Morality* (Grand Rapids, Mich.: Eerdmans, 1983), pp. 124 ff., 263.

53. I agree with Karl Barth that human life needs to be protected, but because human life is not an absolute value, this protection cannot be absolute. Geoffrey Bromiley gives an apt summary of Barth's position on legitimate abortion: "The criteria of legitimate abortion are life for life, scrupulous calculation in responsibility before God, and action in faith." Geoffrey Bromiley, *An Introduction to the Theology of Karl Barth* (Grand Rapids, Mich.: Eerdmans, 1979), p. 168.

54. Even in Roman Catholicism, opposition to abortion is not always unequivocal. According to one Catholic scholar, "Catholic teaching allows abortion for ectopic pregnancies (through removal of part or all of the fallopian tube), uterine cancer (through removal of the uterus), and pregnancy due to rape (through dilation and curettage within a short time after rape). In none of these cases is abortion construed as murder but as a procedure for maintaining the health of a woman by severing the tie between her and a fertilized ovum, embryo or fetus." She goes on to say: "In pregnancies due to rape the dilation and curettage is accomplished before it is known whether the woman is pregnant." See Mary B. Mahowald, "Abortion: Towards Continuing the Dialogue," in *Cross Currents*, Vol. XXIX, No. 3 (Fall 1979), pp. 334, 335.

55. My medical friends tell me that there are some very rare occasions when newly born children might face a very short life in considerable pain, so I am not dealing here with a hypothetical possibility. But neither am I making this a principle that must be adhered to in every case. What I am pleading for is to have each case decided on its own merits; a blanket condemnation of all abortion precludes the remote but still real possibility that permission for an abortion may be included in God's commandment.

I also do not believe that the life of the child should in every case be sacrificed for the life of the mother. Here, too, much wrestling in prayer is necessitated in order to discover the divine commandment.

In comparing abortion with suicide, both fall under the commandment against killing. Yet the Bible gives several examples of where the act of suicide (or an act tantamount to suicide) seems to be in accordance with the will of God (cf. Judg. 16:28–30; Jon. 1:12–16; Dan. 3:16–18).

56. I here have in mind what is called passive euthanasia, in which artificial supports are withdrawn from a life deemed by medical experts as hopeless.

57. J. Van Zytveld calls for a partial disarmament in which America would divest itself of all offensive nuclear weapons. J. Van Zytveld, "Back From the Brink," *The Reformed Journal*, Vol. 32, No. 7 (July 1982), pp. 2, 3. See also Arthur Macy Cox, "Reagan Trading Deterrence Policy for a Chance to Win Nuclear War," *Des Moines Register*

(November 3, 1982), p. 12. A. Cox urges a return to the policy of nuclear deterrence as opposed to a policy of "decapitation," involving the development of first-strike weapons capable of obliterating the entire enemy state. Most nuclear pacifists would support all proposals to pare down our nuclear arsenal provided that they are seen as stepping-stones to universal nuclear disarmament.

58. Jim Wallis, *The Call to Conversion* (San Francisco: Harper & Row, 1981), p. 107.

59. See Jacques Ellul, *To Will and To Do*, trans. C. Edward Hopkin (Philadelphia: Pilgrim Press, 1969), pp. 73–110.

60. See Reinhold Niebuhr, *An Interpretation of Christian Ethics* (New York: Seabury Press, 1979), pp. 84–122; *Discerning the Signs of the Times* (New York: Scribner, 1946), pp. 145–151.

61. Flo Conway and Jim Siegelman, *Holy Terror* (Garden City, N.Y.: Doubleday, 1982).

62. Ibid., p. 347.

63. For a critical appraisal of Moral Majority informed by biblical faith, see Richard Neuhaus, "Religion and . . . : Addressing the Naked Public Square," *Worldview*, Vol. 25, No. 1 (January 1982), pp. 11–12. I have already referred to the timely critiques of Robert Webber and Gabriel Fackre. See pp. 154, 158.

64. See Elémire Zolla, *The Androgyne: Reconciliation of Male and Female* (New York: Crossroad Publishing Co., 1981). Mary Daly defends androgyny in her *Beyond God the Father* (Boston: Beacon Press, 1973), though she later abandons this position. Others who favor an androgynous interpretation include Rosemary Ruether, Helen Luke, Thomas D. Parker, and Matthew Fox. Ruether writes: "Both the woman's movement and the gay movement are moving from the psychology of complementarity to the psychology of androgyny. Although the term itself retains all too clearly its dualistic origins, what it means is that both males and females contain the total human psychic essence." Edward Batchelor, Jr., ed., *Homosexuality and Ethics* (New York: Pilgrim Press, 1980), p. 30.

65. In *The Politics of Jesus* (Grand Rapids, Mich.: Eerdmans, 1978), John Howard Yoder ably demonstrates that the biblical concept of revolutionary subordination is the law of the kingdom of God and is therefore demanded of all Christians. This principle as well as that of representative headship is deeply imbedded in biblical faith, and ideological feminists show their contempt for biblical authority by repudiating both.

66. Loving assistance does not always or necessarily entail obedience. In some cases the wife as a sister in Christ may have to thwart her hus-

band out of concern for his best interests and also out of fidelity to the divine commandment (cf. Gen. 27:1-17).

We should also note that the apostle Paul makes a place for mutual subordination in the framework of holy matrimony. The subordination of the husband to his wife takes the form of his love (see Eph. 5:21-33).

67. Some feminists (albeit a minority) also acknowledge immutable psychic differences between the sexes. See Helen M. Luke, *Woman Earth and Spirit: The Feminine in Symbol and Myth* (New York: Crossroad Publishing Co., 1981), pp. 2, 3. Rita M. Gross takes issue with Luke on this point in her review of Luke's book in *The Christian Century*, Vol. 99, No. 8 (March 10, 1982), pp. 276-279. Yet it should be remembered that Luke also emphasizes androgyny over complementarity. In her view, the woman must be able to live by and for herself before she can relate meaningfully to men.

68. For the biblical and theological basis for women's ordination see Paul K. Jewett, *The Ordination of Women* (Grand Rapids, Mich.: Eerdmans, 1980); and Donald G. Bloesch, *Is the Bible Sexist?: Beyond Feminism and Patriarchalism* (Westchester, Ill.: Crossway Books, 1982), pp. 41-60.

69. Dietrich Bonhoeffer, *Prisoner for God*, ed. Eberhard Bethge, trans. Reginald Fuller (New York: Macmillan, 1954), p. 37.

70. See especially Deut. 32:11, 18; Ps. 131:2; Job 38:29; Isa. 49:14, 15; 42:14; 66:13; Matt. 23:37. Despite his very fine contribution to the discussion on feminism and his defense of biblical language in speaking of God, Vernard Eller fails to consider that in addition to the prevailing masculine symbolism for God in the Bible, there are other forms of symbolism, including the feminine. I also have difficulty with Eller's inclination to view "Father, Son and Spirit" as referring to God only in his relationship to the creature and not also to God as he is in himself. See Vernard Eller, *The Language of Canaan and the Grammar of Feminism* (Grand Rapids, Mich.: Eerdmans, 1982).

71. W. A. Visser't Hooft, *The Fatherhood of God in an Age of Emancipation* (Geneva: World Council of Churches, 1982), p. 133.

72. Ibid.

73. My recommendation is that in public prayers we should generally follow the wisdom of church tradition and address God in the masculine imagery of the Scriptures, in the awareness that the masculine contains the feminine. On the other hand, in private devotions it may be appropriate on occasion to address God in the person of his Word or Spirit as

"Holy Mother, Wisdom of God," or something similar, a practice that has some basis in the church fathers as well as in Scripture.

It is also permissible, in my opinion, to refer to God at times by more inclusive symbolism such as "the all-determining reality" and "infinite ground and depth of all being," but these must always be subordinated to the more personal symbolism of the Bible—Father, Son and Spirit. The latter are closer than the former to the real meaning of who God is.

74. Visser't Hooft points to Anselm's prayer to St. Paul and Jesus as an example of the use of creative imagination in personal devotions. After referring to the apostle as his "sweet nurse, sweet mother," Anselm then asks: "And you Jesus, are you not also a mother? Are you not the mother who like a hen gathers her children under her wings?" He concludes: "Then both of you are mothers. Even if you are fathers, you are also mothers. . . . Fathers by your authority, mothers by your mercy." *The Fatherhood of God*, p. 133. See St. Anselm of Canterbury, *The Prayers and Meditations of St. Anselm*, trans. Benedicta Ward (Harmondsworth, Middlesex: Penguin Books, 1973), pp. 152-155.

75. It is well to note that the conflict with feminism on this point parallels the battle of the Confessing Church with the "German Christians," who sought to accommodate the faith to the ideology of National Socialism. They did not hesitate to reject parts of the Bible they disagreed with and pressed for the resymbolization of the faith.

76. Schleiermacher saw the preacher as a spiritual guide or tutor who enables his hearers to proceed on their mystical journey inward. See Friedrich Schleiermacher, *On Religion: Speeches to its Cultured Despisers*, trans. John Oman (New York: Harper & Row, 1958), pp. 91, 123, 153-155, 173-175.

77. See Myron Simon and Thornton Parsons, eds., *Transcendentalism and Its Legacy* (Ann Arbor, Mich.: University of Michigan Press, 1966); Catherine Albanese, *Corresponding Motion: Transcendental Religion and the New America* (Philadelphia: Temple University Press, 1977); J. Stillson Judah, *The History and Philosophy of the Metaphysical Movements in America* (Philadelphia: Westminster Press, 1967); George F. Whicher, *The Transcendentalist Revolt Against Materialism* (Boston: Heath, 1949); and Charles Braden, *Spirits in Rebellion* (Dallas: Southern Methodist University Press, 1963).

78. James Hastings Nichols, *Corporate Worship in the Reformed Tradition* (Philadelphia: Westminster Press, 1968), p. 32.

79. John R. W. Stott gives eloquent testimony to this theme in his *Between Two Worlds: The Art of Preaching in the Twentieth Century* (Grand Rapids, Mich.: Eerdmans, 1982). Stott contends "that our mes-

sage must be God's Word not ours, our aim Christ's glory not ours, and our confidence the Holy Spirit's power, not ours" (p. 335). Stott is to be commended for his stress on study as a necessary preparation for the preaching of the Word of God.

80. It can be said that Jesus Christ is already Creator-Lord of the universe, but he is Redeemer-Lord only of the church in that this is where his Lordship is acknowledged and confessed. He is Lord of all, but Savior only of some.

81. For a trenchant critique of the popular interpretation of "principalities and powers" as socio-political structures in human society, see Peter O'Brien, "Principalities and Powers and Their Relationship to Structures," *Evangelical Review of Theology*, Vol. 6, No. 1 (April 1982), pp. 50–61.

82. I agree with Emil Brunner that our claim to be Reformed is based not on loyalty to a particular historical tradition but on the fact that the holy catholic faith was rediscovered and proclaimed anew by the Reformers.

83. Philip Schaff declares, "There is, indeed, a negative liberalism which is indifferent to the distinction between truth and error; but there is also a positive liberalism or genuine catholicity which springs from the deep conviction of the infinite grandeur of truth and the inability of any single mind or single church to grasp it in all its fullness and variety of aspects." *Christ and Christianity*, p. 308. Schaff, like Nevin, was not immune to the spell of romantic idealism which dominated that age, but he was able to resist the pull of Romanticism by his deep grounding in biblical faith.

Both Schaff and Nevin often referred favorably to Schleiermacher, but it is unfair to accuse them of being followers of that renowned liberal theologian (as did Charles Hodge). In his preface to his *Anti-Christ: Spirit of Sect and Schism* (Taylor, 1848), John Nevin denied that he was guilty of following the errors of either Schleiermacher or Hegel, notwithstanding the help these men gave to him (p. 4). In his retort to Hodge in a series of articles in the *Messenger* (May 24–August 9, 1848), he made clear that while learning much from Schleiermacher, he objected to the inwardness and subjectivity which characterized Schleiermacher's theology. See Luther J. Binkley, *The Mercersburg Theology* (Lancaster, Pa.: Franklin and Marshall College; Manheim, Pa.: Sentinel Printing House, 1953), p. 99. Significantly Nevin introduced his book *The Mystical Presence* with an essay by Carl Ullman which sought to correct Schleiermacher on sin and forgiveness. *The Mystical Presence: A Vindication of the Reformed or Calvinistic Doctrine of the Holy Eucharist* (Philadelphia, 1846), pp. 26–27.

On Schaff's indebtedness to German idealistic philosophy, particularly as found in Hegel, see Klaus Penzel, "The Reformation Goes West: The Notion of Historical Development in the Thought of Philip Schaff," in *The Journal of Religion*, Vol. 62, No. 3 (July 1982), pp. 219–241. See also Penzel, "Church History in Context: The Case of Philip Schaff," in *Our Common History as Christians*, ed. John Deschner et al. (New York: Oxford University Press, 1975), pp. 217–260. Penzel acknowledges that Schaff severely criticized both Hegel and Richard Rothe for idolizing the state.

84. P. T. Forsyth, *Positive Preaching and the Modern Mind* (London: Independent Press, 1953, 4th impression), p. 143. Forsyth nevertheless affirmed that kind of liberalism characterized by the spirit of self-criticism and willingness to remain open to new truth. He definitely sided with a true liberalism over obscurantism.

85. Philip Schaff, *Christ and Christianity*, p. 152.

86. Ibid., p. 297.

Bibliography of Author's Books

AUTHOR OR EDITOR

Centers of Christian Renewal. Philadelphia: United Church Press, 1964.

The Christian Life and Salvation. Grand Rapids, Mich.: William B. Eerdmans Publishing Co., 1967.

The Crisis of Piety. Grand Rapids, Mich.: William B. Eerdmans Publishing Co., 1968.

The Christian Witness in a Secular Age. Minneapolis, Minn.: Augsburg Publishing House, 1968.

Christian Spirituality East and West. Chicago: Priory Press, 1968. (co-author)

The Reform of the Church. Grand Rapids, Mich.: William B. Eerdmans Publishing Co., 1970.

The Ground of Certainty: Toward an Evangelical Theology of Revelation. Grand Rapids, Mich.: William B. Eerdmans Publishing Co., 1971.

Servants of Christ: Deaconesses in Renewal. Minneapolis, Minn.: Bethany Fellowship, 1971. (editor)

The Evangelical Renaissance. Grand Rapids, Mich.: William B. Eerdmans Publishing Co., 1973. Published in London, England, by Hodder & Stoughton, 1974.

Wellsprings of Renewal: Promise in Christian Communal Life. Grand Rapids, Mich.: William B. Eerdmans Publishing Co., 1974.

Light a Fire. St. Louis, Mo.: Eden Publishing House, 1975.

The Invaded Church. Waco, Texas: Word Books, 1975.

Jesus Is Victor!: Karl Barth's Doctrine of Salvation. Nashville, Tenn.: Abingdon Press, 1976.

The Orthodox Evangelicals. Nashville, Tenn.: Thomas Nelson, 1978. (co-editor)

Essentials of Evangelical Theology: God, Authority and Salvation, Vol. I. San Francisco: Harper & Row, 1978.

Essentials of Evangelical Theology: Life, Ministry and Hope, Vol. II. San Francisco: Harper & Row, 1979.

The Struggle of Prayer. San Francisco: Harper & Row, 1980.

Faith and Its Counterfeits. Downers Grove, Ill.: InterVarsity Press, 1981.

Is the Bible Sexist? Westchester, Ill.: Crossway Books, 1982.

The Future of Evangelical Christianity. Garden City, N.Y.: Doubleday & Company, 1983.

CONTRIBUTOR

"Rethinking the Church's Mission" in *Berufung und Bewährung: Internationale Festschrift für Erick Wickberg*. Geissen, Basel: Brunnen Verlag, 1974. English title: *Vocation and Victory*.

"The Basic Issue," in *Christ Is Victor*. Ed. W. Glyn Evans. Valley Forge, Pa.: Judson Press, 1977 (pp. 27–30).

"A Call to Spirituality," in *The Orthodox Evangelicals*. Ed. Robert Webber and Donald Bloesch. Nashville, Tenn.: Thomas Nelson, 1978 (pp. 146–164).

"The Challenge Facing the Churches" in Peter Williamson and Kevin Perrotta, eds., *Christianity Confronts Modernity*. Ann Arbor, Mich.: Servant Books, 1981 (pp. 205–223).

"Pietism" in *Beacon Hill Dictionary of Theology*. Ed. Richard S. Taylor. Kansas City, Mo.: Beacon Hill Press, 1983.

"A Christological Hermeneutic" in Robert Johnston, ed., *The Use of the Bible in Theology: Evangelical Options*. Atlanta: John Knox Press, 1984.

"Frank Buchman" in *Evangelical Dictionary of Theology*. Ed. Walter Elwell. Grand Rapids, Mich.: Baker Book House, 1984.

"Conversion" in *Evangelical Dictionary of Theology*, 1984.

"Descent into Hell (Hades)" in *Evangelical Dictionary of Theology*, 1984.

"Fate" in *Evangelical Dictionary of Theology*, 1984.

"Peter T. Forsyth" in *Evangelical Dictionary of Theology*, 1984.

"Sin" in *Evangelical Dictionary of Theology*, 1984.

Indexes

SCRIPTURE INDEX